NEW CENTURY BIBLE COMMENTARY

General Editors

RONALD E. CLEMENTS
(Old Testament)

MATTHEW BLACK
(New Testament)

The Pastoral Epistles

THE NEW CENTURY BIBLE COMMENTARIES

EXODUS (J. P. Hyatt)
LEVITICUS AND NUMBERS (N. H. Snaith)*
DEUTERONOMY (A. D. H. Mayes)
JOSHUA, JUDGES AND RUTH (John Gray)*
1 and 2 CHRONICLES (H. G. Williamson)
EZRA, NEHEMIAH AND ESTHER (L. H. Brockington)*
JOB (H. H. Rowley)
PSALMS Volumes 1 and 2 (A. A. Anderson)
ISAIAH 1–39 (R. E. Clements)
ISAIAH 40–66 (R. N. WHYBRAY)
EZEKIEL (John W. Wevers)*
THE GOSPEL OF MATTHEW (David Hill)
THE GOSPEL OF MARK (Hugh Anderson)
THE GOSPEL OF LUKE (E. Earle Ellis)
THE GOSPEL OF JOHN (Barnabas Lindars)
THE ACTS OF THE APOSTLES (William Neil)
ROMANS (Matthew Black)
1 and 2 CORINTHIANS (F. F. Bruce)
GALATIANS (Donald Guthrie)
EPHESIANS (C. Leslie Mitton)
PHILIPPIANS (Ralph P. Martin)
COLOSSIANS AND PHILEMON (Ralph P. Martin)
THE PASTORAL EPISTLES (A. T. Hanson)
1 PETER (Ernest Best)*
THE BOOK OF REVELATION (G. R. Beasley-Murray)

*Not yet available in paperback
Other titles are in preparation

NEW CENTURY BIBLE COMMENTARY

Based on the Revised Standard Version

The Pastoral Epistles

A. T. HANSON

Wm. B. Eerdmans Publ. Co., GRAND RAPIDS

Marshall, Morgan & Scott Publ. Ltd., LONDON

© Marshall Morgan & Scott 1982
First published 1982

All rights reserved
Printed in the United States of America
for
Wm. B. Eerdmans Publishing Company
255 Jefferson Ave. S.E., Grand Rapids, Mich. 49503
and
Marshall Morgan & Scott
1 Bath Street, London EC1V 9LB
ISBN 0 551 00926 8

Reprinted, November 1987

Library of Congress Cataloging in Publication Data

Hanson, Anthony Tyrrell.
The pastoral epistles.

(New century Bible commentary)
Bibliography: p. xi
Includes indexes.
1. Bible. N.T. Pastoral Epistles — Commentaries.
I. Title. II. Series.
BS2735.3.H29   227'.83077   82-1561
ISBN 0-8028-1924-9   AACR2

CONTENTS

PREFACE

When Professor Matthew Black originally invited me to write a commentary on the Pastoral Epistles for the New Century Bible Series, my first impulse was to refuse. This was because I had already written a small commentary on them, and also because two commentaries on the Pastorals have relatively recently appeared in English, each very valuable in its own way, that of Professor C. K. Barrett (Oxford 1963) and that of Principal J. N. D. Kelly (London 1963). Mature reflection however, and the advice of those who were well qualified to speak, persuaded me to change my mind and to attempt the task. A *substantial* commentary on the Pastorals has not appeared in English since Lock's I.C.C. commentary of 1924, and this was not an altogether satisfactory work even in its day. In writing my commentary I have not been disappointed. I have found no difficulty in adding to what I have already written and in some cases modifying it. Perhaps I should acknowledge my indebtedness to the commentary of N. Brox (Regensburg 1969), which seems to me to be the best modern commentary in German. And of course no editor of the Pastorals can ignore the monumental work of Spicq, however much he may disagree with Spicq's theory of Pauline authorship. I would also like to take this opportunity of acknowledging the help and encouragement given me by Professor Black. I am most grateful to my colleague Mr. Lionel North, Barmby Lecturer in the New Testament in the University of Hull, for his aid in reading the proofs, and to my wife for her invaluable help in compiling the indexes.

A. T. Hanson
University of Hull

ABBREVIATIONS

BIBLICAL

OLD TESTAMENT (*OT*)

Gen.	Jg.	1 Chr.	Ps.	Lam.	Ob.	Hag.
Exod.	Ru.	2 Chr.	Prov.	Ezek.	Jon.	Zech.
Lev.	1 Sam.	Ezr.	Ec.	Dan.	Mic.	Mal.
Num.	2 Sam.	Neh.	Ca.	Hos.	Nah.	
Dt.	1 Kg.	Est.	Isa.	Jl.	Hab.	
Jos.	2 Kg.	Job	Jer.	Am.	Zeph.	

APOCRYPHA (*Apoc.*)

1 Esd.	Tob.	Ad. Est.	Sir.	S. 3 Ch.	Bel.	1 Mac.
2 Esd.	Jdt.	Wis.	Bar.	Sus.	Man.	2 Mac.
			Ep. Jer.			

NEW TESTAMENT (*NT*)

Mt.	Ac.	Gal.	1 Th.	Tit.	1 Pet.	3 Jn.
Mk.	Rom.	Eph.	2 Th.	Phm.	2 Pet.	Jude
Lk.	1 C.	Phil.	1 Tim.	Heb.	1 Jn.	Rev.
Jn.	2 C.	Col.	2 Tim.	Jas.	2 Jn.	

GENERAL

Bib	*Biblica*
BibSac	*Bibliotheca Sacra* (Dallas)
BJRL	*Bulletin of John Rylands Library*
BK	*Bibel und Kirche*
BZ	*Biblische Zeitschrift*
CBQ	*Catholic Biblical Quarterly*
CH	*Church History*
CN	*Coniectanea Neotestamentica*
CTJ	*Calvin Theological Journal* (Grand Rapids)
D–C	M. Dibelius (ed. H. Conzelmann), *Die Pastoralbriefe*, Tübingen, 3rd edn, 1955
Did.	*Didache*
Eph.	Ignatius, *Epistle to Ephesians*

ET	English translation
ExpT	*Expository Times*
JAC	*Jahrbuch für Antike und Christentum*
JB	*Jerusalem Bible*
JBL	*Journal of Biblical Literature*
JTS	*Journal of Theological Studies*
LTP	*Laval Théologique Philosophique* (Quebec)
LXX	Septuagint
Mag.	Ignatius, *Epistle to Magnesians*
NEB	*New English Bible*
NovTest	*Novum Testamentum*
ns	new series
NTS	*New Testament Studies*
Philad.	Ignatius, *Epistle to Philadelphians*
Pol.	Ignatius, *Epistle to Polycarp*
Rom.	Ignatius, *Epistle to Romans*
RSR	*Recherches de Science Réligieuse*
RSV	*Revised Standard Version*
ScEsp	*Science et Esprit*
Smyr.	Ignatius, *Epistle to Smyrnaeans*
TDNT	G. Kittel (ed.), *Theological Dictionary of the New Testament*, 1–10 (ET by G. W. Bromiley), Grand Rapids, 1964–76
ThG	*Theologie und Glaube* (Paderborn)
Thl	*Theologische Literaturzeitung*
ThQ	*Theologische Quartalschrift*
ThZ	*Theologische Zeitschrift*
Trall.	Ignatius, *Epistle to Trallians*
TTZ	*Trierer Theologische Zeitschrift*
VC	*Vigiliae Christianae*
VD	*Verbum Domini*
ZNW	*Zeitschrift für die neutestamentliche Wissenschaft*

SELECT BIBLIOGRAPHY

COMMENTARIES

Barrett, C. K., *The Pastoral Epistles* (*New Clarendon Bible*), Oxford, 1963. Probably the best modern commentary in English, but rather brief.

Bernard, J. H., *The Pastoral Epistles* (*Cambridge Greek Testament*), London, 1881.

Brown, E. F., *The Pastoral Epistles*, London, 1917.

Brox, N., *Die Pastoralbriefe* (*Regensburger NT*), Regensburg, 1969. The first Roman Catholic full commentary that wholly disavows Pauline authorship. Probably the best all-round modern commentary.

Bürki, H., *Der erste Brief des Paulus an Timotheus*, Wuppertal, 1974.

Dibelius, M. (ed. H. Conzelmann), *Die Pastoralbriefe* (*Handbuch zum Neuen Testament*), Tübingen, 3rd edn., 1955. Extremely learned, especially in the background of pagan thought and practice. Together with Spicq, one of the two foundation commentaries for the serious student (referred to throughout this Commentary as D–C).

Dornier, P., *Les Épîtres Pastorales* (*Sources Bibliques*), Paris, 1969. Too often a dim echo of Spicq, but occasionally has original and useful suggestions.

Easton, B. S., *The Pastoral Epistles*, London, 1948. A good but brief American commentary.

Falconer, R., *The Pastoral Epistles*, Oxford, 1937.

Gealy, F. D., *The Pastoral Epistles* (*Interpreter's Bible*, Vol. 11), New York, 1955. Dates the Pastorals much later in the second century than do most other scholars.

Guthrie, D., *The Pastoral Epistles* (*Tyndale New Testament Commentaries*), London, 1957. A skilful defence of Pauline authorship from the conservative point of view.

Hasler, V., *Die Briefe an Timotheus und Titus* (*Zuercher Bibel Kommentar*), Zürich, 1978. A short work, but often has original and illuminating comment.

Higgins, A. J. B., 'The Pastoral Epistles', in *Peake's Commentary on the Bible*, London, 1962.

Holtz, G., *Die Pastoralbriefe* (*Theologischer Handkommentar zum NT* 13), 2nd edn., Berlin, 1972. Defends the secretary hypothesis; has a not very convincing theory that there are extensive traces of eucharistic liturgy in the letters.

Houlden, J. L., *The Pastoral Epistles* (*Penguin NT Commentaries*), London, 1976. Within the brief compass allowed by the series, he has written a lively and useful commentary.

Jeremias, J., *Die Briefe an Timotheus und Titus* (*Das Neue Testament Deutsch* 9), Göttingen, 1963. The secretary hypothesis put forward by a veteran expert on the Jewish background to Christianity.

Kelly, J. N. D., *The Pastoral Epistles* (*Black's NT Commentaries*), London, 1963. Those who insist on Pauline authorship will prefer this.

Leaney, A. R. C., *The Epistles to Timothy, Titus, and Philemon*, London, 1960.

Lock, W., *The Pastoral Epistles* (*International Critical Commentary*), Edinburgh, 1924. Full of learned detail, but fatally marred by the author's inability to make up his mind as to whether Paul wrote the Pastorals or not.

Simpson, E. K., *The Pastoral Epistles*, London, 1954.

Spicq, C., *Les Épîtres Pastorales* (*Études Bibliques*), 4th edn. rev., Paris, 1969. An astonishingly learned work, full of interesting information, though much of it irrelevant if one does not accept Pauline authorship. Indispensable for serious students; written in a graceful and witty style.

OTHER BOOKS

Bammel, E., Barrett, C. K., and Davies, W. D. (eds.), *Donum Gentilicum*, Oxford, 1978.

Barnett, A. E., *Paul Becomes a Literary Influence*, Chicago, 1941.

Barrett, C. K. See Bammel, E.

Bartsch, H.-W., *Die Anfänge urchristlicher Rechtsbildungen*, Hamburg, 1965.

Bell, H. I., *Jews and Christians in Egypt*, London, 1924.

Bruce, F. F., *Paul, Apostle of the Free Spirit*, Exeter, 1977.

Cary, E. (ed.), *Dio's Roman History* (Loeb edn.), London, 1925.

Daube, D., *The New Testament and Rabbinic Judaism*, London, 1956.

Davies, W. D. See Bammel, E.

Delorme, J. (ed.), *Le Ministère et les Ministères selon le Nouveau Testament*, Paris, 1974.

Eltester, W. (ed.), *Neutestamentliche Studien für Rudolf Bultmann*, Berlin, 1957.

England, E. B. (ed.), *The Laws of Plato*, Manchester, 1921.

Garzetti, H., *From Tiberius to the Antonines*, ET London, 1974, of Italian ed., Rome, 1960.

Grant, R. M., *A Historical Introduction to the New Testament*, London, 1963.

Haenchen, E., *The Acts of the Apostles*, ET Oxford, 1971, of 14th German edn., Göttingen, 1965.

Hainz, J. (ed.), *Kirche im Werden*, Munich/Paderborn/Vienna, 1976.

Hanson, A. T., *Studies in the Pastoral Epistles*, London, 1968.

Hanson, R. P. C., *The Acts*, Oxford, 1967.

Harrison, P. N., *The Problem of the Pastoral Epistles*, Oxford, 1921.

James, M. R. (ed.), *The Apocryphal New Testament*, Oxford, 1924.

Jewett, R., *Dating Paul's Life*, London, 1979.

Käsemann, E., *Essays on New Testament Themes*, ET London, 1964, of German edn., 1960.

Kertelge, K. (ed.), *Das kirchliche Amt im Neuen Testament*, Darmstadt, 1977.

Knight, G. W., *The Faithful Sayings of the Pastoral Epistles*, Kampen, 1968.

Lemaire, A., *Les Ministères aux Origines de l'Église*, Paris, 1971.

Lestapis, S. de, *L'Énigme des Pastorales de Saint Paul*, Paris, 1976.

McNamara, M., *The New Testament and the Palestinian Targum to the Pentateuch*, Rome, 1966.

Maehlum, H., *Die Vollmacht des Timotheus nach den Pastoralbriefen* (Diss.), Basel, 1969.

Metzger, W., *Die letzte Reise des Apostels Paulus*, Stuttgart, 1976.

Moore, C. (ed.), *Tacitus: The Histories* (Loeb edn.), London, 1962.

Müller, F. (ed.), *Geschichtswirklichkeit und Glaubensbewährung*, Stuttgart, 1967.

Oesterley, W. O. E., *A History of Israel*, Oxford, 1932.

Ogg, G., *The Chronology of the Life of St Paul*, London, 1965.

Pax, E., *Epiphaneia*, Munich, 1955.

Rigaux, B., *St Paul et ses Lettres*, Paris/Bruges, 1962.

Rohde, J., *Urchristliche und frühkatholische Ämter*, Berlin, 1976.

Roller, O., *Das Formular der Paulinischen Briefe*, Stuttgart, 1933.

Roloff, J., *Apostolat – Verkundigung – Kirche*, Gütersloh, 1965.

Sanders, H. A., *A Third Century Papyrus Codex of the Epistles of St Paul*, Ann Arbor, Michigan, 1935.

Schweizer, E., *Church Order in the New Testament*, ET London, 1961, of German edn., Zürich, 1959.

Stauffer, E., *Christ and the Caesars*, ET London, 1955, of German edn., Hamburg, 1952.

Streeter, B. H., *The Primitive Church*, London, 1929.

Sweet, J., *The Revelation*, London, 1979.

Telfer, W., *The Office of a Bishop*, London, 1962.

Townsend, R. B. (ed.), '4 Maccabees', in R. H. Charles (ed.), *Apocrypha and Pseudepigrapha of the Old Testament*, Oxford, 1913.

Trummer, P., *Die Paulustradition der Pastoralbriefe*, Frankfurt/Berne/
Las Vegas, 1978.
Von Campenhausen, H. F., *Kirchliches Amt und geistliche Vollmacht
in der drei ersten Jahrhunderten*, Tübingen, 1953.
Wegenast, K., *Das Verständnis der Tradition bei Paulus und in den
Deutero-Paulinien*, Neukirchen, 1962.
Wilson, S. G., *Luke and the Pastoral Epistles*, London, 1979.

ARTICLES

Barrett, C. K., 'Pauline Controversies in the Post-Pauline Period',
NTS 20, 1973-4, pp. 229-45.
Bell, A. A., 'The Date of John's Apocalypse', *NTS* 25, 1978-9, pp.
93-102.
Beyer, H. W., *'episcopos'*, *TDNT* 2, pp. 608-20.
Binder, H., 'Die historische Situation der Pastoralbriefe', in Müller,
F. (ed.), *Geschichtswirklichkeit und Glaubensbewährung*, Stuttgart,
1967, pp. 70-83.
Bloch, R., 'Note méthodologique pour l'Étude de la Littérature
Rabbinique', *RSR* 43, 1955, pp. 114-225.
Bornkamm, G., *'presbyteros, presbyterion'*, *TDNT* 6, pp. 651-80.
Brox, N., 'Lukas als Verfasser der Pastoralbriefe', *JAC* 13, 1970,
pp. 62-77.
—, 'Pseudo-Paulus und Pseudo-Ignatius', *VC* 30, 1976, pp. 181-8.
—, *'prophēteia* im ersten Timotheusbrief', *BZ* 20, 1976, pp. 229-32.
Büchsel, F., *'palingenesia'*, *TDNT* 1, pp. 686-9.
—, *'antilutron'*, *TDNT* 4, p. 349.
Bultmann, R., *'epignōsis'*, *TDNT* 1, pp. 689-714.
—, *'athanasia'*, *TDNT* 3, pp. 22-5.
Burchard, C., 'Das Lamm in der Waagschale', *ZNW* 57, 1966, pp.
219-28.
Butler, C., 'Was Paul a Male Chauvinist?', *New Blackfriars* 56, 1975,
pp. 174-9.
Collins, R. F., 'The Image of Paul in the Pastorals', *LTP* 2, 1975,
pp. 147-73.
Cousineau, A., 'Le sens de *presbyteros* dans les Pastorales', *ScEsp* 28,
1976, pp. 147-62.
Davies, S. L., 'The Predicament of Ignatius of Antioch', *VC* 30,
1976, pp. 174-80.
Dibelius, M., 'Die Mahl-Gebete der Didache', *ZNW* 37, 1938, pp.
32f.
—, 'Die Stellung des Bischofs in den Pastoralbriefen', in Kertlege,

E. (ed.), *Das kirchliche Amt im Neuen Testament*, Darmstadt, 1977, pp. 470f.

Dornier, P., 'Les Épîtres Pastorales', in Delorme, J., *Le Ministère et les Ministères selon le Nouveau Testament*, Paris, 1974, pp. 94f.

Ehrhardt, A., 'The Beginnings of Episcopacy', *Church Quarterly Review* 280, 1945, pp. 113f.

Elliott, J., 'Ministry and Church Order in the New Testament', *CBQ* 32, 1970, pp. 367–91.

Enslin, M. S., 'Once again, Luke and Paul', *ZNW* 61, 1970, pp. 253–71.

Ernst, J., 'Die Witwenregel des Ersten Timotheusbrief', *ThG* 59, 1969, pp. 434–45.

Ford, J. M., 'The Meaning of "Virgin" ', *NTS* 12, 1965–6, pp. 293–9.

—, 'Proto-Montanism in the Pastoral Epistles', *NTS* 17, 1970–1, pp. 338–46.

Galtier, P., 'La Réconciliation des Pécheurs dans la Première Épître à Timothée', *RSR* 39, 1951–2, pp. 317–20.

Grayston, K., and Herdan, G., 'The Authorship of the Pastorals in the Light of Statistical Linguistics', *NTS* 6, 1959–60, pp. 129f.

Hainz, J., 'Die Anfänge des Bischofs- und Diakonenamtes', in Hainz, J. (ed.), *Kirche im Werden*, Munich/Paderborn/Vienna, 1976, pp. 91–108.

Harrison, P. N., 'The Authorship of the Pastoral Epistles', *ExpT* 67, 1955–6, pp. 77f.

—, 'The Pastoral Epistles and Duncan's Ephesians Theory', *NTS* 2, 1955–6, pp. 250f.

Hegermann, H., 'Der geschichtliche Ort der Pastoralbriefe', in Rogge, J., and Schille, G. (eds), *Theologische Versuche* 2, Berlin, 1970, pp. 47–63.

Herdan, G., *see* Grayston, K.

Hommes, N. J., 'Let Women be Silent in Church', *CTJ* 4, 1969, pp. 5–22.

Hitchcock, F. M., 'The Latinity of the Pastorals', *ExpT* 39, 1927–8, pp. 347f.

Jebb, S., 'A Suggested Interpretation of 1 Timothy 2.15', *ExpT* 81, 1969–70, pp. 221–2.

Karris, R. J., 'The Background and Significance of the Polemic in the Pastoral Epistles', *JBL* 92, 1973, pp. 549–64.

Käsemann, E., 'Das Formular einer Neutestamentlichen Ordinationsparanese', in Eltester, W. (ed.), *Neutestamentliche Studien für Rudolf Bultmann*, Berlin, 1957, pp. 261–8.

Keresztes, D., 'The Jews, the Christians, and the Emperor Domitian', *VC* 27, 1973, pp. 1–28.

Kirk, J. A., 'Did "Officials" in the New Testament Church receive a Salary?', *ExpT* 84, 1972–3, pp. 105–8.

Kuch, K., 'Das Lamm, das Aegypten vernichtet', *ZNW* 57, 1966, pp. 79–93.

Lane, W. L., '1 Tim. 4.1–3: An Early Instance of Over-Realised Eschatology', *NTS* 11, 1964–5, pp. 164–7.

Lemaire, A., 'Pastoral Epistles: Redaction and Theology', *Biblical Theology Bulletin* 2, 1971, pp. 25–42.

Lightman, M., and Zeisel, W., 'Unavira: An Example of Continuity and Change in Roman Society', *CH* 46, 1977, pp. 19–32.

Lohfink, G., 'Die Normativität der Amtsvorstellungen in den Pastoralbriefen', *ThQ* 157, 1977, pp. 93–104.

Lohse, E., 'Die Ordination im Spätjudentum und im Neuen Testament', in Kertelge, K. (ed.), *Das kirchliche Amt im Neuen Testament*, Darmstadt, 1977, pp. 501f.

Lyonnet, S., ' "Unius uxoris vir" in 1 Tim. 3.2, 12; Tit. 1.6', *VD* 45, 1967, pp. 3–10.

McEleney, N. J., 'The Vice Lists in the Pastoral Epistles', *CBQ* 36, 1974, pp. 203–19.

Meier, J. P., '*presbyteros* in the Pastoral Epistles', *CBQ* 35, 1973, pp. 323–45.

Merk, von O., 'Glaube und Tat in den Pastoralbriefen', *ZNW* 66, 1975, pp. 91–112.

Metzger, B. M., 'A Reconsideration of Certain Arguments against the Pauline Authorship of the Pastoral Epistles', *ExpT* 70, 1958–9, pp. 91f.

Michaelis, W., 'Pastoralbriefe und Wortstatistik', *ZNW* 28, 1929, pp. 69f.

—, '*aoratos*', *TDNT* 5, pp. 368–70.

—, '*homologoumenōs*', *TDNT* 5, p. 213.

Moody, D., 'A New Chronology for the Life and Letters of Paul', *Perspectives in Religious Studies* 3, 1976, pp. 248–71.

Mott, S. C., 'Greek Ethics and Christian Conversion: The Philonic Background of Titus 2.10–14 and 3.3–7', *NovTest* 20, 1978, pp. 22–48.

Moule, C. F. D., 'The Problem of the Pastoral Epistles', *BJRL* 47, 1965, pp. 430–52.

Moulton. H. K., 'Scripture Quotations in the Pastoral Epistles', *ExpT* 49, 1937–8, p. 94.

Odeberg, H., '*Iannēs, Iambrēs*', *TDNT* 3, pp. 192f.

Oepke, A., '*henos andros gynē*', *TDNT* 1, p. 788.

—, '*mesitēs*', *TDNT* 4, pp. 598–624.

Oke, G. C., 'A Doxology not to God but to Christ', *ExpT* 67 (1956), pp. 367–8.

Pherigo, L. P., 'Paul's Life after the Close of Acts', *JBL* 70, 1951, pp. 277f.

Quinn, J. D., 'P^{46} – The Pauline Canon', *CBQ* 36, 1974, pp. 379–85.

Reicke, B., 'Les deux fragments grecs onciaux de 1 Tim. appelés 061 publiés', *CN* 11, 1947, pp. 196–206.

—, 'Chronologie der Pastoralbriefe', *ThL* 101, 1976, pp. 81–94.

Roberts, J. W., 'Note on the Adjective after *pas* in 2 Timothy 3. 16', *ExpT* 76, 1964–5, p. 359.

Sand, A., 'Witwenstand und Ämterstrukturen in den urchristlichen Gemeinden', *Bibel und Leben*, March 1971, pp. 186–97.

—, 'Anfänge einer Koordinierung verschiedenen Gemeindeordnung nach den Pastoralbriefen', in Hainz, J. (ed.), *Kirche im Werden*, Munich/Paderborn/Vienna, 1976, pp. 215–37.

Saucy, R. C., 'Husband of One Wife', *BibSac* 131, 1974, pp. 229–40.

Schierse, F. J., 'Kennzeichen gesunder und kranker Lehre', *Diakonia* 4, 1973, pp. 176–86.

Schlier, H., 'Die Ordnung der Kirche nach den Pastoralbriefen', in Kertelge, K., (ed.), *Das kirchliche Amt im Neuen Testament*, Darmstadt, 1977, pp. 478f.

Schweizer, E., '*theopneustos*', *TDNT* 6, pp. 453–5.

Sesboué, B., 'Ministères et Structures de l'Église', in Delorme, J. (ed.), *Le Ministère et les Ministères selon le Nouveau Testament*, Paris, 1974, pp. 380f.

Skeat, T. C., ' "Especially the Parchments": A Note on 2 Tim. 4.13', *JTS* (ns) 30, 1979, pp. 173–7.

Stauffer, E., 'Eine Bemerkung zum griechischen Danieltext', in Bammel, E., *et al.* (eds), *Donum Gentilicum*, Oxford, 1978, pp. 26–39.

Stenger, W., 'Der Christushymnus in 1 Tim. 3.16', *TTZ* 78, 1964, pp. 133–48.

—, 'Timotheus und Titus als literarische Gestalten', *Kairos* 16, 1974, pp. 252–67.

—, 'Textkritik als Schicksal', *BZ* 19, 1975, pp. 204–7.

Strobel, A., 'Schreiben des Lukas? Zum sprachlichen Problem der Pastoralbriefe', *NTS* 15, 1968–9, pp. 191–210.

Synge, F. C., 'Studies in Texts: 1 Timothy 5. 3–16', *Theology* 68, 1965, pp. 200f.

Thornton, T. C. G., 'Satan – God's Agent for Punishing', *ExpT* 83, pp. 151f.

Trummer, P., 'Einehe nach den Pastoralbriefen', *Bib* 51, 1970, pp. 471–84.

—, 'Mantel und Schriften (II Tim. 4.13)', *BZ* 18, 1974, pp. 193–207.

Wake, W. C., 'The Authenticity of the Pastoral Epistles', *Hibbert Journal* 47, 1948–9, pp. 50f.

Windisch, H., 'Zur Christologie der Pastoralbriefe', *ZNW* 34, 1935, pp. 213f.

Zeisel, W. *See* Lightman, M., *above*.

INTRODUCTION

1. AUTHORSHIP

The three letters which comprise the Pastoral Epistles have always stood together as a group on their own. The name 'Pastoral Epistles' seems to have been given them by German scholars in the course of the eighteenth century. But it was not until early in the nineteenth century that *NT* experts began to question the Pauline authorship. Ever since then the problem of their authorship has been hotly debated. It remains the key issue in our understanding of them today. It can safely be said that everyone who attempts a commentary on them must begin by making his position on this question clear, because what he believes about their authorship will condition almost everything else he has to say about them.

Why is there any question about Pauline authorship? They all claim to be written by Paul; they are addressed to two known historical associates of Paul in his work. They mention persons and incidents which we know from Acts and from the undisputed Pauline letters to have been real people and events. The difficulty consists in the differences which we can detect in the Pastorals when we compare them either with the acknowledged Pauline letters (Romans, 1 and 2 Corinthians, Galatians, Philippians, 1 Thessalonians, Philemon), or with the letters that are sometimes called Deutero-Pauline, about whose Pauline authorsip there is some doubt (2 Thessalonians, Colossians, Ephesians). These differences can be summed up under four heads:

1. *Vocabulary*

The author of the Pastoral Epistles uses a number of key words and phrases which are not found at all, or hardly ever occur, in the other Paulines; for example, *eusebeia* (and cognates), 'godliness'; *sōphrosunē*, 'modesty'; *theosebeia*, 'piety, religion'; *semnos* (and cognates), 'serious'; *hygiēs* (and cognates), used of Christian teaching in the sense of 'sound'. This group is all the more significant because it is found in contemporary pagan ethical philosophy. Then there is a group of words which the author uses for God, unparalleled (or very nearly so) in the acknowledged Paulines: *dunastēs*, 'sovereign'; *basileus tōn aiōnōn*, 'King of the ages'; *makarios*, 'blessed'; *Sōtēr*, 'saviour', used indiscriminately of God and Christ; and above all his description of Christ apparently as 'our great God' in Tit. 2:13; with this we can also put the word *epiphaneia*, 'epiphany' (and cognates), which the author uses both of Christ's incarnation and of his parousia. We may add two more quite un-Pauline phrases which the author often employs: 'a good (or clear) conscience', and 'the saying is sure'.

Conversely, we can point to a number of key concepts in Pauline theology which are either absent or apparently misunderstood in the Pastorals. The most startling are *huios*, 'son', which the author never uses for Christ; and the total absence of any mention of the cross, even where the author has Christ's passion in mind, as in 1 Tim. 6:13. C. K. Barrett points out that there is a whole series of words of great importance to Paul which never occur in the Pastorals: *euangelizesthai*, 'evangelise'; *eucharistein*, 'give thanks'; *kauchasthai*, 'boast'; *pneumatikos*, 'spiritual'; *sophia*, 'wisdom'; *sōma*, 'body'; *psychē*, 'self, life'. But the author also shows no signs of holding the Pauline concept of the church as the body of Christ, though he does refer to the church, as in 1 Tim. 3:15. Nor does he seem to use the important phrase *en Christō* ('in Christ') in the mystical way that Paul does. He does not show Paul's concern about the position of the law, and in his one reference to it (1 Tim. 1:8f.), he betrays a complete misunderstanding of Paul's doctrine on the subject. In like manner we can cite a number of important Pauline words which the author seems to use in a non-Pauline sense: *agapē*, 'love', the key virtue in Paul, in the Pastorals is just one virtue among others; *charis*, 'grace', seems to be an exterior aid rather than an interior presence; *pistis*, 'faith', tends to mean 'content of faith', a meaning not absent from Paul; *paideuein* means 'teach' in the Pastorals, not 'discipline' as in Paul; and *mystērion*, 'mystery', is used in the Pastorals as a synonym for the Christian faith as a whole, whereas in Paul it means the saving action of God in Christ revealed to faith.

There is also a marked difference of style. The author of the Pastorals writes good *koinē* Greek, but his prose is pedestrian. He has neither the sparkle nor the depth of Paul.

2. *Theological thought*

We have already touched on this when we pointed out that the words used for God and Christ in the Pastorals are often different from what we encounter in Paul. But we can add that in the Pastorals we have no clear indication of the doctrine of Christ's pre-existence; the incarnation is seen in terms of an epiphany rather than as an act of divine humiliation, as in Paul. Again, there is a very strong emphasis in the Pastorals on the civil virtues (editors often call them 'bourgeois') – temperance, common sense, seriousness, integrity about money, modesty, domestic fidelity, respectability. Dornier's verdict seems well justified: 'The style of the moralist has taken the place of the

style of the prophet.' Editors have also observed that the author of
the Pastorals does not argue with his theological opponents as Paul
does. Almost invariably he is content to abuse them. Certainly Paul
can abuse his opponents soundly, but he always accompanies his
abuse with effective and carefully thought-out arguments. We get
nothing like this in the Pastorals.

It should also be noted under this head that the author of the
Pastorals borrows from contemporary popular philosophy in a way
quite alien to Paul: see particularly 1 Tim. 6:6–10, where he reproduces a series of popular philosophical maxims on wealth; or 2 Tim.
3:13, where he uses language of his opponents which seems to be
drawn from the vocabulary of contemporary pagan philosophical polemic; or Tit. 1:12, where he actually quotes a legendary Cretan poet
in order to blacken his adversaries.

3. *Situation*

Though the Pastorals are ostensibly written in Paul's lifetime to two
of his colleagues, the historical situation which they seem to imply
does not easily tally with this. In the first place, the way in which
Timothy and Titus are addressed is not historically plausible. If 1
and 2 Timothy are to be fitted into Paul's life history, it is very
probable that they came late on in that history. 2 Timothy is by way
of being Paul's last will and testament. But Timothy is still addressed
as a young and inexperienced assistant (1 Tim. 4:12). He needs to be
told how to behave in the church (1 Tim. 3:15). He is warned against
'youthful passions' (2 Tim. 2:22); he is told to be temperate in all
things (2 Tim. 2:5). Similarly Titus has to be given the most elementary instructions about selecting clergy for the church in Crete, and
is told to appoint presbyters in every town at the same time as he is
urged to leave Crete and come quickly to Nicopolis (Tit. 1:5, 6f.;
3:12). This does not seem at all the sort of thing the real Paul would
write to old and trusted colleagues. Again, in the churches which the
Pastorals seem to reflect there is already a clearly established clergy:
presbyters and deacons certainly. There are even signs that monepiscopacy has emerged in some places (1 Tim. 3:1f.; Ti. 1:6, 7f.). But
in Paul's day we do not find anything like a fixed institutional clergy.
The only mention of church officers is in Phil. 1:1, where Paul greets
the Philippian church 'with the bishops and deacons'. It is not clear
what this implies, but it cannot be said to be evidence for the existence
of a regular ordained ministry. Another indication that the Pastorals
are post-Pauline is the existence of an order of widows (1 Tim. 5:3–
16), of which there is no sign in the other Paulines.

Next, we should notice that the author of the Pastorals seems to have an attitude towards doctrine that is not Paul's. For him Christian doctrine is a *parathēkē*, 'what has been entrusted to you' (1 Tim. 6:20). This deposit of faith has been delivered by Paul to Timothy and must be in turn handed on by Timothy to trustworthy successors (2 Tim. 1:13–14; 2:2; 3:14). Quite apart from the fact that for a large part of his ministry Paul was expecting the parousia to take place before his death, and therefore would have seen no point in giving these instructions, this is not the way the historical Paul handles Christian doctrine. It is much more like what one would expect in the record of a third generation of the church. It would also seem that the false teaching which the author condemns so vigorously belongs to a somewhat post-Pauline era. This is not a point which can be pushed too far, since there is a distinct resemblance between this false teaching and that which is condemned in Colossians. If Paul wrote Colossians, then the heresy denounced in the Pastorals is not an anachronism for Paul's day. But did he?

Two more points should be made about the difference of situation: first, there seems to be in the Pastorals an underlying consciousness of the challenge of the official cult of the Roman emperor (see Note at Tit. 2:14). The author uses language of God and Christ which he seems to have taken over from the emperor-cult. He is in fact implying that Christ, not Caesar, is the true God. It cannot be said that there is any trace of this in the acknowledged Paulines. Secondly, the Pastorals, though they refer to the parousia several times, do not seem to have any sense of its imminence. On the contrary, the author seems to be reconciled to a church which must be prepared to go on living in history indefinitely; Christians are to pray for their rulers that all may live a quiet and peaceful life (1 Tim. 2:2; Tit. 3:1): the deposit is to be handed on to successors. It is true that in Ephesians the sense of an imminent parousia is also absent; but then we must ask ourselves even more emphatically than in the case of Colossians, did Paul write Ephesians?

4. *Historical information apparently supplied by the Pastorals*

It is almost impossible to fit the apparently historical details which the Pastorals supply about Paul into the sequence of his life as we know it from his acknowledged letters and from Acts. This is not by any means an insuperable difficulty because our knowledge of Paul's life that comes from these two sources is fragmentary, and ends abruptly when Luke brings him to Rome, probably some time in the early years of Nero's reign, saying that 'he lived there two whole years at his own expense . . . teaching about the Lord Jesus openly and unhindered'. It is possible for anyone who wishes to defend the historicity and authenticity of the Pastorals to maintain that most or all of the details which they give about Paul belong to a period after his first imprisonment in Rome; and in fact most scholars who do defend the historicity of the Pastorals maintain that Paul was released after those two years in Rome and enjoyed another period (perhaps up to four years) of missionary activity during which most of the incidents referred to in the Pastorals took place. This theory has its own problems, and is not held by the majority of scholars today; but it is by no means impossible or even implausible. We discuss it in greater detail in a later section. This fourth consideration, therefore, is not so much an obstacle to belief in the authenticity of the Pastorals. It is rather an indication that those who hold to the authenticity of the Pastorals are obliged to make certain assumptions about the later course of Paul's career.

Faced with these difficulties, modern scholars have offered various solutions. We distinguish here four possible theories, indicating why we think each is mistaken or correct.

1. Some scholars still defend the complete authenticity of the Pastorals. Paul, they maintain, wrote every word of them; or at least was as much the author behind them as he was the author behind any of his undisputed letters. They solve the apparent discrepancies by two arguments. First, different circumstances demand different vocabularies. Among the undisputed letters there is none which falls into exactly the same category as do the Pastorals, which are letters addressed to individuals but also intended for churches (thus the undisputed Philemon is said not to afford a true parallel). The Pastorals simply show us the sort of style, technique, and vocabulary which Paul used when he was writing to colleagues in charge of churches. Secondly, much is made of the fact that the Pastorals, if Pauline, are the last of Paul's letters. The Paul who wrote them was an old man, broken by labours and adversity. His very last letter, 2 Timothy, was written in the harsh conditions of a Roman prison. He had lost his fire, he had realised the value of some pagan philosophy, he had given up the imminent expectation of the parousia. All who defend the authenticity of the Pastorals also maintain the authenticity of Ephesians, so they are able to point to the absence of parousia expectation there. The most distinguished modern champions of this viewpoint are D. Guthrie and J. N. D. Kelly in England, B. Reicke in Denmark, and above all the learned Dominican C. Spicq in France, whose vast two-volume commentary is indispensable for anyone who wishes to study the Pastorals in depth (for details about these commentaries, see the list preceding this Introduction). We might also mention S. de Lestapis, *L'Énigme*. He argues for full authenticity, and places the three Pastoral Letters in the period between the writing

of Romans and the end of Paul's two-year captivity in Rome. But he never faces the problem of the difference of vocabulary and outlook from the authentic Paulines as Spicq does.

These arguments do not convince the present writer. A change of correspondent does not account for so radical a change as that between Paul's profound doctrine of life in Christ and the emphasis on piety, good works, and respectability (*semnotēs*) which we find in the Pastorals. If much is made of the alteration which old age brings, we must reply that if Paul wrote the Pastorals he must have been afflicted with approaching senility. And in this respect Ephesians counts against the authenticity of the Pastorals. Ephesians, if it is by Paul, represents a profound and significant development of his thought. The Pastorals would imply not a development but a deterioration. It is as if someone were to argue that W. B. Yeats, having developed from the poems of the Celtic twilight to the difficult and profound Byzantium poems, ended by writing the poetry of John Betjeman. However much we admire Betjeman, we do not naturally put his work in the same class as that of Yeats.

2. A more popular way of retaining a connection between Paul and the Pastorals is adopted by those who defend the secretary hypothesis. These scholars argue that the Pastorals were not written directly by Paul, but contain Pauline material which has been shaped and expressed by one of Paul's assistants acting as his secretary. Thus the un-Pauline elements can be attributed to the secretary, and anything that seems Pauline, including the apparently historical material, can be attributed to Paul. It is pointed out that Paul certainly used an amanuensis who actually wrote his letters at his dictation. We know the name of one, Tertius, who wrote down Romans (Rom. 16:22; cf. Gal. 6:11; 2 Th. 3:17). Evidence can be brought to show that ancient writers frequently used secretaries for their letters, often allowing them considerable licence in composition (Roller, pp. 17–18). Also, in the case of 2 Timothy, which, if it was written by Paul, was written from strict confinement, we can say that Paul must have given wide powers to a secretary, since he could not have dictated a letter word for word from a Roman gaol. The suggestion is therefore that Paul handed over to a secretary (not necessarily the same man in each case) the task of drafting the letters, contenting himself with telling him what he wanted said, and perhaps looking over the completed work and inserting one or two finishing touches. The most distinguished modern defender of this hypothesis is J. Jeremias; but it was earlier defended by Roller in the work already alluded to, and has more recently been taken up by W. Metzger in Germany in his book *Die letzte Reise des Apostel Paulus* (1976) and by C. F. D. Moule

(though very tentatively) in England. See his article 'The Problem of the Pastoral Epistles: a Reappraisal', in *BJRL* 47 (1965), pp. 450–2.

Most defenders of this theory do not feel obliged to try to guess the identity of the secretary, but some of them have done so. Thus Jeremias thinks he may very well be Tychicus. There is a certain group however who favour Luke. The claims of Luke are strongly urged by Moule, and also by Strobel, who really belongs to the next group of scholars. The difference between Moule and Strobel is that Moule believes Luke acted as Paul's secretary during Paul's lifetime. Strobel thinks he edited Paul after Paul's death. The argument in favour of Luke is largely built on similarities of vocabulary, particularly striking in the case of Ac. 20:18–35 in comparison with 2 Tim. 4:6–8. Compare also 2 Tim. 4:11.

There would seem however to be two very strong objections to the suggestion that Luke wrote, or edited, the Pastorals (quite apart from the general objections to the secretary hypothesis, which we outline immediately below). If there is one thing about Paul that the Pastoral Epistles emphasise, it is his apostleship. But Luke in Acts only once describes him as an apostle and does not rank him with the Twelve (see Ac. 14:4, where Paul and Barnabas are referred to as 'the apostles'). The second objection is well expressed by E. Haenchen in his commentary on Acts. Throughout Acts Luke portrays Paul as a great worker of miracles. But the Paul of the Pastorals makes no allusion to this and claims no such power (thereby actually differing from the historical Paul; see Rom. 15:18–19).

There has recently been published a careful and scholarly attempt to prove the Lucan authorship of the Pastorals by S. G. Wilson (*Luke and the Pastoral Epistles*, 1979). Wilson puts forward the theory that Luke wrote the Pastorals after completing Acts, on the basis of certain 'travel notes' written by Paul which he found, and also by the help of reading certain of Paul's epistles, such as Romans, which he had not read when he wrote Acts. Thus Wilson undertakes the formidable task of combining the Lucan hypothesis with the fragments hypothesis.

I do not find the argument convincing, despite Dr Wilson's moderate and orderly way of setting it forth. In the first place, he never explains that ambiguous phrase 'travel notes' (p. 4). What are they? They seem to have reached Luke undated and unplaced, for on p. 131 he conjectures that 2 Tim. 4:9f., is a genuinely Pauline 'travel note' issued from prison in Caesarea which Luke mistakenly assigned to the Roman imprisonment. This seems to me about the least satisfactory form of the fragments hypothesis that one could imagine.

Next, Wilson's theory requires that Luke wrote first his Gospel, perhaps before AD 85 (see p. 140), then Acts in 85–95, then the

Pastorals in 90–95 (Wilson emphasises that these dates are only guesses). But in that case Luke may very well have known the historical Timothy, or at least lived at a time when oral tradition about him would be fresh and abundant (we see no reason to reject the authenticity of the reference in Heb. 13:23, which must be put at the earliest after AD 70). Can we really imagine Luke writing imaginary letters to a man whom he had known himself? It seems unlikely. Again, two incidents at least which Wilson regards as historical are mentioned in the Pastorals but not in Acts – Timothy's ordination by Paul (2 Tim. 1:6) and Titus' missionary visit to Crete. Why did Luke not mention them in Acts? Wilson's explanation that Luke learned about them only after writing Acts seems contrived.

One could think of other difficulties about Wilson's theory. It seems to me that the rather simple, rule-of-thumb composition of the Pastorals (which we discuss in section 8) is hardly compatible with Luke's highly sophisticated technique of literary composition. In other words, if Luke had intended to write three letters ostensibly in Paul's name he would have made a better hand at it. Nor do I think that Wilson has adequately explained the fact that Luke does have, among other elements in his christology, the concept of Jesus as Son of God, whereas there is no sign whatever of this in the Pastorals. Conversely, epiphany christology is prominent in the Pastorals but absent from Luke-Acts. In short, it seems to me that the most satisfactory way of accounting for the parallels that undoubtedly do exist between Luke-Acts and the Pastorals is to assume that the author of the Pastorals had read Acts (and perhaps Luke's Gospel also), rather than to assume an identity of authorship. J. Rohde (p. 79) actually suggests that the author of the Pastorals did not know Acts, but simply knew something of the tradition about Paul which Luke utilised.

But there are grave difficulties facing the secretary hypothesis. In the first place, how much should be attributed to the secretary? Those who adopt the theory at all thereby admit that there is some material in the Pastorals which Paul could not have written. The more you attribute to the secretary, the less Pauline they are. Most versions of the secretary theory end by representing the Pastorals as much more the work of the secretary than of Paul, thereby largely defeating the purpose of the theory, which was to defend Pauline authorship. Are we to envisage a secretary who wrote largely on his own initiative what he thought Paul would have said? But this is in effect to admit pseudonymity. Or are we asked to believe that Paul could have approved of the contents of the Pastorals?

Another objection to this theory is that it works much better for 2 Timothy than for the other two letters. We can understand why

Paul would have difficulties in writing a letter personally from his last imprisonment, but we have no particular reason for thinking that Paul was in any such difficulties when he wrote 1 Timothy and Titus (if he wrote them). Both Moule and Metzger betray the weakness of their case by suggesting that Paul used a secretary to indite a letter to Titus because he was too busy to write one himself. But why was he any busier then than when he wrote his undoubted letters, when, as he tells us himself, he experienced 'the daily pressure upon me of my anxiety for all the churches' (2 C. 11:28)? The secretary hypothesis raises as many problems as it solves.

3. A third theory is really a variant of the second one, but requires a category of its own: it is the 'Fragments Hypothesis'. According to this theory, an early Christian editor found himself in possession of a number of genuinely Pauline fragments at some period after Paul's death, and published them in the form of three letters, arranging them as if they were genuine Pauline letters, and fitting the fragments into material of his own composition suitable for conditions in his own day. The great champion of this view is P. N. Harrison, whose book *The Problem of the Pastoral Epistles* (Oxford, 1921) marked a milestone in the course of critical study of the Pastorals. On the basis of a very careful and scholarly study of the vocabulary of all the epistles in the Pauline Corpus, he came to the conclusion that the Pastorals were indeed pseudonymous, but that they enshrined a small number of genuinely Pauline fragments, most of them to be found in 2 Timothy (he subsequently modified the list of passages he selected in this book, but that need not concern us). The defenders of this theory can point to the small fragments or interpolations which some scholars have claimed to find in Paul's acknowledged letters, e.g. 2 C. 6:14–7:1, which some editors have described as a completely alien fragment accidentally inserted into 2 Corinthians. Or confirmation for this theory could be found in the way in which Philippians has been divided up into a number of brief epistles by some editors. In the same way, it could be argued, a series of Pauline fragments survived for perhaps a generation after Paul's death and were then incorporated by a later disciple into what we know as the Pastoral Epistles. The chief modern champions of this view are R. Falconer in England, as long ago as 1937, and A. Strobel (*NTS* 15 [1969], pp. 191–210) and G. Holtz in Germany, and P. Dornier in France. Dornier and Holtz believe that the editor of the Pauline fragments had been an actual disciple of Paul, and so are very often able in their commentaries to write as if the author of the Pastorals was Paul himself.

I myself maintained this view in my *Cambridge Bible Commentary* on the Pastorals in 1966, but I have subsequently come to abandon

it. The great difficulty with it consists in explaining how such small
fragments of Pauline material could have survived. Those parts of the
Pastorals which have seemed most Pauline to editors (e.g. 2 Tim.
1:15–18; 4:6–22; Tit. 3:12–14 – the passages which I characterised as
Pauline in my commentary) do not constitute in themselves anything
that could be a letter on its own. In what sort of circumstances could
they have survived? Paul presumably did not send picture postcards
to his friends during his travels! The parallel with 2 Corinthians or
Philippians is not very cogent: the small fragments into which these
epistles are divided by some scholars do nevertheless form quite
plausible letters in themselves. In any case there is nothing like a
consensus among scholars about how 2 Corinthians or Philippians is
to be divided, and many would still hold that there is no need to
divide them at all. It looks as if the 'Fragments Hypothesis' was a
last desperate attempt to retain some Pauline element in the Pastorals.

4. We are left therefore with the fourth solution to the problem of
authorship. The Pastorals have no authentically Pauline elements in
them at all. They are wholly pseudonymous, and were composed by
a writer subsequent to Paul's day who wished to claim Paul's authority
for his material. But this solution leaves open a wide variety of
options. One can hold any view, from the suggestion that the author
was well acquainted with Paul, who had only recently been put to
death, to the theory that the Pastorals are by a comtemporary of
Marcion, who flourished in Rome about AD 140. We shall be attempting to be more precise about the dating in the next section. The most
distinguished modern commentators who defend this fourth view are
in Germany, M. Dibelius and H. Conzelmann (3rd, edn, 1955), and
N. Brox (1969); in Switzerland, V. Hasler (1978); in America, B. S.
Easton (1944) and F. D. Gealy (*Interpreter's Bible*, 1955), and in
Britain, A. J. B. Higgins (*Peake's Bible*, 1962), C. K. Barrett (1963)
and J. H. Houlden (1976). This is the view which is adopted in this
commentary.

2. DATING AND PROVENANCE

We may begin with attestation, starting from the most remote certain
quotations and moving backwards in time. The Muratorian Canon,
which scholars date at the end of the second century AD, states:
  He [Paul] wrote, besides these, one to Philemon, one to Titus,
  and two to Timothy. These were written in personal affection;
  but they have been hallowed by being held in honour by the
  Catholic church for the regulation of church discipline.
One of the early apologists, Athenagoras (wrote AD 177–180) certainly

quotes 1 Tim. 2:2, 'that we may lead a quiet and peacable life'. About
the year AD 160 a certain presbyter of Asia Minor forged a document
which he called *The Acts of Paul*. In these apocryphal *Acts* he introduces various characters who occur only in the Pastorals, such as
Onesiphorus and Hermogenes. Moreover, he represents Demas as
Paul's treacherous enemy; but Demas appears in Col. 4:14 and Phm.
24 as well as in 2 Tim. 4:10, and only in the Pastorals is Demas
presented in a bad light. We must conclude that the author of the
Acts of Paul knew the Pastorals. It seems very likely that Polycarp,
bishop of Smyrna, in his *Letter to the Philippians* 4:1, quotes 1 Tim.
6:10: 'for the love of money is the root of all evils' (Polycarp says
'beginning of all evils'), and 1 Tim. 6:7 'for we brought nothing into
the world and we cannot take anything out of the world'; and in 9:2
he writes of the martyrs, 'for they did not love the present world',
the same phrase as is used of Demas in 2 Tim. 4:10. Some editors
(e.g. Brox) have denied that these quotations prove that Polycarp
knew the Pastorals, since he is only quoting popular philosophical
maxims which he could have derived from the same source as did the
author of the Pastorals; but the similarity of language in all three
passages seems too close to be explained away thus. We must note
however that this brings us down only to about AD 135, since P. N.
Harrison's suggestion that the part of Polycarp's letter which contains
these quotations dates from about then has been widely accepted.

Attempts have been made to show that some early writers rejected
the Pauline authorship of the Pastorals or did not know of them.
Thus Tatian, who founded a heretical sect in Syria on his return from
Rome *c.* AD 172, seems to have rejected 1 and 2 Timothy but accepted
Titus. And Tertullian tells us that Marcion did not accept the Pastorals. But we do not know the precise grounds on which these
writers rejected the Pastorals, and can therefore draw no relevant
conclusions from this. Some play has also been made with the evidence of a fragmentary papyrus MS of the NT, P⁴⁶, which is to be
dated about AD 200. It does not contain the Pastorals – but it does
not contain Philemon either, and J. D. Quinn (*CBQ* 36 [1974], pp.
379–85) has recently argued very effectively that the omission of the
Pastorals and Philemon was deliberate: the MS originally held a collection of Paul's public letters, and never was intended to include his
letters to individuals.

By comparing the Pastorals with the letters of Ignatius of Antioch
we can push the *terminus ante quem* still farther back. In Ignatius'
letters we find that persecution of the church by the Roman authorities is in full swing. Ignatius is travelling as a prisoner from Syria to
Rome, where he expects to be thrown to the beasts. His letters are
full of his approaching martyrdom. But there is no trace of such

persecution in the Pastorals. On the other hand we do find in the Pastorals traces of the emergence of monepiscopacy (evidence will be given in a later section). Now in Ignatius the monepiscopal system seems to be established everywhere in Asia Minor, but to be in need of defence, perhaps because it is a relatively new institution. This would all suggest a date for the Pastorals which is before Ignatius' letters, but not very long before them. S. L. Davies (*VC* 30 [1976], pp. 174–80) has recently argued that Ignatius' arrival in Rome is to be dated AD 113. This is because he must have been sent by the legate of Syria with the recommendation of *damnatio ad bestias* for the emperor's own decision. Trajan was still in Rome in 113, but after that left the capital never to return. She points out that in 112 Pliny as governor of Bithynia suddenly woke up to the fact that the population should be compelled to observe the imperial cult more strictly, and she brings some late evidence to indicate that in 112 Trajan instituted a renewal of the imperial cult throughout the empire. On the other hand, A. Garzetti (*From Tiberius*) suggests that immediately after the murder of Domitian in AD 96, the new regime would by reaction from his severity be less inclined to harry those who had leanings towards either Judaism or Christianity. All this would point towards a date for the composition of the Pastorals between 96 and 110, with perhaps a likelihood of 100–105 being the correct date. We want a period in which persecution was not an immediate threat, but when the emperor-cult was very much in evidence as a source of potential trouble in Christians. As we have seen, this cult does seem to be reflected in the Pastorals in the form of imperial titles which are claimed for Christ.

A *terminus post quem* for the composition of the Pastorals is provided by the fact that the author apparently knew the book of Acts. This is the opinion of Brox (p. 72); it is confirmed by the close agreement of wording between Ac. 20:17–38 and 2 Tim. 4:6–8. We can also point to 2 Tim. 3:11, and the occasional similarities of wording between the two works of which those who defend the theory of Lucan authorship of the Pastorals have made so much. If we put Acts in the 90s, this gives us a very suitable *terminus post quem*. This conclusion carries with it the implication that H. von Campenhausen and W. Bauer were mistaken in putting the Pastorals as late as the time of Marcion, and in attributing the authorship to Polycarp. D–C argue effectively that Polycarp does not need to write in Paul's name, since in his extant letter he quotes Paul directly, and that his style is different from that of the Pastorals. Brox adds that Polycarp did not need to borrow Paul's authority; he could speak *in propria persona* and command a hearing. We may add that 2 Tim. 3:16 is hardly suitable as an answer to Marcionism: it claims that every passage in

Scripture (i.e. the OT) is inspired. This might be valid against someone who took exception to certain passages in the OT, but not against Marcion, who held that the whole OT must be rejected. F. A. Gealy follows von Campenhausen in putting the Pastorals at AD 135–150, but he does not bring any fresh evidence.

All the evidence for the provenance of the Pastorals is internal. They must be written to a group of Pauline churches, We know that it was in Asia Minor that monepiscopacy first evolved, and large parts of Asia Minor were Paul's mission field. Most scholars therefore conclude that the Pastorals were written in Asia Minor, perhaps specifically in Ephesus.

3. HISTORICAL ELEMENTS IN THE PASTORALS

Those who accept the view that the Pastorals are pseudonymous and do not contain any material written by Paul must attempt to answer one question: What are we to make of the apparently historical references that are scattered through the letters? The problem is most acute when we are faced not with references to persons and events which the author could have learned from the acknowledged Paulines and Acts (e.g. 2 Tim. 2:11; 4:11–12), but with people who are mentioned nowhere else in the records and with events for which we have no other evidence in the first century, e.g. Titus' being in Crete; Paul having left his belongings in Troas (2 Tim. 4:13); Onesiphorus' courageous conduct (2 Tim. 1:16). There are in fact only two alternatives as far as this material is concerned: either we say it is all fictional, invented by the author of the Pastorals to give verisimilitude to his narrative; or we admit that some of it may be genuine historical tradition. As a matter of fact very few scholars adopt the first alternative absolutely. For example, D–C (pp. 94f., 107), C. K. Barrett, and N. Brox, all say that some of the material may preserve historical tradition, though they make little or no attempt to distinguish which. However, P. Trummer and V. Hasler regard all the apparently historical material as fictional. Since only Trummer makes any effort to explain why the fiction took the form it did, we may restrict our study to him.

Trummer's examination of the most relevant material is found in his article 'Mantel und Schriften' (*BZ* 18 [1974] pp. 193–207), though his arguments are repeated in his book *Die Paulustradition* (pp. 81f.) In the article he confines himself mostly to one important passage; but it is sufficient to give a good idea of his methods. Trummer thinks that 1 Tim. 1:16 gives us in one phrase the motive behind the invention of all these details: 'for an example to those who were to believe in him'. Thus all the apparently historical details are invented in order to provide a model of how church leaders should live. The request for the cloak, therefore, in 2 Tim. 4:13 is to be regarded as showing how careful Paul was not to buy more clothes than were absolutely necessary. He refers to 1 Tim. 6:8: 'If we have food and clothing, with these we shall be content', and also compares Paul's speech in Ac. 22:33: 'I coveted no one's silver or gold or apparel'. He adds that in any case the apparent circumstances in which this request was made are historically unconvincing. In view of his coming martyrdom Paul would not have had time to receive these goods.

We may take this last point first. In order to defend the historical plausibility of 2 Tim. 4:13 one does not have to argue that it is consistent with 4:6–8. All that we maintain is that the author knew some genuine historical details about Paul's life. We do not need to defend the sequence in which he put them together. 2 Tim. 4:6–8 shows that the author knew that Paul had died as a martyr, and 4:13 suggests that he had access to the tradition of someone (Carpus) with whom Paul once stayed in Troas. De Lestapis' suggestion (*L'Énigme*, p. 236) that Paul had left the cloak (and parchments) in Troas during the visit described in Ac. 20:7–12, hoping to retrieve them on his journey to Rome, is as plausible as any. As for the suggestion that the request for the cloak is intended to show that Paul was content with the barest minimum of clothes, is this not crediting the author with a subtlety which he is very far from betraying in the rest of his work? If he had wanted to make this point, would it not have been more effective to make Paul write: 'Do not concern yourself about the cloak; I can do without it'?

This objection to Trummer's line of argument is even stronger when we examine the way in which he explains the request in the same verse for 'the books, and above all the parchments'. This, says Trummer, referring to 2 Tim. 3:15–17, is to show that the church leader must always have the Scriptures by him and must prize them highly. But here surely Trummer is representing the author as being altogether too subtle: he does not even mention the Scriptures! We are to infer that the books and parchments mean the holy Scriptures. In any case, to represent Paul as leaving his Bible, or part of it, behind in Troas is hardly an indication that Paul was a keen student of the Bible, still less that it was his inseparable companion! We must conclude that Trummer's explanation of why these details are fictional is even more unconvincing than the attempts of some scholars to reconstruct an account of Paul's life that will harmonise all the details given in the Pastoral Epistles.

We conclude, therefore, that we cannot *a priori* rub out all apparent historical references in the Pastorals as fictional, any more than we can *a priori* declare them all to be genuine. We might well consider in this context the strong contrast which scholars have often underlined between the picture of Paul's life and activity given in the Pastorals and that given in the apocryphal *Acts*. An excellent example of this last class is the *Acts of Paul*, an apocryphal account of Paul's activities forged about the year 160 by a presbyter of Asia Minor, who subsequently confessed his offence and was degraded for it. In this work Paul pursues a triumphant career of miracle-working, blasting his opponents and rescuing his friends, only interrupted by a series of uninspiring homilies which the apostle delivers on various occasions. We can say with confidence that the atmosphere of the Pastorals is totally unlike that of the later apocryphal stories of Paul. We might also suggest that there is a certain parallel to be seen between the way in which the Gospel material about the life of Jesus was preserved and the way in which some details of the life of Paul seem to have been preserved in the Pastorals. In each case we have an interval of about forty years during which the material circulates in oral form before being written down, and in each case the person who writes it down seems to have no clear tradition about the exact order in which most of the events took place, or the context, and has to provide his own.

If then some of the apparently historical details may be genuine, how are we to know which they are, and do they tell us anything of value about Paul's life? Some of them obviously are incapable of being dated, like the exhortation that Timothy should not refrain from wine (1 Tim. 5:23), and probably the request for the forwarding of Paul's belongings (2 Tim. 4:13). But some of them have implications for Paul's life-history, such as the alleged connection with Crete in Tit. 1, Onesiphorus' visit to Paul in prison in Rome, Demas' desertion, and Paul's own martyrdom (2 Tim. 1:16; 4:6–10). We shall confine ourselves deliberately to those details which could not be learned from the other Paulines or from Acts, since it is plain that the author was well acquainted with all these documents.

We may begin by laying down the guiding principle that, if any of the more important details are historical, such as those referred to immediately above, then we must assume two imprisonments in Rome. It is true that some scholars have undertaken the heroic task of attempting to fit all the historical references in the Pastorals into the period of Paul's life narrated in Acts. Such a one is H. Binder ('Die historische Situation', pp. 70–83). But the effort involves some truly desperate expedients, such as the assumption that the Cenchreae of Rom. 16:1 and Ac. 18:18 was not the well-known port on the isthmus of Corinth, but a small port near Troas, first mentioned in the 5th century AD; and the even more desperate suggestion that the

phrase describing Demas in 2 Tim. 4:10 should be translated: 'Demas, out of his great love for (the salvation of) the world has left me
(in order to devote himself to the task of evangelism).' This is because
Demas is mentioned not unfavourably in Col. 4:14, which Binder
believes was written after 2 Tim. 4:10. He ignores the fact that both
Polycarp and the author of the *Acts of Paul* understood the phrase in
an unfavourable sense. We need not, therefore, concern ourselves
any more with the possibility that the references in the Pastorals are
compatible with only one Roman imprisonment. It is significant that
N. Brox (p. 29), who does not attempt either to evaluate historically
or to date any of the references to Paul in the Pastorals, nevertheless
concludes that it is very likely that Paul was freed after the two years'
light confinement described in Ac. 28:30.

It must be said that the theory of two Roman imprisonments is not
supported by most scholars today. This may well be because the bulk
of scholarly opinion is now on the side of the view that the Pastorals
are pseudonymous, and with this view goes the natural (but by no
means necessary) assumption that all the apparently historical details
which they supply are fictional. On the other hand, there is nothing
like an agreed dating for the events of Paul's life. The one and only
universally agreed date is the year of Gallio's office as proconsul of
Achaea, AD May 51 to May 52. Other relevant dates are the Neronian
persecution, AD 64–65, and the end of Nero's reign, AD 68. Within
these limits scholars have suggested date-sequences for Paul's life
which differ widely. Thus B. Rigaux (*Saint Paul et ses Lettres*, p. 137)
brings Paul to Rome in February 61, allows him a release from his
first imprisonment from 63 to 66/7, and puts his martyrdom at 67.
E. Haenchen (Commentary, p. 71) brings Paul to Rome in 56, and
believes that after a two-year period of light confinement he was tried,
condemned, and executed in 58. C. K. Barrett (NTS 20 [1973–4],
pp. 229–45) follows a very similar time-table, allowing no second
imprisonment, and suggesting that Paul was executed in 58 or 59. G.
Ogg (*The Chronology of the Life of Paul*, pp. 175–84) agrees that there
was no second imprisonment, but brings Paul to Rome much later
than the two scholars we have first mentioned, in March 62. Two
years later, he believes, Paul was tried, condemned and executed. F.
F. Bruce (*Paul, Apostle of the Free Spirit*, pp. 440f.) inclines to think
that there were two Roman imprisonments; he brings Paul to Rome
in 60. This scheme has the merit of associating Paul's death with the
Neronian persecution. It should be noted that none of these scholars
relies on the evidence of the Pastorals to support his case.

Recently a new and important attempt has been made to fix the
dates of Paul's life. This is R. Jewett's book, *Dating Paul's Life*
(London, 1979). Jewett vigorously and convincingly pursues the

methodology of treating Acts as a secondary witness and giving primary attention to the witness of the acknowledged Paulines. He therefore postulates only three visits by Paul to Jerusalem (as recorded in Paul's letters), not five, as in Acts. He rightly insists that any scientific treatment of the subject must observe certain facts: the pivotal dates, such as AD 37 for the Aretas incident, 51–52 for Gallio's procuratorship, and an arrival in Rome by Paul not later than 61 (after that there were two city prefects, not one, as indicated in the Western Text of Ac. 28:16). He also insists with equal justification that we must allow a full seventeen years between Paul's conversion and his second visit to Jerusalem, as Paul relates in Galatians. A further admirable point he makes is that the long missionary journey from Jerusalem via Asia Minor and northern Greece, to Corinth could not have taken less than three years. We must observe, however, how many of his pivotal dates come from his secondary source. He therefore suggests the following dating: the crucifixion, AD 33; Paul's conversion, 34; the Aretas incident, 37; Paul appears before Gallio, July 51; the apostolic council in Jerusalem, October 51; Paul's arrest in Jerusalem, 57; Felix is replaced by Festus, 59; Paul arrives in Rome, February–March 60; Paul's execution in Rome, 62. Unfortunately he arbitrarily excludes all possible historical evidence from pseudonymous writers apparently just because they are pseudonymous, thereby excluding not only the evidence of the Pastorals but also that of Colossians and Ephesians. One might with equal justification refuse to look for any historical references in the eleventh chapter of the book of Daniel, on the grounds that the chapter was pseudonymous.

He does however produce some positive evidence to shew that Paul was executed in 62. He writes (p. 45): 'A consideration of the redactional evidence suggests that Luke intended to conclude his work on the most positive note he could find, and that the prediction of martyrdom he included in the farewell speech to the Ephesian elders (Ac. 20:24, 38) was intended to indicate what occurred at the end of the two years period.' As additional evidence he points out that the law of *maiestas* (treason) was revived in 62, and that Nero married Poppaea, a Jewess, who might be regarded as an anti-Christian influence, in the same year. But he indicates in a footnote that this last argument is not necessarily supported by the historical evidence. It still seems to me incredible that Luke would have ended a work, which was in part at least an apologia for Christianity to the Roman authorities, just at the point where Paul by due process of law administered by these authorities was put to death on a totally baseless charge.

The great difficulty in deciding whether Paul underwent two trials in Rome lies in the paucity of evidence. Defenders of both views (one trial or two trials) have appealed to the end of Acts to support their case. Assuming that the publication of Acts must be put late in the first century, it does not seem very likely that Luke would bring Paul to Rome and declare that he taught unhindered for two years, if his readers knew perfectly well that at the end of the two years he was unjustly condemned and executed by due process of Roman justice (this is however a conclusion which S. G. Wilson [p. 113] is prepared to accept in the interests of his theory of Lucan authorship of the Pastorals). One of Luke's aims in Acts is to show that Christianity is not a threat to the Roman empire, and that the Roman authorities did not regard Paul as a malefactor. If Paul was actually put to death in the wake of the Neronian persecution which took place in AD 64, that would not injure Luke's case. As R. P. C. Hanson puts it in his commentary on Acts.

> A death under a trumped-up accusation of arson as a result of a despotic emperor's cruelty is very different from death at the end of a trial provoked by the appeal of the accused himself on a perfectly serious charge of provoking a riot. By the time that Luke was writing Acts, Nero had died an ignominious death, outlawed by the Roman Senate . . . To have been put to death by Nero in such circumstances would have seemed no disgrace to many of the educated and sophisticated people . . . for whom Luke was writing.

Indeed the same would apply to anyone executed on a political charge in the latter years of Nero's reign. One might indeed reasonably ask, if Paul at his first trial in Rome was acquitted, why did Luke not say so? It would have supported his argument admirably. We can only answer that possibly he assumed that his readers knew this already. His intention in writing Acts was fulfilled when he had brought Paul to Rome.

If then we may allow the possibility that Paul did enjoy a period of freedom between his first imprisonment in Rome and his second, can we say anything about how he used it? The claim is often made that the first person to mention two imprisonments for Paul in Rome is Eusebius in the fourth century AD. It is true that Eusebius is the first person explicitly to mention two imprisonments, but anyone who holds that Paul carried out his intention, mentioned in Rom. 15:24, to visit Spain must believe in his imprisonments in Rome, and there is much earlier evidence for this belief. The Muratorian Canon at the end of the second century believes that Paul made a journey from Rome to Spain. Likewise an apocryphal document called the *Acts of Peter*, composed in Asia Minor between 150 and 200, represents Paul as visiting Spain. It is even possible that an earlier witness still,

Clement of Rome, held this view. In his letter to the church of
Corinth (*1 Clem.* 5:7) he describes Paul as 'having taught righteousness to the whole world' and as 'having come to the goal of the West'.
His phrase in Greek, *to terma tēs duseōs*, is ambiguous, and could be
construed as referring to Rome itself, 'the goal [of all activity in the
empire] lying in the west [from the point of view of an oriental like
Paul]'. It is true that Ignatius uses language like this specifically
referring to Rome in his *Epistle to the Romans* 3:2: 'May God think
the bishop of Syria worthy of being found in the west, having been
sent for from the east!' But Ignatius was writing in Asia Minor
contemplating a journey westwards to Rome. From the point of view
of someone resident in Rome 'the goal (or end) of the west' would
more naturally refer to Spain, especially as Clement has just described
Paul as preaching to the whole world. Both G. Holtz (p. 18) and N.
Brox (p. 30) believe that Clement means that Paul visited Spain.

But both these scholars put some emphasis on the value of Clement's evidence because it is so early: in company with almost the
whole of the scholarly world they date Clement's letter at *c.* AD 96.
This however is a view which is open to criticism. Two recent articles
have appeared which, apparently quite independently of each other,
have argued that the Clement who wrote on behalf of the church of
Rome to the church of Corinth should be dissociated from the events
connected with the execution of T. Flavius Clemens in AD 95 by
Domitian (P. Keresztes, *VC* 27 [1973], pp. 1–28; A. A. Bell, *NTS*
25 [1978–9], pp. 93–102. But we should note that neither of these
scholars suggests any but the traditional date for Clement.) Compare
also Garzetti, p. 293, where he regards the claim that Flavius Clemens
became a Christian as legendary. If Clement of Rome is thus dissociated from the T. Flavius Clemens affair, he will fit more naturally
into some such date as AD 120, in view of the reference to him in the
Shepherd of Hermas (*Vis.* II.4.3). It should be noted that we are not
necessarily arguing in favour of the view that Paul did visit Spain.
The author of the Pastorals certainly shows no sign of knowing of
such a visit. We are claiming, however, that the belief that Paul was
released after his first imprisonment in Rome can probably be traced
back as early as about AD 120. It seems very likely indeed that this
belief was also held by the author of the Pastorals.

One more objection to the 'two imprisonments in Rome' theory
must be considered. In Ac. 20:25, 38 Paul is represented as telling
the elders of the Ephesian church that he knew they would not see
his face again. We must assume that the author of the Pastorals had
read these words. Does not this imply that Luke did not believe in
any renewed missionary activity on Paul's part in Asia Minor after
his first imprisonment in Rome? And must we not assumed that our

author must have believed this also? This is a formidable objection, but not insuperable. In the first place, Luke does not always represent inspired prophecies as being fulfilled *au pied de la lettre*. In Ac. 21:11, for example, the prophet Agabus ties Paul's feet and hands with Paul's own girdle and prophesies 'so shall the Jews at Jerusalem bind the man who owns this girdle and deliver him into the hands of the Gentiles'. This is not exactly what happened in Luke's own account: it was the Gentiles who bound Paul, to save him from the Jews – the Jews were only too anxious to get him out of the hands of the Gentiles into their own power. Also, the author of the Pastorals may not have regarded Acts as a wholly authoritative document. It had only recently been published and it would certainly not have held for him the same authority as Paul's own letters did. At least it seems very likely indeed that he wishes his readers to believe that Paul did exercise a ministry in Asia Minor after his release from prison in Rome.

We may now briefly review the three letters indicating where we believe there is genuine historical material to be found. Our method is this: where an allusion can be explained by a reference to the Pauline epistles or Acts we shall not seek any further explanation. Where this is not forthcoming, we shall judge each detail on its merits.

We begin with 1 Tim. 1:3, with the reference to Timothy remaining in Ephesus. This at least means that the Pastorals are connected with Ephesus, and it probably implies that Timothy was located there after Paul's death. In Heb. 13:23 we read: 'You should understand that our brother Timothy has been released.' If, as seems likely, Hebrews is written from outside Italy, this implies that Timothy has been in prison somewhere other than Rome, and Ephesus is by far the most likely place. Timothy must have been dead for some time when the Pastorals were written, so this reference cannot be much later than 90, and may be a decade or so earlier. I cannot follow Brox (p. 18) in his doubts about the historicity of this reference. Hebrews is not a pseudonymous work, and the author would seem to have nothing to gain by inventing details about Timothy.

In 1 Tim. 1:20 Hymenaeus and Alexander are described as having erred concerning the faith, and in 2 Tim. 2:17 Philetus is added to their number. These can hardly be contemporaries of the author, as some editors have held, since no one would believe that they had survived since Paul's day. Nor would there be much point in simply inventing names for heretics in Paul's time. They are probably names of actual opponents of Paul in the Ephesian church, who may have had successors teaching in their names in the author's day. This view is adopted by H. F. von Campenhausen (*Kirchliches Amt*, p. 159). Likewise in 2 Tim. 1:15 Phygelus and Hermogenes are described as being among the Asians who abandoned Paul. This may well be genuine tradition from the time of Paul's second arrest, presumably in Asia Minor. We may note that Clement obscurely hints that Paul's martyrdom was caused 'by envy and faction' (*1 Clem.* 5.5). Possibly we should class with this reference the incident of Demas having deserted Paul in 2 Tim. 4:10, but there is more doubt here, since he does occur in Col. 4:14.

There is no reason to doubt the historicity of Eunice and Lois, mother and grandmother of Timothy respectively, in 2 Tim. 1:5, nor the reference to Onesiphorus' courage in visiting Paul in prison in Rome which we meet in 2 Tim. 1:16. He must have come from Ephesus and the tradition of his visit may have been preserved there. Both the reference in 1 Tim. 5:23 to Timothy's weak stomach which needed wine, and the request for Paul's personal belongings in 2 Tim. 4:13 may be taken at their face value. For an interesting suggestion about the relation of the *books* to the *parchments*, see T. C. Skeat, *JTS* (ns) 30 (1979), pp. 123–7. The suggestion (widely supported by editors) that the reference to wine is inserted as a counterblast to the asceticism of the heretics is not very convincing. Surely the obvious way to counter temperance propaganda is to commend wine as a means of comfort and rejoicing, not as a medicine. Even an ascetic might take wine 'for medicinal purposes'. We must conclude that the author had access to genuine traditions about Paul (however trivial) in Ephesus and Asia Minor generally.

We may also believe that the characters referred to in the Pastorals as friends of Paul who do not appear elsewhere are genuine enough, though their mere mention tells us almost nothing about Paul. Such are Crescens in 2 Tim. 4:10 (for his possible connection with Paul, see the Commentary); Eubulus, Pudens, Linus, Claudia in 2 Tim. 4:21; Artemas in Tit. 3:12; and Zenas in Tit. 3:13 (who is probably a jurist not a rabbi: see Commentary).

This leaves us with two more areas of possible historical information. First, the Pastorals are the earliest witness to one important historical event, the martyrdom of Paul (2 Tim. 4:6–8). This is a fact which is not always given the recognition it deserves. Secondly, it seems likely that the connection of Paul's missionary activity with Crete is historical. Not that Paul necessarily visited Crete, but he probably did send one of his co-workers there, possibly Titus. We reach this conclusion because we can think of no more satisfactory answer to the question – why Crete? – a question which those scholars who believe all the apparently historical details in the Pastorals to be fictional too often simply ignore. In AD 105 Crete was sufficiently within the orbit of Asia Minor for it to be impossible for someone to have simply wished Paul upon the Cretan church as their founder;

the Cretan Christians would surely have known who first brought
them Christianity. If the author was merely casting round in his mind
for some suitable mission ground to attribute to Paul, he would well
have chosen Spain, which has the advantage of having been actually
mentioned by Paul and was sufficiently remote from Asia Minor to
preserve the author of the fiction from challenge by Spanish Christians. That he did not do so but fixed on Crete suggests that there was
a real connection between Paul's activity and the church there. It is
remarkable that the author takes more trouble to connect the letter
to Titus with Crete than he does to connect his two other letters with
Ephesus. For speculation about Crete during the author's time, see
the Commentary p.171f.

When we add together all the historical information which we can
glean from the Pastorals, it does not amount to very much. It does
not give us anything like a connected account of Paul's activity after
the point where the book of Acts leaves him. It must not be over-
estimated and above all it may not be used to support Pauline or
quasi-Pauline authorship of the Pastorals. But such as it is, it is worth
reviewing. It does at least suggest that the author of the Pastorals,
though he was writing for a fictional situation, did not confine himself
to using fictional materials. The fictional elements which he introduces (such as his picture of the ordination of Timothy) are more in
the nature of a series of anachronisms, caused by reflecting the conditions of his day back on to Paul's life, than a carefully constructed
piece of deliberate forgery.

A view very similar to that defended here on the historicity of the
Pastorals is to be found in H. Hegermann's article, 'Der geschichtliche Ort' (pp. 47–63). But this scholar would put them a little earlier,
'before the Domitianic persecution' (p. 61). Since I do not believe
there was a Domitianic persecution, I hold to a slightly later date.

4. THE PURPOSE OF THE PASTORAL EPISTLES

Since the Pastorals are not exactly what they claim to be, letters of
advice from Paul to his colleagues, what are they? Why were they
written? We shall answer this dogmatically by saying that the author
had three aims in mind in writing his three letters. He wanted to
provide a solid handbook for church leaders which would strengthen
the authority of the ordained ministers; he wanted to alert church
leaders to the necessity of fighting against growing heresy; and he
wanted to assert what he regarded as the Pauline tradition among the
churches of the Aegean area. We shall examine these three assertions
in order.

The figures of Timothy and Titus in the Pastorals do not correspond to what we know of the historic Timothy and Titus, but they do indicate that there are official leaders in the churches of the author's day who possess very real authority. All the advice which the author offers, whether about appointing clergy, or about how the church leader should behave himself, or about how worship should be conducted, is intended for a real situation in which there are real church leaders. This is why the letters, with their varied, almost miscellaneous, corpus of advice, can be fairly called a handbook for church leaders (Brox, pp. 9–11). Brox remarks that Paul's care for all the churches has become the author's care for individual leaders and their disciples. We must not imagine, however, that Timothy and Titus in the Pastorals represent some sort of 'metropolitan' or 'extra-diocesan' official in the church of the author's day – there is no evidence for the existence of such a figure at the end of the first century (H. Maehlum actually reads this sort of figure into the church of Paul's day; see his book *Die Vollmacht* pp. 95–6). What the author of the Pastorals does is to invest Timothy and Titus with Paul's authority and show them how to exercise it in the local church. In Stenger's words, the author wishes to emphasise 'the living presence and abiding relevance of apostolic origin' (W. Stenger, *Kairos* 16 [1974] p. 262). And P. Trummer (p. 250) says that the author's has made Paul real (*aktualisert*) for a post-Pauline epoch.

One of the most remarkable features about the Pastorals is their single-minded emphasis on Paul's apostolic authority. No other apostles are so much as mentioned. Paul's calling is widened, so that he is 'a teacher of the Gentiles in faith and truth' (1 Tim. 2:7). As R. F. Collins remarks, Paul is the sole source of doctrine for the church ('The Image of Paul', p. 157). J. Roloff (*Apostolat*, p. 249) claims that the author of the Pastorals was not interested in the origin of the apostolic office. It was enough for him that Paul had it and was delegating his authority to the church leaders of his day. A. Sand ('Anfänge . . . Pastoralbriefen', p. 224) rightly points out that Timothy and Titus are represented as fellow-workers with Paul, but they are not fellow-apostles or apostles in succession. They merely wield apostolic authority, and this the church's ministry is intended to do. Similarly Stenger (p. 267) says that the Pastorals do not witness to a doctrine of apostolic succession. Timothy and Titus are so drawn as to witness to an apostolic presence. Their main function is not as links in an apostolic succession, but as guarantors that the apostolic teaching and authority remains intact in the church of the author's day.

This leads us to the second of the author's aims, defence against heresy. Obviously the necessity to repel false teaching was an urgent

task in the author's situation. It is a theme which appears prominently
in all three letters. The precise nature of the false teaching which he
opposes has given rise to much speculation. Scholars who defend
Pauline authorship emphasise its Jewish element (which certainly
cannot be denied: e.g. Tit. 1:14); those who would put the Pastorals
later suggest that the author was facing an early form of Gnosticism.
Thus Spicq underlines the resemblance to Qumran teaching (Introd.,
Vol. 1, p. 2), and Dornier insists that it is pre-Gnostic (Introd., p.
16). Brox draws a parallel with the false teaching attacked in Colossians and suggests there was a docetic element in it, since the author
emphasises at one point 'the man Christ Jesus' (1 Tim. 2:5). He is
able to shew that the false teachers' doctrine to the effect that the
resurrection has already taken place (2 Tim. 2:18) is reproduced in
the *Gospel of Thomas*, certainly a Gnostic work (Brox, Introd., pp.
34, 37). D–C (Introd., pp. 53f.) characterise the heresy as Jewish
proto-Gnosticism. C. K. Barrett (*NTS* 20 [1973–4], pp. 240–1) suggests that the author has lumped together all the heresies he has ever
met. It must be said that one feature of the heresy seems to fit
Gnosticism better than anything else, and that is the references to
genealogies in 1 Tim. 1:4 and Tit. 3:9. The Gnostics did offer long
accounts of the origin and hierarchy of aeons, which often included
stories of how male and female aeons united to produce a litter of
lesser aeons. The only alternative is to adopt Spicq's suggestion that
the genealogies refer to 'haggadic midrashim' (Introd., Vol. 1, p.
101). But it is difficult to see such material as offering a serious threat
to the faith.

We should however pay attention to these scholars who suggest
that the language which the author uses about the heretics is conventional abuse borrowed from the popular philosophy of his day, and
that it does not therefore offer an accurate word-picture of the heretics
themselves. R. J. Karris (*JBL* 92 [1973], pp. 549–64) has shown that
a great deal of the figurative epithets and phrases used by the author
of his opponents can be found in such writers as Philo, Lucian, Dio
Chrysostom and Clement of Alexandria to describe their own philosophical opponents. He therefore discounts a great deal of the des-
criptions of the heretics which we meet in the Pastorals, but certain
elements remain without parallel; among these are the complaint
about 'endless genealogies', and the ascetic and encratite teaching
which formed part of the heretics' doctrine. So 'Jewish proto-Gnosticism' would seem to be the best description of the heresy we can
hope for.

Against this teaching, the author, as we have seen, did not on the
whole employ argument but abuse. However, he does constantly
contrast with the false teaching of the heretics what he calls the

parathēkē, the deposit of sound teaching which Paul has received, which he has passed on to his colleagues, and which they must pass on in their turn to suitable clergy. *Parathēkē* is a word peculiar to the Pastorals in the NT, though he uses synonyms for it, such as 'gospel', 'sound teaching', 'command' (1 Tim. 6:14), 'mystery of piety'. Roloff (pp. 248–50) maintains that the *parathēkē* is something that must be guarded not so much against being forgotten as against being betrayed. Paul moreover is not the guarantor of the *parathēkē*: that is God's role, and *tēn parathēkēn mou* in 2 Tim. 1:12 ('that which has been entrusted to me') is not a genitive of possession. Paul is the guardian of the *parathēkē*. All other details, such as church order, are for the purpose of guarding the *parathēkē*. Trummer (p. 222) rightly emphasises that the *parathēkē* does not apparently consist of set formulae or credal statements; at least the author never explicitly expounds what the *parathēkē* is. It is the content that must be handed on rather than any formula. Thus we have in the Pastorals the paradoxical situation that false teachers are fiercely attacked, but we are left without any very clear picture of their doctrine; and the true teaching is to be carefully guarded, though we are never told precisely what it is.

The author's third aim is to assert the Pauline tradition. He does this partly, as we have seen, by asserting Paul's continuing authority in the church, but also by offering from time to time a sort of commentary on various passages from Paul's letters, a process (as Brox puts it, p. 62) of bringing Paul up to date. We devote the next section to a closer examination of this. In this respect the author may fairly be called a disciple of Paul's. He obviously admires Paul greatly, and believes that he is reproducing Paul's teaching. But he is not a disciple of Paul in the sense in which, for example, the author of Ephesians is. He can hardly be said to be a member of a Pauline school. Trummer uses the ugly but perhaps not inappropriate epithet 'tritopauline' (p. 228). Once the Pastorals are placed in their true historical context at the end of the first century, it can be seen that one theory which once was very popular among scholars will have to be modified. This is the theory that soon after Paul's death his influence ceased and that he was almost forgotten until he was revived in the second century by those who needed him in the fight against heresy. On the contrary, by the end of the first century Paul was revered by the churches round the Aegean as an apostle and martyr. Hasler (Introd., p. 9) suggests that the author of the Pastorals is making a bid for a leading position in the churches in the region of Corinth and Ephesus, and part of his way of achieving this consists in an authoritative appeal to Paul. If this seems not completely warranted by the evidence, we can at least say that the author believed himself to be vindicating the teaching and tradition of Paul.

We can perhaps make an interesting comparison here with Ignatius. On first appearance Ignatius would seem to have very little in common with the author of the Pastorals. He is writing genuine letters, unlike the author; he has a profound theology of his own, which cannot be said for the author. But Ignatius was certainly concerned to commend and defend monepiscopacy as it had recently established itself in Asia Minor and the same concern can be detected in the Pastorals. It is veiled in the Pastorals, because the author knew perfectly well that there had been nothing like monepiscopacy in Paul's day (for details, see Introduction, section 6), so he cannot openly represent Paul as commending exactly the form of ministry which prevailed in Asia Minor. But short of this he does all he can to support the authority of the ordained ministry, and he is as much opposed to sectaries and heretics as Ignatius is. For other resemblances to Ignatius, see Introduction, section 7.

J. Elliott (*CBQ* 32 [1970], pp. 367–91) has suggested that when the Pastorals were written there existed a *Gattung* (literary form) which could be called 'advice to church leaders', and that the Pastorals fits into this. He sees traces of this *Gattung* in 1 Peter. And H. W. Bartsch (*Die Anfänge*) has claimed that the author of the Pastorals, as well as Polycarp and the authors of the later Church Orders, was drawing on an existing document which gave directions on such topics as church discipline and appointment of clergy. We discuss this in greater detail later. But one could equally well maintain that the Pastorals fall into the same category as Jude and 2 Peter and they are pseudonymous documents aimed at repelling contemporary heresy (Brox, Introd., p. 61). The truth is that the Pastorals are *sui generis*. This is because, unlike Ephesians for example, they are not united by one central or developing theme. They are made up of diverse materials because they were intended to accomplish a number of diverse aims.

Those who believe that the Pastorals are authentic letters of Paul carefully distinguish the order in which they were written. 2 Timothy must come last, being largely made up of Paul's last will and testament, and Titus is usually placed between 1 Timothy and 2 Timothy. If one abandons the hypothesis of Pauline authorship, it is much more difficult to see any particular reason why one letter should be put either before or after another. 1 Timothy is more concerned with church order; 2 Timothy has more material personal to Paul, and also more scriptural references; Titus has fewer personal references than the other two and takes no notice of Scripture, though it has all the chief characteristics of the Pastorals, i.e. liturgical fragments,

domestic codes, abuse of heretics. One might tentatively suggest that
by the time the author came to write Titus he was beginning to run
out of material, in which case Titus would be the latest to be written,
and the order of the letters as we have them in our Bibles is the right
one. But there is no great significance in this order of writing. All
three may have been composed and published at the same time.

5. THE AUTHOR'S USE OF PAULINE MATERIAL

The author of the Pastorals was well acquainted with Paul's letters.
I have noted twenty-one places where he is clearly echoing Paul (see
the Appendix at the end of the Commentary) and A. E. Barnett, who
cast his net much wider, has recorded many more (see his book *Paul
Becomes a Literary Influence*, 1941). The author of the Pastorals echoes
every letter in the Pauline corpus (including Ephesians and Philemon)
except 1 and 2 Thessalonians. Sometimes he seems to be merely
borrowing Pauline language (as in 1 Tim. 1:20–1 C. 5:5, and 1 Tim.
4:12–1 C. 16:11). But very often he is consciously reconstructing Paul
to fit his own circumstances. These are the most interesting passages,
since they tell us most about the author's own theology. Indeed, the
adaptation of Pauline material for use in his own day is one of the
author's leading literary characteristics. Together with liturgical fragments, elements of a manual of church order, etc., Pauline material
constitutes one of the main sources of the Pastoral letters. We will
choose four such passages for illustration, one from 1 Timothy and
the rest from 2 Timothy. Both the letters to Timothy are rich in
Pauline echoes, though on the whole those in 2 Timothy have more
theological content. Titus seems to be entirely devoid of Pauline
echoes.

1. *1 Timothy 6:12 = Philippians 3:12–14*

In the 1 Tim. passage Paul is represented as urging Timothy to fight
the good fight of faith, and to lay hold of eternal life, and reminds
him of the confession he has made before many witnesses. The
confession probably refers to the confession made at baptism, renewed at his ordination (this is not to suggest that Timothy necessarily
was ordained by Paul, but it reflects the practice of the author's day).
The Pauline passage refers to Paul's own vocation: he has been
apprehended by Christ; he does not count himself as one who has
already arrived; he presses forward towards the fulfilment of his
vocation. The author has taken the sentiments that Paul expresses
about his own ministry and applied them to that of Timothy. The

two passages have in common the figure of the athletic contest, the thought of eternal life, the note of vocation. The author has dropped Paul's fine paradox of being apprehended by Christ yet not himself fully apprehending, and has substituted a more straightforward, but entirely appropriate, exhortation to lay hold of eternal life, and, with his nervousness about the danger of heresy, has brought in a reference to the content of the faith. This is a good and simple example of theological transposition.

2. 2 Timothy 1:6–9 = Romans 8:12–17

In the 2 Timothy passage Timothy is urged to stir up the charism of God which he has received; he is reminded that he possesses the spirit of power, not of cowardice, and he is recalled to the gospel of the saviour-God. This is certainly based on the Romans passage, in which Paul speaks about life in the Spirit, sonship in Christ, and the right which this gives us to call God 'Father'; he ends with a reference to suffering with Christ and being glorified with him. The author has applied to a church leader what Paul refers to all Christians; the Spirit in the case of Timothy seems to have been conferred in ordination. The author deliberately makes a play on Paul's words. Paul writes, 'the spirit of slavery' (*douleias*); the author changes this to 'the spirit of cowardice' (*deilias*). He omits Paul's reference to sonship; as we shall be seeing, this did not form part of his christology, and his account of the gospel, though it does involve enduring hardship (v. 8), does not seem to include anything so intimate as suffering with Christ (but cf. 2 Tim. 2:11). On the whole he has rather externalised Paul's doctrine, transferring it from the sphere of Christian experience to the function of being a body of belief for which one has to fight.

3. 2 Timothy 3:16–17 = Romans 15:4–6

I have drawn out this comparison in detail in *Studies* (pp. 42–53), but it is worth while reproducing some of it, since the correspondence is so exact. We note the following:

2 Tim. 3:16–17	Rom. 15:4–6
every scripture inspired by God	whatever was written in former
teaching (*didaskalia*)	days
training	teaching (*didaskalia*)
correction	steadfastness
man of God	encouragement
	you

Both authors are saying essentially the same thing, viz. that the

Scriptures (for both writers, of course, what we should call the Old Testament) are a source of instruction and support to the faithful Christian. But the modifications which the author of the Pastorals has made are very significant. Where Paul expects all Christians to make use of the Scriptures, the author is concerned only with their use by the ordained minister (a feature we noted in our last example); where Paul hopes that the whole local church will be built up by study of the Scriptures, the author is primarily interested in their use in an apologetic and polemical context. Moreover the author actually introduces concepts borrowed from Stoic vocabulary:

Epictetus uses *paideia* ('training') and *epanorthōsis* ('correction') as technical terms in moral philosophy. Paul would never have felt the need for this. But the paradox which we have already noted appears here also: Paul, who does not mention refutation of heresy as a use of scripture, nevertheless uses it very effectively elsewhere for this purpose. The author, who explicitly states that this is an end to which Scripture can usefully be put, gives us no examples of doing so. (But G. Lohfink (*ThQ* 157 [1977], pp. 93–104) believes that we get an account of the *parathēkē* in 2 Tim. 1:9–10). Nowhere is the relationship between the genuinely Pauline writings and the Pastorals better illustrated than in this comparison.

4. *2 Timothy 4:6–8 = Philippians 2:16–17*

We could describe the 2 Timothy passage as Phil. 2:16–17 rewritten in the light of Paul's martyrdom. The two passages have much in common. In both Paul is poured out like a libation, both are followed by instructions concerning the movements of colleagues, both contain a reference to Paul's course (*edramon* in Philippians, *dromos* in 2 Timothy); both are concerned with Timothy's work (compare Phil. 2:19 with 2 Tim. 4:9); both expect a judicial decision which may be unfavourable. The passage in 2 Timothy is more confident about Paul's victory and reward, as is natural for someone who is writing with hindsight. The passage shows a largely historical, rather than theological, transposition of a Pauline passage into the terms of the author's day.

This theme could be amply illustrated (see the list of Pauline passages at the end of the Commentary). In *Studies* (pp. 29–41) I have expounded another example, 2 Tim. 2:20–21 Rom. 9:19–24, in which the author of the Pastorals remoulds the sublime but dangerous landscape of the Pauline theology of predestination into the smiling parkland of his own more Pelagian doctrine. The process which the author applies to Paul's letters is essentially that of *midrash*. The aim of *midrash* in Judaism was to expound Scripture in such a way as to make it applicable to the circumstances of each succeeding generation. One can see this happening clearly in the Targums. Where Isaiah writes 'The ox knows its owner and the ass its master's crib; but Israel does not know, my people does not understand', the targumist interprets: 'Israel has not learned to know the fear of me, my people has not considered how to return to my law' (Isa. 1:3). The targumist is adapting Isaiah's words to a period when the written law had become the centre of the people's religion. This is what the author of the Pastorals does, though he is of course spanning a much shorter period of time than was the targumist on Isaiah. But the author is writing in Paul's name and is therefore claiming to interpret Paul's true meaning for his generation. One could be led into some very interesting speculation here. How far are the Pastorals a sort of Mishna on Paul? Why did this process of midrash on the great writers of the NT not continue, as the process continued in Judaism, producing in time both the Mishna and the Talmud? But we must confine ourselves to what we have noted here, being content to observe that, by his successful claim to be writing in Paul's name, the author of the Pastorals has in fact very largely domesticated Paul for the use of succeeding generations.

6. CHURCH ORDER IN THE PASTORALS

One of the distinctive features in the Pastoral Epistles, wherever they differ from all other documents in the NT, is the attention they devote to ordained offices in the church. This in itself marks them as belonging to a later generation than Paul's. In Paul's day there were members of local congregations who had pastoral responsibility over the local church; see 1 Th. 5:12; Rom. 12:8. But 'those who are over you in the Lord' do not seem to be the same as the ordained clergy whom we encounter in the Pastorals. Authority in Paul's day apparently remained with the local church, and there was certainly no suggestion that any of these local functionaries possessed Christ's (or Paul's) authority over against the church in which they served. The only occasion in which we find unmistakeably the names of church offices in Paul is in Phil. 1:1: the letter is directed 'to the saints in Christ Jesus who are in Philippi with the *episkopoi* and *diakonoi*'. This is a mysterious reference, all the more difficult to explain because of its unique character. J. Rohde (pp. 54–5) calls the reference '*ungewöhnlich*' and suggests that in the Philippian church of Paul's day a certain group of Christians were exercising leadership in fact (*episkopoi*) and another were assisting them (*diakonoi*), but that they were not church officers in the later sense. It is true that Luke describes a sort of hierarchy as existing in the church in Jerusalem consisting of the Twelve, with under them a body of 'presbyters' (Ac. 11:30; 15:2). He also represents Paul and Barnabas as appointing presbyters in the churches which they had founded in Cilicia (Ac. 14:23). It is very probable that the church in Jerusalem simply took over from the synagogue the office of elder. Luke seems to have assumed that Paul would appoint elders in his churches, though the term is never used of a church officer in any genuine Pauline letter. By Luke's day the two names *episkopoi* and *presbyteroi* seem to have indicated the same office. See Ac. 20:17, 28, where Paul summons the *presbyteroi* of the Ephesian church to meet him at Miletus and in his subsequent speech refers to them as *episkopoi*.

The word *episkopoi* in secular Greek usage simply meant anyone who had authority to oversee or inspect anything or anyone else. It could be used of someone who had oversight in a religious context, e.g. temple treasurers. But there was no necessarily religious or liturgical meaning belonging to the word (J. Hainz, p. 96). The term *presbyteroi* certainly comes from Judaism. Efforts have been made to connect both *presbyteroi* and *episkopoi* with offices which can be traced in the Qumran community under the name *pāqîd* or *mᵉbaqqer*. This has the authority of J. Jeremias behind it, but is treated with scepticism by most modern editors (H. Beyer, *TDNT* 2, pp. 608ff.). We should probably conclude that the two names for the church officer, *episkopoi* and *presbyteroi*, originated independently in the Pauline and Judaean churches respectively and that by the time of the author of the Pastorals they were everywhere accepted as referring to the same office. In each church would be a group of officials who could be called either *presbyteroi* or *episkopoi*. In secular Greek *diakonoi* means anyone who exercises a subordinate function. Epictetus uses it of the Cynic philosopher, servant-messenger of the gods (A. Lemaire, p. 32). It can apply equally well to a woman. Thus all three traditional offices in the church, bishop, presbyter, and deacon, are indicated by a word which had no necessarily liturgical or cultic associations at all, and above all had no associations whatever with the Jewish cultic system.

But in the Pastorals we cannot be content to say that we find two offices, i.e., bishop-presbyters and deacons, as we do, for example, in *1 Clement*. There are subtle indications that *episkopoi* used in the singular could indicate a bishop with something approaching monepiscopal status such as we find clearly outlined in the letters of Ignatius. This is strenuously denied by all those who advocate Pauline authorship of the Pastorals (e.g. A. Cousineau, *ScEsp* 28 [1976], pp. 147–62) since it is crystal clear that monepiscopacy did not exist in Paul's day. But the evidence on the whole seems to suggest that the

author was aware that in some churches in his day (including those
to whom he was writing) the *episkopoi* had wider authority than had
a mere *episkopos-presbyteros* member of a group of ordained ministers
in the local church. There seems to be an office which can dispose of
wide powers over the local church. The strongest evidence for this
lies in the extent of the authority which the fictional Timothy and
Titus are expected to exercise. We have already disposed of the
suggestion that in actual fact in the author's day there were figures
corresponding to the historical Timothy and Titus, quasi-metropoli-
tans. But the author undoubtedly believes that the church officers to
whom he is writing do have, and should exercise, very much the
authority which we find Ignatius describing as belonging to the bishops of his day. They can ordain clergy, apparently on their own
initiative – see I Tim. 5:22; unless this refers to readmission of
sinners after excommunication; but even that action implies wide
powers. See also I Tim. 5:17, where Timothy seems to have plenary
disciplinary powers, and also seems to be responsible for the financial
affairs of the local church; or Tit. 1:5, where Titus is to appoint
presbyters in each town. Both Timothy and Titus seem to be free to
choose whom they like as church officers, hence the careful test of
qualities necessary for these offices. The two colleagues of Paul are
also told how to conduct public worship (see I Tim. 2:1f.), and they
have full power to entrust the teaching office to those whom they
choose (2 Tim. 2:2). The author would not have given instructions
about how to exercise an office with such wide authority in the local
church unless such an office had actually existed.

The language which the author uses in this context is ambiguous:
see I Tim. 3:1f.; Tit. 1:7f. These are the only references to *episkopoi*
or *episkopē* in the Pastorals. But it is easy to understand why the
author had to use ambiguous language here. He knew, and those to
whom he wrote knew, that in Paul's day there had been nothing
corresponding to the monarchical bishop, and that even at the time
of his writing the office was by no means universal in the church
(there is no evidence for monepiscopacy in Rome, Corinth, or Philippi
till many years later). On the other hand the office was emerging,
probably first of all in the churches of Asia Minor, and the author
wanted to give advice to these newly established bishops. Hence the
ambiguity. It could be said that a consensus on this point among
scholars is emerging, except of course for those who cling to the
theory of Pauline authorship. As long ago as 1929, B. H. Streeter
(*The Primitive Church*, pp. 108, 111) wrote: 'In Asia mon-episcopacy
antedates the writing of the Pastoral Epistles.' G. Bornkamm (*TDNT*
6, pp. 651–80) agrees that in the Pastorals monepiscopacy is emerging. H. von Campenhausen (p. 117) and also A. Ehrhardt (*The

Apostolic Succession, pp. 77f.) had come to the same conclusion. F. D. Gealy in his commentary (1955) takes the same line (p. 345). In 1960 E. Käsemann (*Essays*, p. 87) expressed the view that the monarchical bishop is in the Pastorals depicted under the image of Timothy and Titus. C. K. Barrett in 1963 (Introd. to his comm.), and J. Roloff (p. 251) and H. W. Bartsch (p. 107) in 1965 came to the same conclusion. Bartsch says that in the Pastorals the bishop is on the way towards becoming monarchical, but his position is not yet clearly established. In 1959 E. Schweizer (*Church Order*, p. 84) had already accepted this position, including the suggestion that the author could not openly assume monepiscopacy since he knew it to be an anachronism in Paul's day. Brox (pp. 148f.) in his commentary of 1969 is more cautious. He does not think one can speak of monepiscopacy in the Pastorals, but rather of a group of *episkopoi*, under whom were the presbyters. But Dornier in an article of 1974 ('Les Épitres Pastorales', p. 109) agrees that monepiscopacy was just emerging when the Pastorals were written. J. Rohde (pp. 83–6) will speak only of a tendency towards monarchical leadership of the local church in the Pastorals. Indeed he is more ready to recognise the existence of a quasi-metropolitan office in the author's day than of the monarchical bishop.

There does not seem to be any difference between the functions of the bishop and of the presbyter except that, if we may take it that instructions given ostensibly to Timothy and Titus are really intended for bishops, the bishop has wider authority. Lemaire ('Les Ministères', in Delorme, p. 107) rightly emphasises the strong family atmosphere of the local church. It is still very much of a house church. The bishop must be a good family man, ready to entertain visiting Christians (see 1 Tim. 3:2–7; 2 Tim. 2:24; Tit. 1:6–9).

Schlier (p. 486) distinguishes four functions of the *episkopos-presbyteros* in the Pastorals: 1. He must teach the deposit of faith and defend it against heresy. This function is common to all orders of the minority in the Pastorals, even the deacons; see 1 Tim. 3:9; 4:11–3; 5:17; 2 Tim. 2:2; 3:16–17; Tit. 1:9; 2:1; 2:15. 2. He arranges for worship and for the church's social activities (1 Tim. 2:1f.; 2:8; 5:3–16). 3. He exercises penitential discipline over the members of the community; for this see 1 Tim. 5:20, 22. Timothy seems to be in a position to discipline presbyters, which looks very like the situation of a monarchical bishop. Whether v. 22 refers to ordination (as the *Book of Common Prayer* takes it) or to readmission of sinners to communion, is not clear (for the latter view see P. Galtier, *RSR* 39 [1951], pp. 317–20). 4. He ordains his representatives and successors. We discuss ordination further below.

The actual functions of deacons are nowhere specified in the Pas-

torals. There is a hint that well-behaved deacons can expect promotion (1 Tim. 3:10, 13). Bartsch (p. 91), relying on the evidence of
later church orders, maintains that the deacon is 'the potential bishop'. Mere presbyters remained in that order all their lives. But he
may be anticipating later developments.

We have in the Pastorals no fewer than three passages in which the
qualities necessary for admission to the various orders are listed: 1
Tim. 3:2–7 3:8–10; Tit. 1:6–9. When we compare these lists with a
list of qualities desirable in older men (laymen), as one finds in Tit.
2:2, it is surprising to find very little difference. Indeed the qualities
requisite in a church leader seem to have very little in them that
marks out the clergyman as the priest at all. No particular ability in
cultic matters is demanded, no training in prayer, very little that
distinguishes the minister from any respectable member of society.

This impression is increased when we compare the list of qualities
requisite in a bishop with a document written in Greek by a writer
called Onosander in about AD 50. He lists the qualities requisite in a
good general, and they bear a striking resemblance to what the author
of the Pastorals requires of a bishop. Onosander demands that his
successful general must be self-restrained, moderate, respectable,
sober, frugal, able to speak well, no lover of money, a family man,
tough (*diaponos*), intelligent, and neither a youth nor too elderly (the
passage can be found in D–C, pp. 117–18). About the only qualities
required in a bishop that are not needed in a general are ability to
teach and willingness to give hospitality. Indeed we may well regret
that the author of the Pastorals did not take his cue from Onosander
and have toughness as a quality that bishops should possess! What
we can conclude from this remarkably 'secular' or 'civil' view of the
bishop which we find in the Pastorals is, not that the author was
copying Onosander, but that when the Pastorals were written the
ministry had not yet become the cultic, separated, professionalised
superior caste which it became later in the history of the church.
Some scholars have suggested, on the basis of 1 Tim. 5:17, that there
was within the presbyterate an inner circle of those who were competent to teach and to preside, and even that the monarchical bishop
emerged out of this circle. But it does not seem to us that such a
conclusion is justified by the evidence.

Undoubtedly when the Pastorals were written ordination of new
ministers by the laying on of hands of the local group of bishop-
presbyters was the practice; see 1 Tim. 4:14; 2 Tim. 1:6. On the face
of it there appears to be a contradiction here. Was Timothy ordained
by the group of presbyters or by Paul? In fact however these passages
do not tell us anything about Timothy's own ordination. The author
is reading into the conditions in Paul's day the custom of his own

time. David Daube in a famous article has tried to resolve the apparent contradiction by claiming that in 1 Tim. 4:14 the phrase translated in *RSV* 'when the elders laid their hands upon you' should be rendered 'by the laying on of hands for the office of eldership', and that the Greek *epithesis tōn cheirōn tou presbyteriou* corresponds to a rite witnessed to in rabbinic literature called *Simkat Z^eqenîm*, whereby a man was appointed rabbi (see his book *The New Testament and Rabbinic Judaism*, pp. 224–48). This view has been adopted by many scholars, especially by those who wish to defend Pauline authorship of the Pastorals, since the closer the practice witnessed to in the Pastorals proves to be to Judaism the more likely they are to be by Paul. W. Nauck, who greatly underlines the Jewish character of the Pastorals, welcomes this sort of explanation (see his Dissertation, 'Der Herkunft des Verfassers der Pastoralbriefe', Göttingen, 1950, p. 71).

But we should hesitate to adopt so relatively complicated an explanation for a passage which admits of a simpler solution. In the author's day ordination was by the laying on of the hands of the local group of presbyters, and the reference in 2 Tim. 1:6 to Paul ordaining is part of the author's historical window-dressing. Only a few years later Ignatius uses *presbyterion* to mean the group of presbyters in a local church, not 'the office of presbyter'. In any case it is by no means clear that the rite of *Simkat Z^eqenîm* had actually yet come into use among Jewish rabbis by the end of the first century AD. E. Lohse (in Kertelge, p. 518) claims that ordination in the Pastorals is essentially an act of authorisation. The newly ordained is authorised to handle, to guard, to pass on the deposit of faith. G. Lohfink (p. 102) considers that the author of the Pastorals was not interested in the ministry as such, only in its capacity to guard the deposit, and that there is no sign of a hierarchy in the Pastorals. Schlier (pp. 483, 488–9) emphasises rather more the authority that Timothy has received. He has a charisma which marks him off from the laity, and one can point to a long list of verbs which the author uses to describe what Timothy must do, all carrying a strong overtone of authority: proclaim, do the work of an evangelist, teach, affirm, convey to the brethren, remind them, exhort, rebuke, testify, refute, teach the opponents, etc. Roloff (p. 262) maintains on the basis of 1 Tim. 4:14, 6:11–14 that in the author's time ordination took place before the whole local church, was something that could not be called back (only denied), and was mediated by persons in authority who had either themselves been ordained or who held office in the local church.

We may legitimately conclude that when the Pastorals were written the ordained ministry was very securely established and was growing in authority as a bulwark against false teaching (Käsemann, *Essays*,

p. 85). The distinction between lay and ordained was quite clear, but had not yet been given a sacramental (still less a sacerdotal) significance. The notion of succession in the ministry was certainly present, but was regarded primarily as a succession of teaching or tradition rather than as an 'apostolic succession' of ordination reaching back to the apostles (see 2 Tim. 2:2). It is still the gospel and not the office that is the norm for the church. The church officer has not yet monopolised all church activity and his task is not yet defined in sacral or cultic terms (Lohfink, p. 105; Trummer, p. 223).

We must refer to two more classes of persons who may have appeared to be constituting an order, widows and prophets. The passage on widows is confined to 1 Tim 5:3–16. It is confused because the author is probably dealing with a confused situation, and perhaps because he is using some sort of a rule for widows as one of his sources. The difficulty lies in deciding what the author means by the phrase 'widows who are real widows' (1 Tim. 5:3; 5:16). Some scholars have suggested that this phrase is used to distinguish genuine widows from consecrated virgins, and have pointed to a curious phrase used by Ignatius in his letter to the Smyrnaeans 13.1: 'the virgins who are called widows'. (See J. Ernst, *ThG* 59 (1969), pp. 434–45). On the other hand J. Massingberd Ford (*NTS* 12 [1965–6], pp. 292–9) has suggested that the contrast may be between genuine widows and girls who were married and who have become widows before puberty, a possibility which is envisaged in rabbinic law. Most modern editors conclude that there was an order of widows and that those who entered it took some sort of a vow (so Schlier, p. 498; Trummer, p. 219). Bartsch p. 116 suggests that widows were making a bid to be recognised as church officers, and that the author wishes to curb their ambitions. This was certainly the case in the later church. But several scholars deprecate the idea that at this early stage there could be anything in the nature of a vow (A. Sand, *Bibel und Leben* [March, 1971], p. 196). Rohde (pp. 97–7) distinguishes three categories: young widows, who ought to remarry; middle-aged widows (aetat. 45–60), who should make themselves useful in the social activities of the church; and elderly widows (60+), who could claim full support from the church. But this seems to be too specific.

We may reasonably draw four conclusions about the status of widows in the church to which our author is writing: 1. There was an order which certain widows could join after taking a vow of constancy. But any Christian widow was not ipso facto eligible to join; a candidate had to be genuinely destitute and have reached sixty years of age. 2. Any really destitute Christian widow of any age would probably receive some support from the church. 3. The author does not disapprove of remarriage for widows on principle (he recommends it in certain cases; see I Tim. 5:14). 4. The author has tried the experiment of admitting younger widows to the order but it has not been a success.

Prophecy is only mentioned twice in the Pastorals, each time in connection with Timothy's ordination or at least vocation (I Tim. 1:18; 4:14). There can be no doubt but that prophets played an important part in the life of the church in the period of our author. A few years later we find Ignatius, himself a monarchical bishop, claiming in effect to be a prophet (*Philad*, 7.1); and the author of the *Didache* has actually to plead on behalf of the bishops and deacons in each local church that they should be given as much honour as the prophets receive (see *Did*. 15.1–2). The suggestion has been made that in I Tim. 4:14 the reference to prophecy actually means the words used in the ceremony of laying on of hands, but this seems unlikely (see N. Brox, *BZ* 20 (1976), pp. 229–32). We may not conclude anything from these two references about what actually happened as far as an ordination for Timothy is concerned, but it does seem clear that prophecy was a normal accompaniment of the appointment and ordination of clergy when the Pastorals were written. Probably the Christian prophet or prophets would indicate whom God had chosen for the ordained ministry, and the chosen men would then be ordained. There is no trace in the Pastorals of any tension between prophets and ordained ministers. Indeed there is no reason why a church officer should not himself be a prophet. Thus we have no justification for speaking of 'an order of prophets'. At the time when the Pastorals were written, prophecy was a charisma not an office.

7. THE CHRISTOLOGY OF THE PASTORALS

In 1935 H. Windisch (*ZNW* 34, pp. 213f.) wrote about the author of the Pastorals: 'He has no theological christology, but only teaching about Christ in the form of statements, formulas, and hymns which spring from various circles of teaching and teaching material'. This gives us the key to the author's christology. He does not have any doctrine of his own, but makes use of whatever comes to him in the sources which he uses. Indeed one could legitimately claim that his way of teaching doctrine is to quote liturgical and confessional formulae. It is true that Paul did this also; in several places scholars are convinced that Paul is using confessional or liturgical material, e.g. Phil. 2:6–11; Rom. 1:3–4; I Th. 1:9–10. We find it also in deutero-Pauline letters, e.g. Col. 1:15–19; Eph. 5:14. But in all these cases the material is integrated into the context of the argument and if necessary adapted to the writer's theology. Not so with the Pastorals. Here the material is simply presented with its implied christology and no attempt is made to work it into a consistent doctrine.

The consequence is that we find several different ways of expressing the significance of Christ in the Pastorals, not all consistent with each other. Several editors for example have found an epiphany christology in the Pastorals: the appearance of Jesus on earth is described in terms of an epiphany of God; see 1 Tim. 3:16, **He was manifested in the flesh**; see also 2 Tim. 1:10; Tit. 2:11, 3:4. D–C and Pax both speak of an epiphany christology (see E. Pax's book, *Epiphaneia*, p. 246). But Windisch prefers to speak of adoptionism or even a 'servant of God' (*pais theou*) christology, even though the author never uses the phrase. He thinks that the author is actually reverting to a very early pre-Pauline christology: but Trummer (pp. 193, 204), probably rightly, denies this. He prefers to speak of a 'title christology'. This is because the author certainly expresses his doctrine of Christ by using titles for him rather than by expounding an ontological or soteriological theory. His two favourite titles are *kurios* ('lord') and *sōtēr* ('saviour'). There can be little doubt but that this latter title has been deliberately borrowed from the imperial cult (see detached Note at Tit. 2:14). The remarkable feature of these two titles is that the author uses them interchangeably for God and Christ (*kurios* for Christ is too frequent to need illustration; he applies the title to God in 1 Tim. 6:15, and probably 2 Tim. 1:18. He uses *sōtēr* of God in 1 Tim. 1:1; 2:3; 4:10; Tit. 1:3; 2:10; 3:4; and he uses it of Christ in 2 Tim. 1:10; Tit. 1:4; 2:13; 3:6).

Even more surprising is the fact that the author uses *theos*, 'God', of Christ as well as of the Father. This seems to be the natural interpretation of Tit. 2:13, **the appearing of the glory of our great God and saviour Jesus Christ**, though some editors prefer to translate 'of the great God and our saviour Jesus Christ'. But Pax (p. 242) insists that we must adopt the first translation, and C. C. Oke (*ExpT* 57 [1956], pp. 367–8) has even suggested that the author uses *theos* of Christ in 1 Tim. 1:17, since he believes that the context requires that 'the King of ages, immortal, invisible, the only God' be Christ and not the Father. This is not an unparalleled usage. Only a few years later Ignatius freely applies the word *theos* to Christ. See, for example, his letter *Eph.* 7.2, where Christ is called 'God in man'; see also 18.2, 'our God Jesus Christ'; *Rom.* 6.3, 'the passion of my God'; *Smyr.* 1.1, 'Jesus Christ, the God who has made us thus wise'; *Pol.* 8.3, 'I pray that you may always flourish in our God Jesus Christ'. We should note of course that Ignatius always qualifies *theos* when he applies the title to Christ: he is 'our God' or 'my God', etc. And indeed the author of the Pastorals follows this rule too. To call Jesus

Christ God in so many words is to involve oneself deep in theological doctrine. The question must arise: if Jesus Christ is God and the Father is God, are there then two gods? Ignatius avoids this difficulty by openly espousing a Logos doctrine. Jesus Christ is the 'Word proceeding from silence' (*Mag.* 8.2). But our author is quite innocent of such theological profundity. He therefore leaves himself open to the charge of virtual Ditheism, though we may be quite sure that any such doctrine was far from his conscious mind.

D–C claim that there is an element of subordination present in the christology of the Pastorals, chiefly on the strength of the confessional formula which is quoted in 1 Tim. 2:5–6. They think that **one mediator between God and man, the man Christ Jesus** implies subordination. I have suggested in *Studies* (pp. 56f.) that this phrase originated in a Christian midrash on Job 9:32–33 LXX. But I agree that the phrase, if taken in its full implications, would lead to an Arian doctrine of Christ. The author of the Pastorals however must not be held to be conscious of everything that his christological language implies. He did not invent it himself; he took it over together with the material in which it was enshrined. His *lex orandi* was his *lex credendi*, and he did not indulge in christological speculation.

Most editors deny that he has any notion of the pre-existence of Christ (this is Windisch's view). This seems correct, though Stenger (*TTZ* 78 [1964], p. 44) rightly observes that in 1 Tim. 3:16 'the christology here has cosmic dimensions'.

We must also conclude on the basis of his own expressions that the author of the Pastorals was a Binitarian rather than a Trinitarian in his theology. In three places (1 Tim. 5:21; and 2 Tim. 4:1) Paul is represented as solemnly adjuring Timothy in the name of God, and in all of them God and Christ appear but not the Holy Spirit. Against this could be put Tit. 3:4–6, where in a liturgical passage, God, Christ, and the Spirit are all mentioned. G. W. Knight (p. 91) calls this 'a Trinitarian statement'. So it is, but it is doubtful if it represents the author's own theology as clearly as do the passages where he is using his own language. For a vindication of the view that his theology is Binitarian (this writer strangely spells it as 'binatarian'), see R. F. Collins, *LTP* 2, 1975, p. 163.

The only other references to the Spirit in the Pastorals occur in 1 Tim. 3:16, where Christ is described as 'vindicated in the Spirit'. This is certainly a quotation from an early Christian hymn. Then there is 2 Tim. 4:1, which is a reference to prophetic utterance in the Spirit; and 2 Tim. 1:7, which, as we have seen is based on Rom. 8:15, and therefore hardly tells us much about the author's own doctrine of the Spirit. Finally, there is 2 Tim. 1:14: **guard the truth that has been entrusted to you by the Holy Spirit who dwells within**

us. This certainly suggests a fuller doctrine of the Spirit, but can hardly outweigh the rest of the evidence. In the Pastorals the Holy Spirit does not seem to be integrated into the being of God.

It has been claimed that the author of the Pastorals regards faith (*pistis*) more as the content of the gospel than as personal trust in God (von O. Mark, *ZNW* 66 [1975], pp. 91–102). Of course Paul can use *pistis* to mean the content of faith as well as the act of trusting, but the tendency of the author of the Pastorals seems to be to put the emphasis on that which is to be believed. This is no doubt because in his day the gospel needed to be defended against incipient Gnosticism. He seems to use *pistis* to mean 'the content of faith' in the following places 1 Tim. 1:2, 4, 19; 3:9, 13; 4:1, 6; 5:8; 6:10, 12, 21; 2 Tim. 2:18; 3:8; 4:7; Tit. 1:1, 4, 13; 2:2. Against this we can put several places where *pistis* must mean 'trust': 1 Tim. 1:5, 14, 19; 2:7, 15; 4:12; 6:11; 2 Tim. 1:5, 13; 2:22; 3:10; Tit. 3:15. Thus the author cannot be accused of ignoring the subjective side of faith. But he certainly does objectify the faith in a way which is foreign to Paul. It has become a body of doctrine which must be guarded and handed on. As Merk says (p. 94), faith has its substance in the gospel, so that the mere fact that the heretic has fallen away from the faith shows him up as self-condemned (1 Tim. 1:19; 6:10, 21). The central message of the gospel is that Christ has come into the world to save sinners (1 Tim. 1:15). Through the continuity of the gospel the salvation offered becomes available for the church's life, and the continuing presence of the gospel is ensured by the institutions which the author commends, the ministry, rules for church order, etc. (Merk, pp. 98–9). Something of Paul's intimate attachment to the person of the risen Lord has been lost, but the author's emphasis on the gospel implies an emphasis on Jesus and his history.

We must finally notice one more interesting feature of the author's christology. He has what Brox calls a '*Leidenstheologie*', a theology of suffering (see Brox on 2 Tim. 3:11). It is centred on Paul, who is the great example of suffering and martyrdom. See 2 Tim. 1:12; 2:8–9, 10; 3:11; 4:6. Paul suffers ill-treatment, imprisonment, and finally death because of the gospel with which he has been entrusted. Persecution has always been his lot ever since his conversion. But this is not confined to Paul. Because Timothy also has been entrusted with the gospel, he too must be prepared to suffer hardship and persecution: 1 Tim. 1:18; 4:10; 6:12. Timothy must 'wage the good warfare'; he and Paul must 'toil and strive'. Timothy must 'fight the good fight of faith'; he must be prepared to 'take his share of suffering'. These words are ostensibly addressed to Timothy, but they are certainly intended for all church leaders. The role of suffering is not however to be confined to them. The author of the Pastorals extends this duty to embrace all faithful Christians. The great principle is stated in 2 Tim. 3:12: all who desire to live a godly life in Christ Jesus will be persecuted. We find the same note in the hymn quoted in 2 Tim. 2:11–12:

If we have died with him, we shall also live with him;
if we endure, we shall also reign with him.

This is remarkable, and reminds one of Paul's doctrine that Christians are to reproduce in their own lives the sufferings, death, and resurrection of Jesus. But it is connected to Jesus at one remove: we are to suffer hardship and persecution because of our service to the gospel of Jesus Christ. What is really astonishing is the total absence of any reference whatever to the cross of Christ. Indeed, even if one only contemplated the absence of the cross and of the title 'Son' for Christ from the Pastorals, and considered no other evidence, one would be driven to the conclusion that Paul could not have written them. Even when the author mentions the witness of Jesus Christ before Pontius Pilate, as in 1 Tim. 6:13, he does not go on to mention the cross. It may be implied, but if so it remains implicit throughout the Pastorals. One cannot help suspecting that Paul's profound doctrine of the cross was simply too deep for the author of the Pastorals. We may surely conclude that this theology of suffering is the author's own creation. He did not get this from his sources. It is no doubt the product of his own experience.

8. TECHNIQUE OF COMPOSITION

The Pastorals are made up of a miscellaneous collection of material. They have no unifying theme; there is no development of thought. We can therefore make a reasonable estimate of the various materials which they contain and of how the author has linked them together. We can isolate the following nine distinct types of material (I have marked with an asterisk those elements which seem to have been largely the author's own composition):

1. *Extracts from a church order*

H. W. Bartsch (pp. 11–13) insists that the author had access to an already existing document that gave rules about church order. He claims that Polycarp later drew from the same document, and that much later church orders, such as the *Didascalia Apostolorum* (early 3rd cent.), are based on this document also. We do not need to follow him in his speculations about the later orders, but we may well agree that the author of the Pastorals had some sort of a church order as one of his sources. Bartsch points to a series of introductory phrases, which, he claims, betrays the presence of a regulative document; e.g. sentences beginning with 'if', as used in case-law or casuistry, 1 Tim. 5:4, 9; 'if anyone' in 1 Tim. 3:1. He also emphasises the case of the more formal imperative in 1 Tim. 5:4: *manthanetōsan* ('**let them first learn**'), and *axiousthōsan* ('**let [the elders] be considered worthy**') in 1 Tim. 5:17. And he underlines the very authoritative style of *boulomai* ('**I desire**') in 1 Tim. 2:8; 5:14 ('**I would have**' – the same word in Greek); or *diatassomai* ('**as I directed you**') in Tit. 1:15. He compares also the use of *dei* ('**it is necessary**') in such passages as 1 Tim. 3:2; Tit. 1:7 (in each case *RSV* has translated with 'must be'). These elements of a church order document are most apparent in 1 Timothy: see 3:1–7 (bishops); 3:8–13 (deacons); 5:3–16 (widows); 5:17–24 (payment and discipline of presbyters). They do not appear at all in 2 Timothy, but are present in Titus: see 1:5–9 (bishops). We have here then the first faint beginnings of canon law, that body of church law that was to grow to such massive proportions centuries later in the West.

2. *Domestic Codes*

This means lists of various groups in the community with a description of the conduct which is appropriate to them. These groups are mostly natural ones, such as husbands and wives, fathers and children, older people and younger people. But it also includes at least one purely social group, slaves and slave-owners. The occurrence of these domestic codes is a feature of the later part of the *NT*. We find them in Col. 3:18–4:1; Eph. 5:22–6:9; 1 Pet. 2:18–37; 5:1–6. Indeed these other books of the *NT*, give us a fuller development of the domestic codes than what we find in the Pastorals. But they are undoubtedly present in the Pastorals; see 1 Tim. 2:9–15 (women); 6:1–2 (slaves); Tit. 2:1–10 (older men, older women, younger women, younger men, slaves). It is very likely that the author of the Pastorals was drawing on a domestic code document of which we can find traces in Ephesians and 1 Peter, and also in the *Didache*, Ignatius, and the *Epistle of Barnabas* (see Bartsch, pp. 146–7, and my *Studies*, pp. 86f.). Here then we seem to have identified a second written source for the Pastorals. The domestic code did not originate in Christianity. It can be paralleled in contemporary pagan literature. But, though borrowed from pagan sources, it was thoroughly Christianised, as the contents of the codes in the *NT* demonstrate.

3. *Liturgical fragments*

This is so obvious, it hardly needs illustration. It will be quite enough to point to one outstanding example from each letter: 1 Tim. 3:16; 2 Tim. 2:11–13; Tit. 2:11–14 and 3:3–7 (originally one source, no doubt). We should not try to be too well-informed about the exact origin of these passages. We do not know enough about early Christian hymnology to be dogmatic. Some of these passages no doubt represent hymns sung by Christians at worship; such would be 1 Tim. 3:16 and 2 Tim. 2:11–13. Others may be extracts from the thanksgiving prayer in the eucharist. This would probably best describe the two fragments in Tit. 2–3. At this period there was nothing like a fixed liturgy: he who presided at worship was free to use his own language. But not all presbyters or bishops were equally well endowed with ability to speak well, and it was natural that certain outstanding individuals should influence others in the language they used in worship, and thus a liturgical tradition would grow up. I have suggested in *Studies* (chs. 7 and 8) that one can find traces of both a baptismal and a eucharistic liturgy in the Pastorals which has connections with other books inside (and outside) the *NT*. Incidentally, if there is any value in my conclusions, this could help to fix the date of the Pastorals to approximately the end of the first century or the first years of the second. Of course at that period we must not try too sharply to distinguish a baptismal from a eucharistic liturgy. Justin, writing fifty years later, makes it clear that baptisms were normally conducted at a eucharistic celebration.

4. *Confessional or homiletic statements*

These are not so easy to distinguish, but virtually all editors agree that they are to be found in the Pastorals. An obvious example occurs in 1 Tim. 2:4–6; 6:13 also seems to be a quotation from a creed. But several editors claim that 6:11–16 is an extract from an ordination homily; vv. 15–16, however, sound much more like a liturgical prayer. Of course using confessional material was a well-attested habit of Paul's, as we have already noticed.

5. *Lists of sinners or sins*

We meet such lists in 1 Tim. 1:9–10; 6:4–5; 2 Tim. 3:2–5; Tit. 3:3. This is a feature of the *NT* generally; cf. Mk 7:21–22 (parallel Mt. 15:19). We also meet a list of sinners in Paul (Rom. 1:29–31), a list which the author of Pastorals has certainly used as his inspiration. But, for the length of his work, the author makes far greater use of these 'vice-lists'. He was probably also to some extent influenced by contemporary pagan usage in this respect. Such lists of vices or sinners are to be found in contemporary popular philosophical debate.

6. *Historical details about Paul's life*

We have already identified and discussed these in a previous section. The author of the Pastorals uses them primarily to give historical verisimilitude to his work, not because he had any particular concern to reconstruct or represent Paul's life-history.

*7. *Pauline passages transposed*

These we have already dealt with, and see the complete list in the Appendix at the end of the Commentary. Here however we may detect more than a mere desire to make the letters appear Pauline. The author genuinely believed that Paul had a message for his generation, and attempts to transmit that message in terms more appropriate to his own day. He was a writer of *midrash*, not a mere imitator of Paul.

*8. *Midrash or Haggada on Scripture*

By this I mean those passages in which the author of the Pastorals is explicitly or implicitly expounding Scripture (which meant for him of course what we would call the Old Testament). For a fuller discussion of those passages, see the detached Note at 2 Tim. 2:21. We can identify six places where the author is basing himself on the *OT*: 1 Tim 1:13–16 (Exod. 34:6); 2:3–4 (Isa. 45:21–22); 3:15 (1 Kg. 8:12); 2 Tim. 2:19 (Num. 16:5; Isa. 52:11; see my *Studies*, pp. 29–41); 3:7 (*Haggada* on Exod. 8:18–19); and 2 Tim. 4:16–18 (probably Ps. 22). How far any of these expositions is the author's own is discussed in the Note mentioned above. But these examples do at least show that the charge often brought against the author that he virtually ignores the *OT* is not justified. He could handle it with skill.

*9. *Direct exhortation and instruction*

There is so much of this it does not need illustration. Here the author gives his own sentiments unvarnished; here we find what he thinks of heretics and how he believes a church leader ought to behave. We can perhaps distinguish instruction about how to behave in special circumstances from more general exhortation about life-style, etc. He seems to be giving instruction in 1 Tim. 2:1f. (how public worship should be conducted); also 2:8–9; 5:1–2 (how a church leader should behave towards various age-groups in the local church); 2 Tim. 2:2 (direction to hand on the *parathēkē*); 3:16 (the uses of Scripture); Tit. 1:5 (instruction to appoint presbyters in every local church); 3:10 (how to treat a heretic). This advice is sometimes seasoned with material taken from contemporary popular philosophy. The most outstanding example occurs in 1 Tim. 6:6–10, which is full of popular saws about riches; see also 6:17–19 on the same theme. We can find a trace in 2 Tim. 3:16; *epanorthōsis* ('correction') and *paideia* ('training') are used together in Stoic moral philosophy. Then in Tit. 1:12 the author quotes a line from a pagan poet to prove his contention that Cretans are a bad lot; and in Tit. 1:14 we may have another echo of popular philosophy. We may pause to ask, why did the author need to draw on the resources of pagan thought in this way? Probably because he had only limited Christian resources on which to draw, not being an original theologian himself, and he decided to make what use he could of his secular education, which probably did not extend beyond the equivalent of our modern university entrance level.

These materials, then, the author skilfully formed together to make up what we know as the Pastoral Epistles. He carefully alternated his materials. It would not have done to put all his church order material, or all his Pauline transpositions, or all his liturgical material together in one block. That would have looked too like a manual of church order, or an exposition of Paul, or a book of worship, and he wanted to give the impression that he was writing letters. This explains that peculiar feature which runs all through the three epistles, his habit of beginning a theme, dropping it, and then resuming it. We can illustrate it thus:

Theme	Begun	Resumed
false doctrine	1 Tim. 1:3–7	1:18–20
public prayer	2:1–3	2:8
life style for a church leader	6:6–10	6:17–19
guarding the deposit	2 Tim. 1:11–14	2:1–7
movements of colleagues	4:9–15	4:19–21
liturgical fragment	Tit. 2:11–14	3:3–7
false teachers	1:10–16	3:9–11
good works	3:8	3:14

A consequence of this technique is that the author has often to switch from one topic to another for no reason that arises from the nature of the material itself. He has therefore devised a whole series of connecting words or phrases that help to smooth the transition from one to another. The most remarkable of these is **the saying is sure**, which occurs five times (though see the detached Note on these 'faithful sayings' at 1 Tim. 1:17).

But we can point to many others. They are not always obvious in the English, because they do not always come at the beginning of a sentence; but in Greek they do, and are therefore all the more emphatic. See **I am writing these instructions to you** (only three words in Greek), 1 Tim. 3:14; **if you put these instructions before the brethren** (four words in Greek), 4:6; **Command and teach these things**, 4:11; **teach and urge these duties**, 6:2*b*; **but as for you**, 6:11 (also 2 Tim. 3:10; Tit. 2:1, the same phrase in Greek; and compare **you then**, in 2 Tim. 2:1); **You are aware that**, 2 Tim. 1:15; **remind them of this**, 2:14; **but understand this**, 3:1; **declare these things**, Tit. 2:15; **remind them**, Tit. 3:1. These connecting phrases serve to bind the material together and make it seem more like a letter with certain definite themes. His book certainly does include several themes, but when we analyse it we find that it does not naturally fall into the category of genuine correspondence. If we compare any of the Pastorals with 1 Corinthians, for example, the difference must strike us at once. 1 Corinthians contains a number of diverse topics, because Paul has to deal both with questions which the Corinthians have asked him and with problems that he knows have arisen in the life of the church. But he deals with one topic after another in order, and there is no trace of this peculiar feature of the taking up, dropping, and resumption of themes that we find in the Pastorals. 1 Corinthians is a genuine letter; each of the Pastorals is an ingenious pastiche.

The conclusion seems to be that the Pastorals were all written at much the same time; the themes and technique we have outlined above are common to all of them. Once give up the notion that they are genuine letters, and there seems to be no particular reason to place the writing of Titus between that of 1 and 2 Timothy, as many editors do. It is true that we can find certain features that are more prominent in 1 Timothy and others in 2 Timothy. Thus 1 Timothy is the epistle of church order *par excellence*, and 2 Timothy is primarily the letter of Paul's last will and testament. There seems to be nothing very distinctive about Titus, unless it be the negative feature that it has no Pauline transposition and no scriptural *midrash*. This is why one is led to suspect that Titus was written last of all and that the author was beginning to run short of material.

9. THE SIGNIFICANCE OF THE PASTORALS

The accusation has been made against the Pastorals, mostly by Lutheran scholars, that they exhibit clear signs of 'early Catholicism' and therefore represent a sad falling away from the Pauline doctrine centred on the justification of sinners by faith in Christ. It is not appropriate in this Commentary to pass moral judgments on Paul or the author of the Pastorals, but we may certainly admit that in fact the Pastorals do show signs of 'early Catholicism', if by that is meant the pattern and structure of church life which grew up during the second, third and fourth centuries, and which eventually developed into the Catholic Church (both Eastern and Western) of the Middle Ages. Thus, in the Pastorals we do encounter a clearly defined ordained ministry, which claims wide authority over the church. We do find the beginnings of church order: rules and regulations about the ordering of church life are already in use and are being elaborated. We do find for the first time the concept of ordination to the sacred ministry as conferring a charisma. The clergy are undoubtedly marked off from the laity by means of ordination. Likewise we meet a strong emphasis on the necessity for preserving the orthodox faith over against heresy (that word 'heretic' occurs for the first time in the sense of 'misbeliever' in Tit. 3:10). And we see the beginning of that violent emotional reaction against heresy that is a notable feature of the Catholic tradition throughout the ages. We can also see the beginning of the process whereby the clergy monopolise all activity and decision making in the church. Paul's belief that each local church is, as a representative of the church as a whole, responsible for its own life and discipline seems to be disappearing. We can also detect in 2 Tim. 3:14 a distancing between Scripture and tradition which later on was to become a burning issue (we discuss this further below). And it might be said with some justice that in the Pastorals there first appears a certain tendency to turn Christianity into a sanctified moralism which is markedly different from Paul's brilliant assertion of the primacy of free grace, but which certainly is a characteristic of the early church.

On the other hand, it would be a great mistake to regard the Pastoral Epistles simply as documents illustrating the emergence of early Catholicism. There are certain features in them that seem quite contrary to the very essence of what is normally associated with Catholicism. For example, the author of the Pastorals, far from desiring a celibate clergy, takes it for granted that bishops, presbyters, and deacons will be married, and makes some suggestion as to how they should manage their families. The stress on virginity, and the downgrading of the married state, which so strongly marked the

church from the fourth century onwards, are totally opposed to the
spirit of the Pastorals. Again, we do not find in the Pastorals any
claim to the 'apostolic succession'. The succession of orthodox teaching must be maintained, but there is no stress on succession by
ordination; and the only apostle is Paul. Above all, the ministry is
not defined in cultic or sacral terms. It is related to the gospel and
the preservation of the deposit of faith, not to the eucharist or the
conduct of worship. One could add that there is no great emphasis
on the sacraments in the Pastorals. But in fact one can probably find
excerpts from both baptismal and eucharistic liturgies in the Pastorals, and there is one clear reference to baptism (Tit. 3:5). Above all,
the gospel is still the test or norm of the church's life and belief, and
the ministry and all other institutions exist in order to serve it. So,
whether early Catholicism was a healthy or an unhealthy development
in the church's life, the Pastorals do not give an unambiguous witness
to its emergence.

The fact that the author of the Pastorals wrote pseudonymously
has sometimes been brought as an accusation against him. Or else
the Pauline authorship has been defended on the grounds that we do
not find any pseudonymous Christian literature till much later.
Neither argument is very convincing. We must not apply modern
ideas about authorship to the practice of the ancient world. The
contemporaries of the author of the Pastorals would not have condemned him for claiming Paul's authority for his work. Nor can it be
easily maintained that there are no other pseudonymous books in the
NT. We can point to the 'Deutero-Paulines' in the first place. Very
many scholars deny the Pauline authorship of Ephesians. And both
Colossians and 2 Thessalonians are doubted. It must however be
allowed that these three letters are much closer to Paul than are the
Pastorals – hence the name 'Deutero-Pauline', and even the epithet
'Trito-Pauline' which Trummer has invented for the Pastorals. Beyond this, it is very likely indeed that 1 Peter is pseudonymous, and
quite certain that 2 Peter is. To these examples we can add that of
Jude, which few scholars today believe to have been written by Jude
the Apostle.

We can see from the witness of 2 Peter 3:16 that the Pauline
epistles were causing some difficulties in the church of the early
second century. The author of 2 Peter writes: 'There are some things
in them hard to understand, which the ignorant and unstable twist
to their own destruction.' The author of the Pastorals had, as one of
his aims in writing, the desire to make Paul more intelligible to his
own generation. Not that Paul needed rehabilitation, but he did need
being brought into relation to a later time. As Brox writes (Introd.,

p. 71), it was not to rehabilitate Paul that the author wrote, but to show that Paul stood behind orthodox doctrine.

Certainly the author of the Pastorals falls far short of Paul in almost every respect. But it is not with Paul that we ought to compare him; the comparison should rather be with his own contemporaries and immediate successors. Compared with Jude and 2 Peter he emerges very much the superior; he does not have their pretentiousness or their bombastic style. Compared with Clement of Rome, though there is much in common, on the whole the author of the Pastorals should be allowed to be more modest, less moralistic, less unfortunately ambitious in his use of Scripture. When we go farther afield and compare him with Hermas, or the authors of the apocryphal *Acts* and *Epistles*, the author of the Pastorals must bear off the palm. He is no profound theologian, but he does not descend to Hermas' level of appalling theological muddle, and he does not give us a legendary or incredible picture of his master. The two contemporaries who certainly excell him are the author of 1 Peter and Ignatius – the first because he has retained a vein of pure, early Christian insight, the second because he is altogether a deeper theologian.

We ought to be grateful to the author of the Pastorals when we understand the circumstances in which he wrote. At that epoch the church needed to strengthen the authority of the ministry, and to marshal its forces both institutional and intellectual against the mortal threat of Gnosticism. The author of the Pastorals could not do much at the intellectual level, but he could and did help to strengthen the institution. The intellectual battle was being maintained by others. Indeed one might reasonably claim that the author of the Pastorals achieved at the institutional level what the author of the Fourth Gospel achieved at the level of high theology. He defended the church against a form of Christianity that would have proved fatal in a couple of centuries. In doing so he decided to claim the patronage of Paul, but his picture of Paul is neither legendary nor sentimental. We should applaud his intention; his execution is by no means despicable.

We could point to two more virtues which he evinces. The first is his emphasis on the universal love of God. God wills that *all men* should be saved. In this respect he might almost be said to have excelled his master. Paul was so much preoccupied with the question of the Jews that perhaps the full range of the scope of God's love did not always occupy him as it might have. In the time of the author of the Pastorals the possibility that the Jews might join the church in any number was past. He is able to view the truly catholic range of the church's vocation more fully; see 1 Tim. 1:16, 24; 2 Tim. 2:25–6; 4:17.

The other virtue we have already referred to in connection with 2

Tim. 3:16. In that passage the author outlines the uses of Scripture. It is useful for teaching, for rebuke, for reformation, for training. This implies that Scripture and the *parathēkē* are not identical. Scripture is to be the foundation on which the *parathēkē* is built, the means by which the *parathēkē* is to be proved and defended. Admittedly there is little evidence that the author of the Pastorals would himself be very competent if he were ever to be required to prove or defend the Christian tradition from Scripture, but he has got the relation of the two right. The old maxim, 'the church to teach, the Bible to prove', would receive full approbation from the author of the Pastorals. In our own day that principle has been revindicated in a remarkable way by the *aggiornamento* in the Roman Catholic Church. It is good to know that the Pastoral Epistles are entirely in line with this understanding of the role of Scripture.

I do not think I should want to alter what I wrote about the Pastorals in 1968 (*Studies*, p. 120): 'If they are Pauline, they represent a dismal conclusion to Paul's writings; if they are post-Pauline, they are an admirable and indispensable illustration of the state of the Church at the end of the first century.' In fact it is pretty plain by now that they are not Pauline. In them we see the church as it sets out into the second century, tackling its practical problems with vigour and success.

THE FIRST EPISTLE TO TIMOTHY

THE CONTENTS OF 1 TIMOTHY

GREETING

1:1–2

In vv. 1 and 2 the author observes the formula for the opening greeting of a Pauline letter, as he does in his other two letters also. It takes the form (1) superscription (2) addressee (3) salutation. Only three of the Pauline corpus of seventeen letters lack a thanksgiving, of which this and Titus are two. The third is Galatians, but Paul had special reasons for not giving thanks there (Roller, pp. 55, 65).

1. The phrase **by command of God our Saviour** marks the letter as un-Pauline. In acknowledged Paulines the phrase 'according to the command of the eternal God' occurs, but there are good textual and stylistic reasons for doubting whether Rom. 16:26 was actually written by Paul. It is more probably part of a final ascription of praise added by a later editor. Also Paul never uses the word *sōtēr* (**Saviour**) of God and only once absolutely of Christ (Phil. 3:20) – the author of the Pastorals uses it freely of both God and Christ. But only in Tit. 3:6 is the title applied to Christ quite independently of God, and even there God has been called **Saviour** in v. 4, which forms part of the same liturgical fragment. In all other places the author uses it either of God alone or of Christ in close association with God (see 1 Tim. 2:3; 4:10; Tit. 1:3; 2:10 – for God; and 2 Tim. 1:10 for Christ, in the same formula as the phrase 'God who saved us' in vv. 8–9; see also Tit. 1:4; 2:13, as used of Christ). This usage is somewhat different from that of two other writers who probably wrote a little later, the author of 2 Peter and Ignatius. These two Christian authors use **Saviour** quite freely of Christ without associating him in the same passage with God. See 2 Pet. 1:1, 11; 2:20; 3:2, 18; Ignatius, *Eph.* 1.1; *Philad.* 9.2. The title Saviour was freely applied to rulers in the Hellenistic world, especially to the Ptolemies, and it was a favourite epithet of the divine emperor in the emperor cult. But it could also be applied in an inscription to a citizen who had supplied oil free to the gymnasium! (For references see Spicq.) One might perhaps conclude from his use of the term that the author did not want Christ to be regarded as a Saviour-God on the analogy of Hercules, Orpheus, Adonis, or the Roman emperor. But he did want to emphasise that salvation is to be found in God in Christ rather than in the emperor (see *Note on the Imperial Cult*, under Tit. 2:14).

Christ Jesus our hope: this may be an echo of Ps. 65:5: 'O God of our salvation, who art the hope of all the ends of the earth'. Paul speaks of 'the God of hope' in Rom. 15:13, and in Col. 1:27 'this mystery' (i.e. the contents of the gospel) is described as 'Christ in you the hope of glory'. Ignatius calls Christ 'our hope' in *Mag.* 11, and 'our common hope' in *Eph.* 21.2. See also Tit. 1:2; 2:13; 3:7, in all of which passages the hope refers to eternal life after death or to the parousia. To call Jesus Christ **our hope** without qualification seems to be the mark of third-generation Christianity.

2. My true child in the faith: perhaps an echo of Phil. 4:3, 'true yokefellow' (the adjective *gnēsios* is common to both passages). It is not clear to whom Paul is referring in Phil. 4:3. One theory is that he means Timothy, so it is just possible that the author of the Pastorals took this interpretation and that is why he uses the adjective here. D–C quote a phrase from the *Corpus Hermeticum* where the devotee is called a 'true son' of the deity. Brox suggests that the author wishes to underline the legitimacy of Timothy's position in the Ephesian church. Perhaps Paul's warm and intimate relation to Timothy is meant as an example of what relations among the ministers of the church should be. The phrase **in the faith** means the Christian religion. Dornier well compares 1 C. 4:17, where Timothy is called 'my beloved and faithful child in the Lord'. Verse 20 here could be called a gloss on that phrase.

Grace, mercy, and peace: Compare Gal. 6:16; Rom. 1:7. The combination of the three words recurs in 2 Tim. 1:2 and in 2 Jn 3. Spicq is ready to associate it with Asia Minor.

WARNING AGAINST FALSE DOCTRINE

1:3–7

The author loses no time in bringing in one of his main themes in all three letters. He is plainly very much alarmed by the threat of heresy.

3. As I urged you: *RSV* has corrected the author's syntax by making **remain at Ephesus** the apodosis of the opening phrase **As I urged you**. But it is more probable that the author wrote 'As I urged you to remain at Ephesus', without supplying any main verb, thus providing an anacoluthon at the very beginning of his work. Spicq regards this as a sign of authenticity, because Paul is quite capable of writing unfinished sentences (but with him they are the mark of passages of high emotional tension, which cannot be said of this one). Alternatively Spicq suggests that the apodosis is to be found in the words **that you may charge certain persons**, but this is grammatically very strange, or even in v. 18, **this charge I commit to you** – but that is a desperate remedy. It is more likely that the author uses *kathōs* (**as**) because it is a favourite word with Paul and adds a certain solemnity to his first charge to Timothy. In 2 Pet. 1:3 we meet a very similar use of *hōs* (omitted in *RSV*), with no doubt a very similar motive. A good parallel can be found in Ignatius *Eph.* 1.3, where he uses a clause beginning with *epei* ('since') without any apodosis. Compare also the speech of the small-town lawyer Tertullus in Ac. 24:2–4, where we have a similar anacoluthon. But Luke may well be faintly making fun of small-town lawyers there. Holtz suggests that Paul was dictating in a hurry, hence the confusion. But his own theory demands the presence of a secretary who carried out a thorough revision at his leisure.

Not to teach any different doctrine represents two words in Greek, *mē heterodidaskalein*; this is a very rare word, used by Ignatius in *Pol.* 3:1; some believe Ignatius has taken the word from this passage – there, as here, it refers not to heretics who attack the church from outside, but Christians who spread false doctrine from inside. D–C

suggest that the description of the doctrine is deliberately left vague
so as to cover a wide range of teaching.

4. The phrase **myths and endless genealogies** has given rise to
much debate. Those who defend Pauline authorship make it refer to
Jewish *haggada*, such as we find in the book of *Jubilees* or the literature of Hellenistic Judaism. But it is very doubtful if our author
would have seen very much wrong in this literature. He himself
knows the *haggada* about Jannes and Jambres (see 2 Tim. 3:8), and
is probably acquainted with the *haggada* which we meet in the *Book
of Adam and Eve* (see on 2:13–15). And he was acquainted with 4
Mac. Hence it is more likely that he has in mind a form of Jewish
Gnosticism, and the **myths and endless genealogies** will refer to the
accounts of the movements and couplings of the various aeons as
described in this or that Gnostic system. So generally D–C and Brox;
the latter suggests that the author is thinking of a Gnostic treatment
of the *OT*. The word translated **speculations** (*ekzētēseis*) occurs
absolutely nowhere else in Greek literature, but there is a variant
reading *zētēseis*, which would mean 'philosophical enquiries'. The
phrase **the divine training that is in faith** is somewhat ambiguous in
Greek. The word **training** translates *oikonomian*, and it is followed by
theou, 'of God'. Now the 'economy of God' is the great theme of
Ephesians, where it means God's whole cosmic scheme of redemption
in Christ. It is tempting to conclude that the author had this in mind,
for he certainly knew Ephesians. But it is more likely that he is
contrasting elaborate intellectual speculations with the simple faith
which is the best training for the Christian. There is an alternative
reading *oikodomēn*, which would mean 'building up' in faith. As
often happens, an alternative reading offers a gloss, but here probably
a correct gloss.

5. **whereas the aim of our charge is love that issues from a pure
heart.** Love as the aim of the proclamation is genuinely Pauline but
what does **charge** (*parangelia*) refer to? It is difficult not to connect
it with the verb **charge** in the previous verse (same root in Greek
also). In 1 Th. 4:2 the word is used of Christian moral exhortation,
and in v. 18 below of Paul's moral advice to Timothy. The sense will
then be that exposition of the Christian faith is not meant to create
endless discussion groups; rather the moral exhortation that goes with
the teaching will always be intended to create love, etc. The phrases
a pure heart and a good conscience and sincere faith seem to take
one into a sphere very different from the lofty atmosphere of Paul's
life lived as a justified sinner. It is very doubtful if Paul would have
recognised any of these as the elements of the Christian life. Houlden
describes **a good conscience** as 'a tamed equivalent for Paul's justification by faith'. Here is moralism taking the place of theology. It

is possible that **sincere faith** refers to the content of the faith rather than to the mode of believing, in which case it might mean orthodox belief contrasted with the false teaching of the heretics (so D–C).

6. by swerving from these: Epictetus, an outstanding Stoic philosopher of the second half of the first century *AD*, uses this verb (*ektrepein*) of turning out of the right way in moral philosophy. The word translated **vain discussion** (*mataiologia*) is used by Plutarch and by Vettius Valens, an astronomical writer of the second century *AD*. See Tit. 1:10 'empty talkers', which is *mataiologoi*. Both D–C and Houlden note that the author is more concerned with abusing his opponents than with refuting their doctrine. Dornier compares Rom. 1:21–22, where the pagan world is described by Paul as having 'become futile'. The first verb is *mataiousthai*, of the same root as the word which the author uses here. But Paul's approach is significantly different. Paul says they lapsed into wrong thinking, polytheism and idolatry. The author here says that their talk is silly and meaningless. Paul proceeds to supply the right theology, but the author of the Pastorals does not attempt to understand or refute his opponents.

7. teachers of the law: does this mean mere Judaisers, or does it imply some sort of Gnostic use of the *OT*? A certain Jewish element there must be, in view of Tit. 1:14; 3:9. D–C emphasise the significance of 'certain persons' in 6; they say it indicates that the opponents have not yet broken with the Catholic Church, and hence the author does not wish to name them, and they well compare Ignatius' use of 'certain persons' in *Philad.* 8.2, where Ignatius' adversaries seem to be Christians who have not shaken off the yoke of Judaism. A. E. Barnett (p. 253) makes the interesting suggestion that the author calls the trouble-makers **teachers of the law** because he wishes to bring them under Paul's condemnation. We should probably regard them as Gnostic Jewish Christians. They **make assertions** about their hierarchies of aeons, whose names they take from the *OT*.

THE USE OF THE LAW

1:8–11

8. The author seems to be echoing Rom. 7:14 when he writes **Now we know that the law is good**. In Rom. 2:16 Paul actually uses the same word *kalos* (**good**) for the law. But the author betrays his imperfect grasp of Pauline thought when he adds **if any one uses it lawfully**. A better translation is that offered by C. K. Barrett: 'correctly'. And for the author, using the law correctly simply means being a law-abiding citizen. Spicq points out the *nomimōs* (**lawfully**) is often used in Jewish literature for observance of the Torah, precisely what Paul regarded as impossible. D–C well comment that 'in the Pastorals the law does not serve to uncover the paradoxical situation of unbelieving men', as it does in Paul.

9–10. the law is not laid down for the just, a moralistic misunderstanding of Paul. Now follows an apparently miscellaneous list of sinners. It is vaguely (though not exactly) reminiscent of Paul's list in Rom. 1:29–31. There Paul is giving a general indictment of the pagan world. The author does not appear to be doing this – he is ostensibly giving some examples of those against whom the law is directed. Scholars have made strenuous efforts to calibrate this list with the Decalogue, notably Nauck and Dornier, but without notable success. We have noted in the Introduction that lists of vices or sinners constitute one element in the materials which the author includes in his letters. Brox suggests that he is using the list here as a way of smearing his opponents. The law, says the author, **is laid down . . . for the ungodly and sinners.** Paul in Rom. 4:5 describes God as 'justifying the ungodly'; but that does not make him 'godly', but 'holy, elect, called'. There is not a single item in this list that would not have been condemned just as vigorously in most contemporary pagan moral codes. N. J. McEleney (*CBQ* 36 [1974], p. 209) suggests that the phrase **murderers of fathers and murderers of mothers** is a hit at the false teachers who were ruining homes by their teaching. F. M. Hitchcock (*ExpT* 39 [1927–8], pp. 347f.) romantically apprehends here a reference to Nero's murder of his mother! The appearance of **sodomites** has been linked with Ephesus. Philostratus claims that when Apollonius of Tyana passed through Ephesus (some time in the second half of the first century *AD*) he found it full of homosexuals. It is slightly strange to meet **kidnappers** in this list. Lock points out that, though slavery is not condemned, slave trading is. D–C add that slave trading is thought of as robbery rather than as an invasion of human rights. The final clause **and whatever else is contrary to sound doctrine** is a rather lame ending. By **sound doctrine** the author means orthodox teaching, but the phrase has an overtone of 'commonsense morality' about it. Epictetus uses it to mean 'reasonable opinion'. With **and whatever else,** etc., Dornier well compares Rom. 13:9. From the point of view of syntax this passage begins with what is really an anacoluthon, since **understanding this** in v. 9 is in the singular and has no exact subject preceding it. The phrase may be a technique for introducing an already existing vice-list.

11. in accordance with the glorious gospel of the blessed God: literally translated this would be 'in accordance with the gospel of the glory of the blessed God'. It is therefore a Semitism and as such is quite reminiscent of Paul; cf. 2 C. 4:6 and Rom. 9:5*b*. But the author gives himself away by his use of the phrase **the blessed** (*makarios*)

God. This is an epithet that Paul never uses of God. It came originally from pagan Greek literature (Homer calls the gods 'blessed'), and was adopted by Hellenistic Judaism, which is no doubt how it entered the vocabulary of the author of the Pastorals. D–C, rightly no doubt, see here traces of a liturgical style.

GOD'S MERCY SHOWN IN PAUL'S LIFE

1:12–17

In this passage we see the author at his best. His genuine admiration for his master shines through it, and so does his conviction of the universal scope of God's love. The same theme is treated in Eph. 3:7–8. If, as seems very likely, Ephesians is not by Paul, we have there and in this passage two accounts of Paul's conversion and call by writers later than Paul. The Ephesians passage could be described as a poetic version as compared with the prose account here.

12. I thank him: the Greek *charin echō* is not a Pauline phrase. Spicq calls it a Latinism. **who has given me strength** certainly echoes Phil. 4:13, 'I can do all things in him who strengthens me'; the alternative reading in 1 Tim. 1:12, 'who gives me strength', shows that an early copyist recognised the quotation. But D–C are no doubt right in pointing to 1 C. 7:25 as another passage that lies behind this one. Indeed one could almost call these verses a cento of Pauline phrases. Spicq well quotes Augustine: 'God does not choose anyone who is worthy, but in choosing him renders him worthy'.

13. though I formerly blasphemed and persecuted and insulted him: *RSV* has turned three nouns into verbs and has assumed that the object of Paul's blasphemous and insulting behaviour was Christ (cf. Ac. 9:5). It does not seem very likely that the historical Paul would have described himself before his conversion as 'a blasphemer'; on the contrary, he thought that he was doing God service (cf. Jn 16:2; and see Phil. 3:5–7, which hardly looks like blasphemy in the religious sense). Paul certainly would have called himself a persecutor; see 1 C. 15:9. Whether he would have described himself as 'a man of violence' (which is what the Greek *hubristēs* means) is debatable. Spicq points to 1 Th. 2:2, where he uses the verb to describe the violence he encountered at Philippi, and also to 2 C. 12:10, where 'insults' (*hubresin*) are listed among the hardships he endures for Christ's sake. The word suggests violent, insolent, reckless behaviour, which hardly fits into the picture of Paul the enthusiastic Pharisee. R. F. Collins (p. 167) agrees that it is unlikely that the historical Paul would have described himself in these terms. Brox also says that it is unlikely that Paul regarded himself as having been converted from blasphemy and unbelief. **I received mercy because I had acted**

ignorantly: this seems an un-Pauline sentiment. Paul's view would be that Christ had called him *despite* his ignorance.

14. the grace of our Lord overflowed: the word translated **over-flowed**, *hyperepleonasen*, is a very rare one. The author is echoing such passages as Rom. 5:20; 6:1; 2 C. 4:15. **with the faith and love that are in Christ Jesus** is a vague phrase using Pauline language, but leaving the exact sense uncertain. Is it Christ's love for Paul, or the mutual love of those who are 'in Christ'? The variety of translations witnesses to the difficulty of extracting the precise meaning. The author probably thought that such words would appear appropriate in this context, without reflecting very deeply on what exactly he wished to convey.

15. The saying is sure and worthy of full acceptance: this is the first of the 'faithful sayings'. For a discussion of their significance as a whole, see the Note after v. 17. This entire formula only recurs at 4:9, but **the saying is sure** occurs in four other places in the Pastorals. There is a strange variant reading for *pistos* (**sure**); it is *anthrōpinos*, which would mean 'human, natural, popular'. It has probably been inserted from 3:1, q.v. Whatever we may conclude about the other four 'faithful sayings', this one is undoubtedly a quasi-credal formula, which the author took from his own church tradition. Editors have compared Lk. 19:10, and no doubt both sayings represent the same original logion. A good parallel can be found in the realtion of 1 Tim. 2:6 to Mk 10:45. The phrase **worthy of acceptance** is almost a cliché in near-contemporary Greek literature and inscriptions. Here **worthy of full acceptance** could mean either 'worthy of acceptance by all' (which is how the *Book of Common Prayer* takes it) or 'worthy of whole-hearted acceptance'. In view of the parallel in 1 Tim. 6:1, **worthy of all honour**, the latter is probably right. **Christ Jesus came into the world**: only the author of the Fourth Gospel uses similar language, and the logion may have come to the author of the Pastorals via the school of the Fourth Gospel. The phrase does seem to imply a doctrine of pre-existence (so G. W. Knight, p. 37); but this does not mean that the author of the Pastorals consciously held a doctrine of pre-existence. Spicq says that *apodochē* (**acceptance**) means 'welcome' not just passive reception. **And I am the foremost of sinners** must echo 1 C. 15:9; Eph. 3:8. The author probably means **foremost** in gravity rather than in chronology. Spicq well points out that Paul is represented as saying **I am** not 'I was', a truly Pauline touch.

16. Here we have one of the finest original insights of the author of the Pastorals. Just because he is not inhibited by Paul's very Jewish belief about God's predestination, he is able to express the universal saving intention of God in Christ more boldly and simply than Paul could. No doubt he is also motivated by a desire to oppose the

Gnostic teachers, who tended to hold that only the élite could hope for salvation. The word translated **example**, *hypotupōsis*, normally means 'an imperfect sketch' in contemporary secular Greek, but **example** must be the right meaning here. Editors compare Jas 5:10 and 2 Pet. 2:6, where a similar word, *hupodeigma*, is used, though in the latter passage the sense may be nearer that of 'type'. Spicq quotes a good comment by Thomas Aquinas on his perfect patience: 'perfect because, though provoked he did not punish, but rather exalted his adversary, and that to our benefit'. **foremost** in this verse, as contrasted with v. 15, does mean 'first in time' (Spicq). D–C refer to *Barnabas* 5.9: 'When he chose his own apostles, who were destined to proclaim his gospel, they were more lawless than any sinners, in order that he might show that he came not to call the righteous but sinners'.

17. All editors agree that this is a liturgical fragment, brought in here to round off the section. Brox remarks that this whole description of Paul is important for the author, as it fixes the image of Paul for the rest of the three letters. But Brox adds, rightly no doubt, that there is not much historical plausibility in Paul discussing his conversion so long ago with an old and tried colleague. D–C believe that this verse was originally a Jewish formula, since it breathes the air of Hellenistic Judaism (for a discussion of Oke's thesis that the verse actually refers to Christ, see Introduction, section 7; it is quite possible that the author did not stop to ask himself whether the formula referred to God or Christ). We may note the alternative reading 'immortal' (*athanatōi*) for 'invisible' (the word rendered **immortal** by RSV is properly 'incorruptible'). This is the only passage in the entire NT in which God is described as invisible without the accompanying assertion that he has made himself known in Christ or in his works of creation. Compare 6:16, where the invisibility of God is strongly emphasised, but his intention of manifesting Christ at the parousia is also asserted. Compare Rom. 1:20; Col. 1:15; Jn 1:18; 6:46. This is no doubt an oversight on the author's part; he was no great theologian.

It seems possible that behind vv. 14–17 lies a midrash on Exod. 34:6. In that passage the invisible God makes himself known as 'the God of grace and truth' to Moses. It was a revelation of basic importance to Judaism and was incorporated into his prologue by the author of the Fourth Gospel (see my *The New Testament Interpretation of Scripture* [London, 1979], ch. 3). We could draw the following parallel:

Exod. 34:6	*1 Tim. 1:14–17*
A God merciful and	the grace of our Lord
gracious	
slow to anger	overflowed . . . with
	faith
abounding in steadfast *love*	and *love*
and *faithfulness*	I received *mercy* . . .
	his perfect patience

Where there are identical words in the Greek of the *LXX* of Exod. 34:6 and the Greek of 1:14–17, the text has been underlined. (This has been more fully worked out in my book *Grace and Truth* [London, 1975], pp. 15–16). This suggests that the author could compose effective Christian midrash on the *OT*, although his formulated theology cannot compare with Paul's.

Note on the 'faithful sayings' in the Pastorals
Five times the phrase *pistos ho logos* occurs (always rendered by *RSV* **the saying is sure**); besides this passage, 1 Tim. 3:1; 4:9; 2 Tim. 2:11; Tit. 3:8. As we have noted, the additional phrase **and worthy of full acceptance** also occurs at 1 Tim. 4:9. Naturally this striking feature of the Pastoral Epistles has drawn the attention of scholars. The longest treatment is in the scholarly book of G. W. Knight referred to under v. 15. An attempt has been made to connect the phrase with something similar in the Qumran documents. 'The word is sure to come to pass and the prophecy is true' (see D. Barthélemy and J. T. Milik, *Discoveries in the Judaean Desert* [Oxford, 1965], p. 103, for the Hebrew text). But this refers to the fulfilment of prophecy and has really no connection with the way the phrase is used on the Pastorals. Editors have tried to find some all-embracing category which will cover all five contexts – no easy task. Perhaps Nauck (pp. 46f.) is the most convincing; he claims that in all five places it is connected with *sōtēr* (**saviour**) or *sōzein* (**save**). But this can only be maintained by insisting that the phrase in 1 Tim. 3:1 refers to 2:15 and in Tit. 3:8 refers to 3:7, neither of which is at all an obvious conclusion. Besides, though some sort of a reference to salvation can be found in all five contexts by this means, in some of them it seems pretty casual, i.e. Tit. 3:7–8. Spicq (p. 277, h.) claims that the formula 'introduces an article of faith or a liturgical sentence universally diffused'. This can hardly apply to 1 Tim. 3:1, even if it is taken with 2:15. D–C are uncertain whether the formula is intended to introduce citations or statements. At any rate the author uses it in connection with credal, cultic, and church-order material. He employs it to link traditional material with his present situation. Since the three categories they mention cover so large a proportion of the

material which the author uses, this does not tell us very much about the purpose of the sayings.

H. Bürki (*Der erste Brief*) says that the phrase marks 'a formulated statement of early Christianity, perhaps of liturgical origin'. But this will not apply to 1 Tim. 3:1, however it is understood. A. Lemaire (p. 132) cautiously describes the phrase as belonging to 'community sayings' which only means that the author used it to mark material not of his own composition (but not *all* material not of his own composition). Bartsch (pp. 77, 161–2) claims that the sayings belong only to teaching and proverbial utterances, never to church rules (but does 1 Tim. 3:1 accord with this?). He thinks they are used to turn a mere statement into a rule for the church. But it would be difficult to apply this to Tit. 3:8. Compare also the claim of K. Wegenast (p. 157) that the 'faithful' words are always connected with the *parathēkē*, the deposit of faith.

The truth is that, whatever generalisation one likes to make about the role of the 'faithful sayings', it will always be found that it cannot apply to all five contexts, whether we say with Houlden that they mark 'key doctrinal statement', or with Holtz that they are always accompanied by a quotation, or with Brox that they mark 'basic normative maxims'. We cannot claim that they always accompany a credal statement (1 Tim. 3:1 and 4:9 do not fall into this category), nor a liturgical (once more these two are the exceptions), nor even a statement of basic belief, for it is difficult to see how 1 Tim. 3:1 could be classified thus, whether it refers to what precedes or to what follows. Our conclusion must be that it is useless to try to identify one class of statement which the formula marks. Trummer (p. 204) has come nearest the truth when he says that it is in fact 'a formula of asseveration'. The author uses the 'faithful saying' formula to give emphasis and solemnity to some statement, no matter what its origin or contents. As we observed in section 8 of the Introduction, it serves to link together the disparate elements in his letters, and to add a touch of solemnity to the tone of his work.

THE THEME OF FALSE DOCTRINE RESUMED

1:18–20

18. This charge must refer to the letter as a whole, since the immediately preceding verses do not contain any charge; cf. Heb. 13:22, where the author of Hebrews calls his work a 'word of exhortation'. **in accordance with the prophetic utterances that pointed to you** is probably the best way of understanding a phrase which literally means 'according to the prophecies which led the way beforehand on you'. Jeremias insists that this must refer to the fact that

Timothy was first marked out by various **prophetic utterances** as a
suitable candidate for the ministry and was then ordained. Lock
believes that Paul himself was the author of **the prophetic utterances**.
Others would tie the incident more closely to the actual ordination
service. Houlden well compares *Philad.* 7.1, where Ignatius reminds
the Philadelphians that he had cried out 'with the voice of God': he
had urged them to 'pay attention to the bishop and to the members
of presbytery and the deacons'. This incident probably took place
during worship and Ignatius regarded his utterance as prophetic. A.
Lemaire (in Delorme, p. 104) takes the view that **the prophetic
utterances** are the actual words of ordination of Timothy uttered by
the prophetically inspired Paul, a theory which Brox rightly rejects.
Others take the phrase more literally, e.g. C. K. Barrett renders it
'the prophecies leading me towards you' and compares Ac. 13:1–3.
H. Bürki takes it still more generally as the often repeated commis-
sionings and encouragements received by Timothy during his
ministry.

We must be careful to view it in the context of the author's day,
not Paul's. As such it no doubt gives us a picture of how candidates
for ordination were selected. A Christian prophet (whether ordained
or not) would probably have some part in declaring who should be
ordained, and may have participated in the ordination service, though
we certainly cannot identify the **prophetic utterances** with any formula of ordination. D–C say that the military metaphor in **wage the
good warfare** smacks of the contemporary diatribe: the philosopher
also, it is claimed, has a fight to wage for truth. The words **inspired
by them** renders a phrase which means literally 'in them' (a Semitism,
according to Nauck, p. 22), but editors are unanimous in understanding it in some such way as *RSV* suggests.

19–20. We note that the Christian faith and moral rectitude are
closely allied and that heretics are moral failures. It looks as if the
author has used *pistis* (**faith**) in two senses in the same sentence; the
first time it occurs it seems to mean 'trust in God' (subjective) and
the second time 'correct belief' (objective). D–C claim that the **ship-
wreck** metaphor comes from contemporary moral philosophy. They
believe that **Hymenaeus and Alexander** are contemporaries of the
author. But surely the author's readers could not be so simple-minded
as to believe that persons living in their own day could have been
alive and active forty years previously when Paul was still living? It
is much more likely that they are known opponents of Paul; they may
have had successors in the author's day who claimed the authority of
their masters (so C. K. Barrett and Brox). Hymenaeus appears again
at 2 Tim. 2:17. Brox justly remarks that the real Paul does not
characterise Christians as possessing **a good conscience**. There has

been some debate as to whether this **Alexander** is the same as 'Alexander the coppersmith' in 2 Tim. 4:14. On the whole it seems unlikely. **whom I have delivered to Satan that they may learn not to blaspheme** probably implies that Paul excommunicated them (or that the author thought Paul ought to have excommunicated them); see 1 C. 5:5. This conclusion is accepted by C. K. Barrett (pp. 254-5), D-C, and Schlier (p. 482). T. C. G. Thornton (*ExpT* 83 [1971-2], pp. 151-2) has suggested that Satan is here regarded as God's agent, as in the book of Job. But this is certainly not the role he assumes in the rest of the letters. The association of blasphemy with false teaching is a mark of some of the works of the second half of the *NT*; cf. Jude and 2 Peter. On the other hand when we read Revelation we learn what true blasphemy means; see Rev. 13:1-6; 17:3.

HOW TO CONDUCT PUBLIC PRAYER

2:1-3

In *Studies* (pp. 62-4) I have argued that the author of the Pastorals in these verses and Clement in his *Letter to the Corinthians* 59-61 are making use of the same document, relating to church worship. The fact that at the end of each passage a formula about the mediatorial function of Christ comes is very significant. *1 Clem.* 61.3 calls Christ 'high priest and guardian of our souls'. Clement seems to be reproducing material from the form of eucharistic prayer which he uses. It seems therefore very likely that the author of the Pastorals is giving us here an outline of what was regarded as essential for public worship in the tradition of his church. It is not likely that he composed any of it himself. If it is correct that Clement in fact lived later than the author, this makes it all the more likely that the author is giving the outline of the tradition and Clement is clothing it with flesh. Holtz agrees that vv. 1-7 are part of a eucharistic prayer. Bartsch (p. 57) agrees that the Pastorals are earlier than *1 Clem.*

1. **supplications, prayers, intercessions and thanksgivings:** We should not try to distinguish the different meanings of the first three words too meticulously (D-C). Brox suggests that the emphasis on praying for **all men** may be to counter a Gnostic tendency towards esotericism. We note the authoritative overtone in **I urge** (*parakalō*). There is an alternative reading *parakalei*, which would give the imperative 'urge that prayers should be made'. But the parallel with 'I desire' in v. 8 makes this seem less likely.

2. **for kings:** the plural has caused some comment here; 1 Pet. 2:13 only refers to 'the king'. The reference is of course to the emperor; only in Rome itself was there an inhibition against describing the emperor as 'king'. In Asia Minor there would be nothing

strange about it. Certain editors have even claimed that this plural is
an indication of date; it must be, they say, after AD 137, when Hadrian
nominated his successors and gave them quasi-imperial status. But
this is quite unnecessary; the plural is used to make the reference less
specific. Nor can we claim, as Spicq does, that the words imply that
the author was living in a client kingdom, of which there were more
extant in Paul's day than forty years later. Neither the author nor
Clement prays for the conversion of the rulers. Whether public prayer
should be made for non-Christian rulers was something of an issue
in the Indian church when India received independence in 1947.
With the phrase **godly and respectful in every way** we encounter
two nouns that are favourites with the author; they recur frequently
throughout all three letters. The two nouns never appear in any of
the acknowledged Pauline letters. They are *eusebeia* and *semnotēs*. C.
K. Barrett's translation of this second noun, 'high standards of morality', exactly conveys the sense. We are dealing with a writer devoid
of Paul's insights into the nature of Christian ethics, and with a
church that has to settle down to meet the exigencies of life in the
provinces during the opening years of the second century.

3. There may be echoes in these verses of some *OT* passages, such
as Dt. 12:25 ('when you do what is right in the sight of the Lord'),
or even the famous prophecy in Mal. 1:11 of the 'pure sacrifice' which
is offered in every place (so Bartsch pp. 30, 52); Malachi's phrase is
a favourite proof-text for the eucharist with later writers, e.g. Justin
Martyr. It is first explicitly met with in this connection in the *Didache*.
But if there is an echo of Deuteronomy or Malachi here, the references
are unconsciously inherited by the author in the material he is using.
God our Saviour is a striking phrase, never used by Paul. It has an
ancestry in Judaism. Compare especially Isa. 45:21, which in LXX
runs:

   I am God, and there is none other beside me;
   Righteous and a saviour, there is none besides me.
And v. 22 follows on with:
   Turn to me and be saved, you who come from the end of the earth.
   There is evidence that the rabbis understood Isa. 45:22 as indicating the eventual conversion of the Gentiles to Judaism (see W. G.
Braude, *The Midrash on the Psalms* [New Haven, 1959], Vol. I, p.
142 and Vol. II, p. 146). Thus the liturgical material in vv. 4–5 here
may originally have formed a sort of Christian midrash on Isa. 45:21–
22. But whether the author of the Pastorals himself composed the
midrash must be doubtful.

A CREDO AND A COMMISSION

2:4-7

4. who desires all men to be saved: this noble statement of the universality of God's love runs directly counter to the strict predestinarian tradition in Christianity which Augustine so emphatically championed, and Calvin, eleven hundred years later, reaffirmed. Consequently both Augustine and Calvin had to evade the obvious meaning of these words by saying that it means God chooses his elect from all classes of men. The author probably wishes to take his stand against the esoteric Gnosticism of his day, which tended to restrict the possibility of salvation to the élite. **to come to the knowledge of the truth** means in effect to accept Christianity. The word for **knowledge** is *epignōsis*. Lock calls it 'a technical term for the intellectual acceptance of Christianity'. It is contrasted with *gnōsis*, which the author uses in a depreciatory sense in 1 Tim. 6:20 because of its frequent use by the Gnostics. Dornier makes the nice distinction that *gnōsis* is ordinary knowledge, whereas *epignōsis* is revealed knowledge. Compare Heb. 10:26, where exactly the same phrase **knowledge of the truth** is used of the formal acceptance of Christianity.

5. Here begins a credal formula which continues to the end of v. 6. Barnett (pp. 255-6) thinks that **one God** is a conscious echo of Eph. 4:5. The phrase **one mediator between God and men, the man Christ Jesus** is a striking one. Editors have suggested that the humanity of Christ is emphasised over against the Docetism of the Gnostics. The use of *mesitēs* (**mediator**) has occasioned much debate; the word is used by Paul only once, in Gal. 3:19-20, where it refers to Moses, and the fact that the law needed a mediator in order to convey it to Israel on Sinai is cited as an indication of the inferiority of the whole legal dispensation. The word is applied to Christ three times in Heb. 8:6; 9:15; 12:24 (and the cognate verb in 6:17); but there he is described as the mediator of a new covenant, in obvious contrast to Moses, the mediator of the old covenant. Here in Pastorals **mediator** is used of Christ absolutely, and he is mediator **between God and men**. I have suggested in *Studies* (pp. 56-62) that the origin of the use of *mesitēs* is to be found in the LXX version of Job 9:32-33. In that passage Job expresses the wish that there was a mediator between God and man, though he has no belief that such a mediator actually exists. But LXX has somewhat mistranslated the Hebrew so as to give this sense:

I wish there were our mediator and reprover
And one to hear the case between us both.

A Christian reading his Job in LXX could easily take this as a prophecy of the mediator who was to come. Clement shows great interest in the book of Job (*1 Clem.* 17.1–4; 26.3; 66.3–6). So there is nothing surprising that Christians in the first century should see Job as a prophet of Christ. E. K. Simpson comments: 'Job's pathetic cry . . . has been answered'; but in fact the situation is not quite as simple as that. What Job was asking for was an arbitrator between God and man who could negotiate between them. But an arbitrator must be neutral. He cannot afford therefore to be either completely God or completely man. The sort of ontological mediator which this phrase describes is much more likely to turn out to be an Arian Christ, neither adequately God nor adequately man. Not, of course, that our author had any such consequence in mind, but an Arian Christ is the logical conclusion of the mediator-christology which we have here. It is not Pauline at all. It probably got enshrined in the formula before the author used it. He is very unlikely to have been the person who found it in LXX of Job. J. Daniélou (*Théologie du Judéo-Christianisme* [Paris, 1957], p. 175) quotes a passage from the *Testament of Dan* in which the angel Michael is described as 'a mediator between God and man'. This would point very much in the Arian direction when applied to Christ. As a credal confession this formula is marked by that binitarianism that we have noted already (see Introduction, section 7). There is no mention of the Spirit here.

6. who gave himself as a ransom for all: this is undoubtedly an alternative form of the saying which we meet in Mk 10:45 'to give his life as a ransom for many'. D–C describe it as 'a Hellenistically coloured variant of Mk. 10:45'. The word for **ransom** is *antilutron*. It may have been influenced by the use of *antipsuchon* in 4 Mac. 6:29, a book which there is reason to believe our author had read. There the aged Eleazar prays that his life offered in martyrdom may be a 'counterweight' for the sins of Israel. The phrase in 6*b* which *RSV* renders with **the testimony to which was borne at the proper time** is very obscure. Spicq describes it as being 'so elliptical as to be almost unintelligible'. The most satisfactory interpretation is to take it as meaning that the sacrificial death of Christ was a fulfilment of God's promises in God's good time. So *NEB* with its translation 'so providing at the fitting time proof of the divine purpose'. J. N. D. Kelly also takes it in this sense. In other words it is an allusion to salvation history. Others take it of Jesus' own witness. Knox readers: 'At the appointed time, he bore his witness'. Dornier understands it as a reference to the love of the Father and of the Son. Brox comments that here Christ is certainly viewed as possessing divine rank, though pre-existence is not implied. He takes the witness to be Christ's own witness in dying, as contrasted with the witness of the Father in vv. 4–5, and of the church in v. 7. But he admits that the *Heilsplan* is certainly implied here.

• **7. a preacher:** literally 'a herald'. The same word *kēryx* is applied to Paul in *1 Clem.* 5.6, and in 2 Pet. 2:5 the phrase 'herald of righteousness' is used of Noah. D–C compare Eph. 3:7, where Paul is called 'a minister of the gospel according to God's grace'. Trummer (p. 122) sees a link with Eph. 4:7, where the account of the various ministries which God has given the church immediately follows what looks like a credal formula. (**I am telling the truth, I am not lying**): Why this parenthesis? Why should anyone doubt that Paul was a genuine apostle? The answer is probably that the author has Rom. 9:1 in mind, where Paul, protesting that he has a genuine concern for his fellow Jews, writes: 'I am speaking the truth in Christ, I am not lying'. This no doubt accounts for the variant reading in our text here: 'I am speaking the truth in Christ'. The author is trying (not very successfully) to impart some of Paul's liveliness to his own style by using Paul's words of protest.

a teacher of the Gentiles: by the time the author wrote, the church was overwhelmingly Gentile in composition. In his lifetime Paul had been regarded as an apostle, but he is seen by a later generation as *the* apostle because it is the churches founded by him that have survived and increased. Spicq actually compares the title of the founding father of the Qumran sect, 'the teacher of righteousness' (which should be understood in the sense 'the divinely authorised teacher'). Collins (p. 154) suggests that this phrase is used of Paul in order to emphasise his authority over against the false teacher. **in faith and truth** is one of these vague phrases which the author likes to use. It probably means that Paul teaches the Gentiles in a faithful and true manner rather than that he teaches them faith and truth. Compare Rev. 3:14, where Christ is called 'the faithful and true witness'. Houlden well points out that the historical Timothy would hardly have required the assurances which we meet in this verse.

THEME OF PRAYER RESUMED

2:8

8. I desire then: Spicq comments on the strong authoritative tone. **in every place:** because of this phrase a number of editors have claimed that there is here an echo of the famous passage in Mal. 1:11: 'in every place incense is offered to my name, and a pure offering' (so D–C, Bartsch [p. 13], Houlden, Brox). If so, it is very likely that the prayer of the eucharist is intended, because in *Didache*, Justin Martyr, and frequently afterwards, Mal. 1:11 is taken as a prophecy of the eucharist (see on 2:3). **men should pray;** the Greek means 'men not women'. E. Schweizer (p. 86) claims that this indicates that in the author's day any male member of the congregation could lead the church's prayers in worship. **lifting up holy hands:** a very similar phrase is used in *1 Clem.* 29.1. It is more likely that the author and Clement are using the same church order document as a source than that Clement is copying Pastorals. Compare also Jas 4:8.

quarrelling: if the reading behind *RSV* is the word *dialogismou*, it would be better translated 'argument'. But if *RSV* follows the alternative reading *dialogismōn*, the plural of the noun, then **quarrelling** is probably accurate enough. The author dislikes arguing about anything, unlike Paul.

HOW WOMEN SHOULD BEHAVE, AND THE SCRIPTURAL AUTHORITY FOR THIS ADVICE

2:9-15

9-10. women should adorn themselves modestly and sensibly: there is a very similar passage in 1 Pet. 3:3-5. Both passages no doubt come from a domestic code (see Introduction, section 8). The phrase **by good deeds** probably means that women's best adornment is the good deeds they perform rather than cosmetics or jewelry. This is certainly the sentiment of 1 Pet. 3:4-5. One could claim that the author of Pastorals is fond of the expression **good deeds**; he uses it also in 1 Tim. 3:1; 5:10, 25; 6:18; 2 Tim. 3:21, 17; Tit. 2:7-14; 3:1, 8, 14. Paul does not use the expression at all. The nearest he gets is Rom. 2:7, 'in well-doing', and compare Col. 1:10, 'in every good work'. The plural seems to give an overtone of someone piling up a credit balance. By the time we reach v. 10 the context of worship has been forgotten and the author is giving advice to women about their behaviour in general.

as befits women who profess religion: the word translated **religion** is *theosebeia*, a word never used by Paul, one which would be very familiar in the popular non-Christian religious background of the author's day. Philo actually uses the phrase 'those who profess religion'. Spicq justifiably points out that, despite the restrictions on women's activity in the church which this passage imposes, Christianity had already given women a fuller part in worship than Judaism ever did, or indeed than orthodox Judaism does to this day. Brox conjectures that women may have been more vulnerable to the attacks of the false teachers, and therefore needed to be more carefully restricted.

11-12. Spicq believes that the relative abruptness with which this verse begins shows that the author is reverting to the original subject of this section, how women should behave during worship. **with all submissiveness:** this injunction is already met with in Col. 3:18; in this respect both Jewish and Hellenistic moral standards agreed.

Woman was inferior to man, and the wife's duty was to submit to her husband. The author of Ephesians has enlarged on this theme in Eph. 5:22-33, but the differences between that passage and 1 Tim. 2:11-15 are remarkable. In the Ephesians passage the relation of husband to wife is connected with the relation of Christ to the church, and is thereby deepened and spiritualised. In Ephesians, as in Colossians, the man's duty to love his wife is emphasised. There is no sign of that in 1 Timothy. In Ephesians the scriptural warrant is found in Gen. 2:24, which very much follows Jesus' line (see Mk 10:4f.), not in a forced interpretation of the garden of Eden story. And in Ephesians the whole relation is governed by the injunction 'Be subject to one another out of reverence for Christ' (Eph. 5:21). In other words, the Ephesians passage is much more profound, spiritual and human than what the author of the Pastorals writes.

I permit no woman to teach or to have authority over men: the authoritative note is markedly stronger than that which the authentic Paul employs. *RSV*'s rendering is a little misleading here. The literal meaning is 'have authority over man', which no doubt means the woman's husband. The author seems to associate a woman teaching in the church with wives lording it over their husbands (see N. J. Hommes, *TJ* 4 (1969) pp. 5-22). We should bear in mind that the Gnostics in all probability encouraged women to take a leading part in both worship and preaching. Brox suggests that the Gnostics, because of their dislike of the physical, were too ready to ignore the physical differences between men and women. Spicq, on the basis of 1 C. 14:34-35, claims that this is one of the most authentically Pauline passages in the Pastorals. But there is in fact some reason for believing that that passage in 1 Corinthians may be an interpolation. In some MSS it is displaced, which is often a sign of interpolation. It seems to be hardly consistent with 1 C. 11:5, where Paul appears to assume that a woman praying in church worship is quite a normal phenomenon. It has even been suggested that 1 C. 14:34-35 is an interpolation inserted by the author of the Pastorals in order to support his case. But this is very speculative indeed. A Lemaire (in Delorme, p. 116, footnote) describes the passage as 'probably post-Pauline'. Hence we cannot reasonably claim that the author of the Pastorals is merely being faithful to his master Paul in vv. 11-12.

13-15. We have here a treatment by the author of the Pastorals of a piece of *Haggada* which also appears in the authentic Pauline writings. It concerns the way in which Eve was tempted and fell (see my *Studies*, ch. 6). There was a tendency in later commentary on the story of the fall in Genesis to represent Eve as having been sexually seduced by the serpent, who disguised himself as an angel. Paul's treatment of the theme is found in 2 C. 11:2-3, 14. There Paul

compares the Corinthian church to a virgin espoused to Christ; he
fears lest Satan may have deceived them, and he shows that he is
aware of the legend that Satan disguised himself as an angel of light.
There is evidence to suggest that the Greek word for deceived in 2
C. 11:3 carried the overtone of 'seduced'. It is the same word as the
author uses in 1 Tim. 2:14. But Paul does not make any theological
capital out of this legend. He merely uses it as an analogy for the way
in which he fears Satan has seduced the Corinthian church.

   The author of the Pastorals is undoubtedly rehandling this passage
in 2 Corinthians, but, unlike Paul, he draws a number of theological
(or at least anthropological) conclusions from it. First of all, as Brox
points out, he regards the fact that Adam was created before Eve as
a sign of man's superiority to woman (here Paul would have agreed;
see 1 C. 11:8-9). Then he concludes that woman is naturally more
easily deceived than man, a point in which both Judaism and Hellenistic thought would have agreed with him. Paul probably would not:
he seems to describe Adam as having been deceived also; see Rom.
7:11. The original transgression, according to the author of the Pastorals, seems to have been sexual. This seems to be implied by **the
woman was deceived and became a transgressor.** Here again Paul
would certainly have disagreed: the original sin was disobedience,
according to Paul (see Rom. 5:19). Finally, the author of the Pastorals
believes that women can be rehabilitated through carrying out the
duties of a wife and mother. Here he is being true to the tradition of
Judaism. Both of the more ancient Targums on Gen. 3:16 interpret
the verse so as to mean that because of her sin the woman is to be
totally subordinate to her husband for good or evil, and to find in
that her God-given vocation. This would not at all accord with Paul's
view of salvation; he would not have held that we can be saved by
anything that we do or suffer. Thus we have in this short passage a
clear indication of the difference of theological outlook between Paul
and the author of the Pastorals. Few will doubt that Paul must be
judged to be infinitely the deeper theologian. It is surely significant
that a number of those scholars who defend the Pauline authorship
of the Pastorals attempt to avoid attributing all of this passage to him.
Thus Spicq suggests that v. 15 is a gloss; and Holtz believes that both
this passage and 1 C. 14:34-35 are not from Paul's pen. We may
however appreciate the intention with which the author undertook
this transposition of a Pauline passage. The Gnostic teachers probably
held that marriage was invented by Satan. To be born into this world
was to be damned. The author replies (says Brox) that on the contrary
the process of salvation begins with the event of procreation and
birth.

   The first phrase in v. 15 is ambiguous. It is literally 'she will be saved through the childbearing'. The alternative translation in *RSV* margin is 'by the birth of the child'. Some editors have seen here a reference to the birth of Jesus and have claimed that we have here the origin of the idea later elaborated by Irenaeus and others that Mary is the counterpart to Eve as Christ is the counterpart to Adam. But the Greek will hardly allow this sense, and the interpretation is more romantic than convincing. Others, such as Nauck (p. 100) would translate the phrase 'by accepting childbearing with meekness she will come through (the experience of childbearing) safely'. But this is difficult to extract from the Greek. S. Jebb (*ExpT* 81 [1969–70], pp. 221–2) has suggested that the true meaning is 'she will be saved from the error of lording it over her husband by devoting herself to bearing and bringing up children'. But v. 15 is rather too far away from v. 12 to make this plausible. The natural interpretation is that woman, a weak, gullible creature, should find her natural vocation in a life of domesticity in subordination to her husband (so Bürki, Bartsch [p. 71], Brox, Hasler). There is also a problem in v. 15*b* with **if she continues**. As *RSV* margin points out, the Greek is **if they continue**. The question is, to whom does **they** refer? Some editors (e.g. Spicq, Brox) take it as referring to man and wife, who after all must co-operate in the procreation of children. But the author is not here concerned with the salvation of Adam; the verb **will be saved** in 15*a* is singular. We may well accept Bartsch's suggestion (p. 73) that the author uses the plural in v. 15*b* because he is quoting from a source-document on church order. Spicq well points out that the reference to **holiness** at the end of the verse shows that the author held the married state to be quite compatible with a life of Christian sanctity. This is a principle which the church very largely ignored from the fourth century onwards.

QUALIFICATIONS FOR A BISHOP

3:1–7

For comment on the remarkably unsacerdotal character of the list of qualities requisite in a bishop, see Introduction, section 6.

1. **The saying is sure**: this is the second of the 'faithful sayings'. For a note on the sayings as a whole, see above on 1:17. There is an interesting alternative reading here for *pistos* (**sure**); it is *anthrōpinos*. This word normally means merely 'human', but Paul uses it to mean 'natural' or 'in accordance with fallen human nature' (see Rom. 6:19; 1 C. 2:13; 4:3; 10:13). Some editors have therefore accepted this reading as original and translated 'there is a popular saying "To aspire to leadership, etc" '. This is in fact the *NEB* rendering. Both Knight (p. 48) and Barrett would translate *anthrōpinos* as 'popular', though

neither considers it the original reading. It is not by any means clear, however, that *anthrōpinos* can mean 'popular'. Barrett suggests that it could mean 'in general use', but even this is doubtful. On the whole therefore it seems more likely that the original reading was *pistos*, **sure**, and that *anthrōpinos* was substituted, or crept in from the margin, because there did not seem to be any statement in the context which merited the dignity of being called a 'sure saying'. In fact editors have been much exercised as to which is the statement that the author so designates here. D–C think it refers to what precedes in 2:15. We have seen that this is also the way Nauck takes it. J. N. D. Kelly solves the problem by suggesting that the phrase here is a gloss. If we must make up our minds between the two, it seems more likely that the phrase refers to what follows than to what precedes, but, as we have indicated in the Note at 1:17, it is not necessary to plump for one or the other. The author uses the phrase to give solemnity to an otherwise pedestrian text. **the office of bishop** translates one word in Greek, *episkopē*. Knight (op. ct. 51) points out that this word in profane Greek only occurs in contexts later than the first century AD. But it does occur in LXX with the meaning 'office', and is quoted as such of Judas' office in Ac. 1:20. It may seem surprising that the author should have to encourage people to aspire to church office; but there is evidence in the *Didache* that in the first or early second century the charismatic offices, such as prophet, exercised more attraction. We also find younger men being appointed to the monarchical episcopate in Ignatius. There is some hint of this perhaps in the injunction in 4:12 that no one should despise Timothy's youthfulness (N. Brox, *VC* 30, [1976], p. 183). Hasler well observes that the phrase **If any one** in this verse indicates that the author is quoting from a church-order document which he uses as one of his sources.

2. the husband of one wife: this phrase has given rise to much debate. See the Note at 3:7 below, where the issues involved are discussed. We take it to mean 'not someone who has been divorced'. **hospitable** suggests the strongly domestic nature of the church to which the author is writing. Christianity had not yet advanced beyond the stage of the house-church. **an apt teacher** also indicates one of the most essential qualities of the early bishop. Most of the outstanding theologians of the first four centuries were bishops. The author emphasises this quality all the more because of the need to counter the false teaching of the Gnostics.

3. no drunkard and **not violent** may strike us as surprising, especially as there is nothing exactly corresponding to these qualities in Onosander's list. Perhaps the predominantly lower-class character of the church in Asia Minor made such precautions necessary. **gentle**

translates *epieikē*. Spicq's description of what this word means is '*un sympathique equilibre*'. The abstract noun cognate to it is applied by Paul to Christ in 2 C. 10:1. Brox well compares Tit. 1:7 'The bishop, as God's steward, must be blameless'. It is therefore quite appropriate to expect the bishop to display the quality which God has so signally displayed in Christ.

4–5. The language used here very much suggests a church presided over by one man rather than by a group of presbyters. Houlden claims that here we can see the church in process of developing from a household church to a more public institution. The author likes this household simile for the church; see 3:15; 2 Tim. 2:19–21. It is also met with in Paul (Gal. 6:10; Eph. 3:15). The sentiment expressed here is not particularly Christian. One could cite many examples from secular Greek literature of the maxim 'he who rules his household well can rule the state well'. Brox claims that this shows how far specifically Christian virtues are rooted in natural virtues. The phrase **God's church** appears to be a coinage of the author's: cf. 3:15. Of course in the *OT* Israel was often called God's people. In the light of the subsequent development of the ordained ministry, it is remarkable that here where the office of bishop first emerges into the light of history, it should be taken for granted that he will be a married man.

6. a recent convert: this is undoubtedly the right translation for the Greek *neophuton* (from which we get the English 'neophyte'). If this rule had been strictly observed, Cyprian would never have been made bishop of Carthage. He was converted to Christianity about AD 246, and within two years was elected bishop. **puffed up** is a mistranslation. As Spicq points out, there is no lexicographical justification for translating the Greek word *tuphōtheis* as **puffed up**. The correct meaning is 'blinded' or 'beclouded' (so also Brox). The phrase **and fall into the condemnation of the devil** is obscure in Greek. There are four possible translations: (a) that offered by *RSV*: he incurs the same condemnation as the devil incurred for the sin of pride; (b) the judgment and doom which the devil has contrived for him by tempting him to become proud; (c) the punishment which the devil as God's agent inflicts on him (cf. 1:20); (d) the condemnation pronounced by the slanderer, i.e. the pagan critic (see *RSV* marg.). Of these (b) seems to be on the whole the most likely. In the very next verse we have a reference to the snare which the devil has prepared. Compare also 2 Tim. 2:26. Brox opts for (a) above and Spicq for (c).

7. outsiders, says Spicq, is originally a Jewish term. There is a strange repetition here of what we have already met in v. 6: there the **condemnation of the devil**; here **the snare of the devil**. But in v. 7 the **reproach** must be the bad opinion of non-Christians, of which

there is no mention in v. 6. **the snare of the devil** recurs in 2 Tim.
2:26. As in the previous verse, so here, *RSV* margin's rendering 'the
slanderer' can hardly be right. The pagan critic would not set a snare.
Just as v. 6 would have disqualified Cyprian for episcopal office, so
this verse would have disqualified Augustine, the converted
profligate.

Note on **husband of one wife** *and* **having been the wife of one
husband** (5:9)
These phrases also occur in 3:12; Tit. 1:6. The traditional explanation
of both these phrases is that the author prohibits second marriages
after the death of the spouse. The later church tended to frown on
such marriages, especially for clergy, and many scholars hold that
this is the right interpretation. This view is held by Spicq (though he
shows some leaning towards the fourth interpretation outlined below),
J. N. D. Kelly, Dornier, Brox, and Hasler. In Graeco-Roman society
the woman who had remained with one husband all her life, or who
when widowed had not remarried, was honoured. The epithet *unavira*
('married to one man only') is often found on epitaphs. (See M.
Lightman and M. Ziesel, *CH* 46 [1977], pp. 19–32.) The difficulty
with this view is that the author himself urges remarriage for younger
widows in 5:14.
    A second view therefore has been put forward that the author
simply requires fidelity within marriage from the bishop, and in 5:9
from the widow who is to receive support from the church. To the
objection that this is perfectly obvious, a basic Christian assumption,
S. Lyonnet (*VD* 45 [1967], pp. 3–10) replies that equally obvious
basic qualifications for episcopal office are found in the same passage,
such as that he must not be a heavy drinker or a brawler. Some of
the early Fathers, particularly of the Antiochene school, took it in
this sense. It seems nevertheless that the objection which Lyonnet
attempts to meet is a formidable one: all Christian husbands should
be 'husbands of one wife' in this sense. Even R. L. Saucy's modification (*BibSac* 131 [1974], pp. 229–40), to the effect that it means
'faithful to one wife since his conversion', will hardly serve as support.
This interpretation is nevertheless accepted by Holtz, Houlden, and
Trummer (*Bib.* 51 [1970], pp. 471–84). Hasler, who tends towards
the first view, shows also some sympathy towards this one.
    A third, and rather surprising interpretation is that **husband of
one wife** is intended to prohibit polygamy for the bishop. Some
evidence can be brought to show that polygamy was not completely
unknown in Judaism at this period. D–C actually support this interpretation. They suggest that the list of qualifications came originally from a pagan source and that the prohibition of polygamy was

carried over when the author of the Pastorals adopted it. This view is also supported by B. S. Easton, E. K. Simpson, and J. Rohde (p. 92). We must however surely dismiss it as being the most unlikely of all the interpretations. Anything approaching polygamy would have been abhorrent to the strict moral standards of the church of the time. Even if the phrase is interpreted to mean 'not keeping concubines', it is particularly inappropriate. Besides it will not apply to the widows mentioned in 5:9. Whatever evidence there be for polygamy in Jewish or pagan society at the end of the first century, there is none at all for polyandry.

We turn therefore to the fourth possible interpretation. The phrase could mean that the bishop must not be one who has divorced a previous wife and remarried. This view is defended by Jeremias, Holtz and Bartsch (p. 130), and both Spicq and Brox admit that it is a possible interpretation. It fits a Jewish background, in the sense that a Jewish husband could very easily divorce his wife and remarry. A Jewish wife had no such freedom, though in certain circumstances she could more or less compel her husband to divorce her. Similarly in Hellenistic society a husband could divorce his wife and remarry without difficulty. In Roman society divorce initiated by either spouse was notoriously easy. The chief objection to this is Jesus' total prohibition of divorce (Mk. 10:2–12). But many of those who support this objection are quite ready to imagine a situation in which a candidate for church leadership is disqualified because of infidelity within marriage, something which Jesus condemned just as severely. In any case we know that in the Matthean church Jesus' absolute prohibition of divorce had already been modified (see Mt. 5:32), so it does not seem at all improbable that there existed in the church to whom the author is writing a situation whereby prominent church members might have been divorced, even after conversion. This would apply equally to either partner.

QUALIFICATIONS FOR DEACONS

3:8–13

We now have a section on the qualities needed for deacons. Deacons are clearly by this time members of the ordained ministry. We get almost no information about their duties. The fact that they must not be **greedy for gain** (v. 8) would suggest that they had some financial responsibility. Perhaps they administered the church's fund for the needy. But the really remarkable feature of this list of qualifications is the extent to which it coincides with the list of qualifications needed for a bishop in 3:1–7. Of the nine qualifications drawn up for a deacon, only two cannot be paralleled in the list of bishop's qualifi-

cations (if we may allow that **they must hold the mystery of the faith**
in 3:9 is roughly equivalent to **an apt teacher** in 3:2). One of these
two refers to the need for a probationary period, which could hardly
apply to a bishop. The most probable conclusion is that both lists are
drawn from some common source, in which perhaps neither bishop
nor deacon was mentioned.

8. serious: this is omitted by some MSS but is probably original.
not double-tongued: this is the most likely translation of the Greek
dilogous. The word does not occur in Greek literature before this, but
the verb *dilogein* and the noun *dilogia* mean 'to be repetitious' and
'repetitiveness' respectively. On the other hand Polycarp (*Phil.* 5.2),
in a passage where he is probably echoing this one, says of the deacons
that they are not to be 'slanderous, *dilogoi*, or greedy for gain'. Spicq
thinks *dilogous* here means 'envious critics'; but Chrysostom says it
means one who says on thing and thinks another. Theodoret, rather
more accurately perhaps, says it means one who says one thing to A
and another to B. Holtz, pursuing his peculiar theory that there are
frequent cryptic references to the eucharist in the Pastorals, claims
that the bishop's task was to look after the house-church, whereas
the deacon had charge of the eucharist.

9. The author of the Pastorals has a talent for using apparently
straightforward phrases the precise meaning of which is obscure.
Does this mean that deacons are unfeignedly to believe the Christian
faith? Or does it mean that they are to combine a good grasp of
Christian theology with a morally blameless life? It is quite likely that
the author is here echoing I C. 4:1, where Paul describes himself and
his fellow-workers as 'stewards of the mysteries of God'. In the
authentic writings of Paul **mystery** means generally God's saving
action is Christ revealed to faith. In the deutero-Pauline writings
(including Rom. 16:25) the emphasis shifts onto the hiddenness, so
that the mystery is God's design of salvation, present in the mind of
God since the creation of the world but only revealed in Christ. In
the book of Revelation it means a symbol (almost 'a cipher') in 1:20
and 17:5-7, and in 10:7 it means 'God's mysterious design'. D–C say
that the phrase the **mystery of faith** was a formal one, current in the
church of the author's day, which seems most probable. They add
that the emphasis here is more on the necessity for a clear conscience
than on the content of the faith. Kelly paraphrases with 'the totality
of hidden truths, inaccessible to reason, and made known only by
divine revelation', which is perhaps to credit the author with more
intellectual acumen than he actually possessed. Dornier thinks the
mystery is a body of doctrine and says that moral faults often lead to
intellectual deviations. In fact however the author seems to believe
that it is the other way round: if a man is a heretic he must be a

moral reprobate as well. We may conclude that what is required of deacons is a combination of correct doctrine and pure life. This suggests that deacons did have a teaching function. In the later church the phrase in this verse came to be applied to the consecrated elements, which it was the deacon's task to carry to the sick.

10. There is a small problem here: RSV translates 10b with **let them serve as deacons**. The Greek is *diakoneitōsan*. But this verb, even in the Pastorals, can mean merely 'carry out Christian ministry', as in the case of Onesiphorus in 2 Tim. 1:18. The point is that, if we translate *diakoneitōsan* as 'serve as deacons' in this verse, are we to give the same rendering in v. 13 to the same verb, as RSV does? If so, we are committed to the assumption that the diaconate is regarded in the Pastorals as a probationary ministry, probably for the episcopate rather than the presbyterate. This conclusion is accepted by Bartsch (p. 91): '*Der Diakon in den Past ist der mögliche Bischof*'. This was certainly the situation in the later church, but many editors would hesitate to read it into the Pastorals, suggesting as it does something of a graded hierarchy. On the whole it seems safer to accept that the verb *diakonein* is used in two different senses in vv. 10 and 13. In v. 10 it means **serve as deacons** and in v. 13 simply **those who serve well**. Brox well points out that this precaution about a probationary period for deacons fits in well with the prohibition of the appointment of recent converts to church office. It looks very much as if the whole local church had a say in the appointment of deacons, a primitive feature.

11. We have another problem here. Are **the women** in this verse deacons' wives or women ministrants of some sort, deaconesses perhaps? The majority of modern scholars opt for the second alternative: Bernard, Lock, Kelly, Spicq, Barrett, Dornier, Bürki, Brox, Lemaire (in Delorme, p. 114). Their arguments are that if the author had meant to indicate the deacons' wives he would have said something about their families. But he does in the next verse, and in the ancient world it was the father who was considered responsible for the conduct of the children. Dornier says that he means deaconesses, but has no specific word to use for them, since *diakonissa* had not yet been coined and *diakonos* has no female equivalent. Pliny, writing probably in AD 112, knows of certain women in Christian congregations whom he calls *ancillae*, 'handmaids', and *ministrae*, 'women ministrants'. Brox, after a judicious discussion, opts for 'deaconesses'. If the author had meant deacons' wives, he could have written 'their wives'. But Brox admits it is an open question. D–C reserve judgment, pointing out that the author has adapted his source rather unskilfully in this passage. In favour of the meaning being 'deacons' wives', it can be said that this list of requisite qualities has much in

common with the list requisite for older women in Tit. 2:3, where
there is no question of deaconesses. Indeed there is one detail in that
passage, **they are to teach what is good**, which would seem to be
more appropriate to deaconesses than any of the qualities listed in v.
11 here. A further argument in favour of deaconesses being referred
to is that the author says nothing anywhere about the qualities desirable in a bishop's wife. Why then should he take the trouble to say
what deacons' wives should be like? But presumably the wife of a
prospective bishop would be an older woman and therefore better
known to the local church. Deacons might be more recently married,
and their wives unknown and perhaps more inclined to unsuitable
behaviour. We conclude that on the whole it is more likely that the
author is referring to the wives of deacons here. This view is supported by Easton, Jeremias, Higgins, and Houlden. It looks as if the
author had a document before him which gave a list of desirable
qualities for any office holder. He applies it to bishops and then
decides it could be used for deacons and their wives also. Verses 8,
10-11, and 13 represent his attempt to adapt it for this purpose.

12. This verse simply continues the application of the list to the
deacons. It is a mere repetition of elements in 3:2, 4.

13. a good standing: the word for standing is *bathmos*, literally
'step'. The temptation is strong to conclude that this means a good
position as regards promotion to the episcopate (this is how Bartsch
takes it: see on v. 10). Spicq actually accepts this suggestion, though
one would have thought that this would be pretty conclusive proof
of non-Pauline authorship. But most editors, rightly no doubt, are
unwilling to translate *bathmos* here as 'step'. We should compare
5:17, **the elders who rule well**, where there is no suggestion of
promotion. D-C, who scout the notion that there is any question of
possible promotion for deacons in this verse, suggest that deacons
had more to do with encountering pagans on behalf of the church
and that is why they need **great confidence in the faith**. The word
for **confidence** is *parrhēsia*, a word which literally means 'confident,
free speech'. It is used in this sense frequently in Acts (see Ac. 2:29;
4:13, 29, 31; 28:31). Paul uses it to mean a confident attitude, expressed no doubt in frank speaking (see 2 C. 3:12; 7:4; Phil. 1:20).
In Ephesians and Hebrews it can mean 'confident bearing' (see Eph.
3:12; Heb. 3:6; 4:16; 10:19, 35), though it can refer to speech also
(Eph. 6:19). Lemaire (Les Ministères, p. 135) agrees that the confidence in the faith refers to the deacons' dealings with pagans. Brox
notes that **the faith which is in Christ Jesus** is not a Pauline phrase.

A MIDRASH AND A HYMN

3:14-16

This is one of the most interesting passages in the Pastorals, for here the author draws on his extensive storehouse of exegetic and liturgical material. But first he must introduce it plausibly into the text of his letter.

14. I hope to come to you soon: almost an epistolary cliché. See W. Stenger, *Kairos* 16, 1974, p. 256. It seems very unlikely that the authentic Paul would need at this stage of their acquaintanceship to give Timothy such very elementary instruction. Spicq claims that **I am writing these instructions to you** refers to the contents of the entire epistle. Brox writes, 'In the church's tradition one possesses the word of the absent apostle'; and Houlden adds that Paul's death is to be no obstacle to the continuance of his authority. We could well compare the way in which the author claims to speak in Paul's name with the way in which much later successive bishops of Rome claimed to speak in the name of Peter. It is a dangerous precedent which the author of the Pastorals set, no matter how unexceptionable were his motives in setting it.

15. how one ought to behave in the house of God: it is not clear whether this means the temple of God or the household of God. It is quite possible that the author did not know himself. Lock and D–C insist that it means 'family, household', not a building. We can of course cite 2 Tim. 2:20–21 for the household figure (though there the word is *oikia* not *oikos* as here). In 1 C. 6:19 the bodies of Christians are a shrine for the Holy Spirit (the word is *naos*, a term not found in the Pastorals). In both Ac. 7:49 and Jn 2:13–22 the implication is that God's true temple is Jesus Christ. In Eph. 2:19–22 Christ and the church make up a whole building, a shrine (*naos*) to be a dwelling for God in the Spirit. In Heb. 3:6 faithful Christians are God's house (see also Heb. 10:21). In Rev. 3:12 those who overcome are to be pillars in the shrine (*naos*) of God. The only place in the *OT* where Israel is called God's house is Num. 12:7.

the church of the living God: this phrase is apparently unique; we cannot help suspecting that it has a liturgical origin.

the pillar and bulwark of the truth: bulwark here is a mistranslation. The Greek word is *hedraiōma*, a word not hitherto met with in Greek literature. There is however a cognate word *hedrasma*, which means 'foundation'. This is a word used in the Greek translation of 1 Kg. 8:13*b* (8:53 in *LXX*) for Solomon's temple, where it certainly means 'foundation'. (I have explored this passage more fully in *Studies*, ch. 1.) The concept of the elect community as 'a foundation of truth' is found in the Qumran writings. See 1QS 8.7f., where the sect is described as 'a foundation of truth in Israel for the community of the eternal covenant'. This in its turn probably goes back to Isa. 28:16, where we learn of 'a precious cornerstone, a sure foundation'. This is in fact God's promise that 'he who believes will not be in haste', but the Qumran sectaries interpreted it as applying to their community. It is a popular messianic text in the *NT* ; cf. Rom. 9:33; 1 Pet. 2:6. Once we have established that the church here is called the 'foundation of truth' in association with Solomon's temple, we can turn back to the first figure in the phrase, **the pillar**. Despite all apparent associations with Paul's description of James, Peter and John as 'pillars of the church', or even with the text in Rev. 3:12 already referred to, the context rather suggests the pillar of cloud, the visible manifestation of God in the wilderness, which was traditionally identified with the cloud which filled Solomon's temple at its dedication (1 Kg. 8:10–11, where the cloud is identified with God's glory). Thus what this densely packed phrase means is that the Christian church is the true temple of God, the place where his presence is to be found. The only modern editor who insists on translating *hedraiōma* as 'bulwark' is Hasler. D–C say that the phrase is 'deliberately composed liturgical speech'. In view of the very deep roots which it has in scriptural tradition, it seems more likely that the phrase was originally based on a midrash on Scripture, on exegesis rather than on liturgical composition. It seems unlikely that the author of Pastorals himself originated the midrash, so it may have come to him through his liturgical tradition.

16. Great indeed, we confess, is the mystery of our religion: *RSV* is not altogether satisfactory here. It is more like a paraphrase. In the first place **we confess** renders one word in Greek, a word which has no reference to the first person plural. It is *homologoumenōs*. This is an unusual word with strong philosophic overtones. The Stoics said one should live conformably (*homologoumenōs*) to nature. It could suggest an adversative sense 'admittedly', or some such translation, but there is no trace in the context of either philosophy or of an argument. Several editors (e.g. Easton, Holtz) seize on the apparent connection with *homologein*, which means 'confess' and claim that the author is using the word to introduce his credo (this is of course how *RSV* takes it). The true solution, we believe, is to be found in 4 Maccabees, a work known to our author, where *homologoumenōs* occurs three times, always in connection with *ho eusebēs logismos*, which means 'rational piety'. Indeed it could be said that the theme of 4 Maccabees is expressed in the passage where this word first occurs, 6:31: 'Rational piety is thus demonstrably the master of the passions'. See also 4 Mac. 7:16; 16:1. This book is ostensibly a quasi-philosophical discourse; the level of philosophical thought is just about equal to the capacity of the author of the Pastorals. It seems therefore that the author has lifted this word from 4 Maccabees. We note the connection between rational piety (*ho eusebēs logismos*) and *to mystērion tēs eusebeias*, literally 'the mystery of piety' in v. 16 here. *Homologoumenōs* is an academic word, well rendered by 'demonstrably'. Our author has used it, not because he is demonstrating anything, but because he thinks his text will be improved by a good highbrow word (see my *Studies*, pp. 21–4). The alternative reading *homologoumen hōs* ('we confess that') is obviously secondary. **the mystery of our religion** is, as we have seen, to be literally translated, 'the mystery of piety'. We have here the author's favourite word *eusebeia*. It means exactly the same as **the mystery of faith** in v. 9 above. *RSV* is therefore quite correct in interpreting *eusebeia* here as 'our religion', but it is an interpretation rather than an accurate translation. The author of the *Epistle to Diognetus* (second or third century AD) describes the Jews' religion as 'the mystery of their own cult' ('cult' is *theosebeia*). The author uses this sentence with its impressive quasi-philosophic vocabulary as a way of introducing the hymn that follows.

We must begin by noting a textual difficulty. There are three possible alternatives for the first word of the first line of the hymn: *hos*, which means 'who', and must refer to Christ; or *ho*, which means 'which'; or *theos*, which means 'God'. *RSV* has put all three alternatives in the margin and translated a text which does not exist, since no MS simply begins with the verb **he was manifested**. Of these three, *hos*, 'who', has the best MS backing, and is intrinsically likely, since other credal or hymnic formulas in the *NT* begin with this word, applying of course to Christ; see Phil. 2:6; Col. 1:15. The reading *ho*, 'which', would represent an attempt by a later scribe to smooth out the grammar by making the 'mystery of piety' the subject referred to. B. Reicke (*CN* 11 [1947], pp. 196–206) actually thinks that *ho* is original. The third reading, *theos*, probably originated from a misreading of *hos* as if it had been the contracted form of *theos*. It does have some sort of backing in Greek minuscules and the Fathers. These variant readings have played a dramatic part at certain points in the history of the church. Macedonius II, patriarch of Constantinople, was dethroned, excommunicated, and probably executed in 511, on a charge of Nestorianism. Liberatus, writing in the middle of the sixth century, claims that he was accused of changing *hos* to *theos* in this verse in the interests of his heresy. More than a thousand years later, however, the reading *theos* was cherished by the champions of orthodoxy. Théodore de Bèze himself warmly defended this reading. He wrote, 'Since there is hardly any other passage in which all the mysteries of our redemption are more magnificently or plainly set out, it is not surprising that this passage has been foully corrupted by the devil.' And in 1730 J. J. Wettstein was dismissed from the ministry and from academic office in the University of Basel because he read *hos* instead of *theos* in his edition of the Greek *NT*. He was accused of deliberately tampering with the sacred text in order to support Socinianism. See an interesting art. 'Textkritik als Schicksal', by W. Stenger in *BZ* 19 (1975), pp. 204–7.

Next we must consider the form of the hymn. *RSV* points it in two stanzas of three lines each; but a careful consideration of the contents would seem to suggest that it was intended to be cast in three stanzas of two lines each (so Jeremias). This gives us in each stanza a contrast between the two realms, the realm of the flesh and the realm of the spirit, or the realm of earth and the realm of heaven. There is a certain chiasmus, but that would be deliberate. It could run this:

(a)	*He was manifested in the flesh,*	Earth
	vindicated in the Spirit,	Heaven
(b)	*seen by angels,*	Heaven
	preached among the nations,	Earth
(c)	*believed on in the world,*	Earth
	taken up in glory.	Heaven

This flesh-spirit contrast is also found in what many scholars believe is an early credal formula quoted by Paul in Rom. 1:3–4, and also in 1 Pet. 3:18, 'being put to death in the flesh but made alive in the spirit'. The whole hymn is a sort of creed in that it details what are regarded as the essential facts about Christ. It is surprising that there is no reference to Christ's death; but we may compare Rev. 12:1–5, where in a vision John the Divine sees a child born to a woman who is adorned by sun and moon. When the child is born he is snatched up to heaven. This also sketchily outlines the career of Christ without mentioning his death.

manifested in the flesh probably refers to the incarnation, in which case pre-existence is certainly implied, though the author of Pastorals may not have been aware of this. Dornier also takes this view, though D–C are more doubtful; but Brox is definite that both incarnation and pre-existence are implied here. The alternative view, defended by Spicq in his latest edition and on the whole by W. Stenger (*TTZ* 78 [1964], p. 37), is that the clause refers to the appearances of the risen Lord. One could compare Mk 16:12, where *ephanerōthē* occurs, the same word that *RSV* has here rendered **he was manifested**. But the contrast seems to require that the first line should refer to the incarnation and the second, **vindicated in the Spirit**, to the resurrection. The word **vindicated** no doubt correctly translates the

Greek *edikaiōthē*, which in another more Pauline context could mean 'justified'. **seen by angels** will then refer to the triumph which the risen Christ enjoyed over all the powers in the universe, good and bad alike; cf. 1 Pet. 3:22. The third stanza, **believed on in the world, taken up in glory**, is the nearest this hymn gets to providing an eschatology. There is a certain cosmic element in the hymn which seems to be characteristic of the deutero-Pauline literature. J. Kremer (*BK* 20 [1965], pp. 33–7) assimilates **taken up in glory** to the passages in the authentic Paulines and deutero-Paulines where the exaltation of Christ is referred to. He thereby presents a uniform, Pauline, doctrine. But he never even considers that the Pastorals may not be authentic and therefore never faces the problems that his theory has to encounter.

Some editors maintain that we have here a very old pre-Pauline christology. Jeremias, followed by Stenger (*TTZ* 78 [1964], p. 36), finds here a pattern of exaltation, presentation, inthronisation. But this seems rather overelaborate. Windisch certainly believed we have a pre-Pauline christology in the hymn (see Introduction, section 7); and Brox calls it 'a very old christology'. It is certainly nothing like a Pauline christology that we encounter here, but one might hesitate to call it 'pre-Pauline': it is not Adoptionist, and its links seem to be rather with 1 Peter and Revelation. C. K. Barrett (*NTS* 20 [1973–4], p. 242) is however surely right in saying that it dates from a time when the Gnostic threat was not yet apparent, because as it stands this hymn seems to offer too many hostages to Gnosticism.

Editors have speculated as to how far the author of Pastorals has adapted the original hymn. Hasler thinks he may have put together the hymn himself from various miscellaneous materials at his disposal, a suggestion which hardly fits the relative uniformity of the hymn. Lock conjectures that it may come from the same hymn as that quoted in Eph. 5:14. But this hardly seems justified unless one is determined to make Paul the author of both works. Bürki and Holtz believe that the hymn was composed in order to be sung at the eucharist. Certainly the author introduces it here in order to give a brief and striking expression of what he means by the **mystery of our religion**, i.e. the content of the Christian faith. It is characteristic of him that he does not attempt to put it in his own words, but draws instead on the liturgical tradition of his church.

RENEWED WARNING AGAINST FALSE TEACHERS

4:1–5

1. Now the Spirit expressly says: naturally we ask how and when the Spirit says this. We must remember that the author is presenting this statement as an utterance of Paul. It is very probable therefore that the **later times** to which he refers are intended to be the period at which the author was actually writing. Thus he is using the same technique as the author of the book of Daniel, prophecy after the event; compare Ac. 20:29–30, where Paul is represented as warning the Ephesian elders against the false teachers who would appear after his death. They were probably already at work when Luke was writing Acts. The **later times** of this verse are no doubt to be identified with the **last days** of 2 Tim. 3:1. Thus this is not really a strongly eschatological prophecy and it does not suggest that the author had a vivid sense of the imminence of the parousia. If we ask how the Spirit made this explicit prophecy, we are probably to imagine it as having been made by some Christian prophet of Paul's day, perhaps in a context of worship. Holtz calls it 'an apocalyptic utterance' and Hasler 'a prophetic revelation formula', but we must ask ourselves whether it ever actually took place. Is it not more likely to be the sort of thing that the author imagined must have happened during Paul's lifetime? **doctrines of demons** is quite in line with Pauline thinking: he did see the activity of Satan behind the work of his opponents in Corinth (cf. 2 C. 11:3, 13–15). R. J. Karris (*JBL* 92 [1973], p. 549) well points out that this is the only passage in which the author actually argues with his opponents.

2. **liars whose consciences are seared**: the word translated **seared** here *kekaustēriasmenōn* is one which was applied to the practice of cauterising human flesh. But this cauterising could have one of two very different purposes, either to brandmark the flesh (as was done with slaves and criminals), or to heal the flesh, to some extent rendering it anaesthetic. The great majority of editors accept the first of these two meanings: in some way the conscience of these heretics has been marked (so Lock, Easton, D–C, Kelly, Brox). Some editors even talk about an 'invisible mark', which seems a contradiction in terms. Anyway it is not clear what it means to say that they are 'brandmarked in their consciences'. Does it mean that in their heart of hearts they know that they belong to the devil? But this seems somewhat irrelevant to the author's purpose. If however we paraphrase *kekaustēriasmenōn* with 'anaesthetised (because cauterised)', we can make excellent sense of the verse. The false teachers are liars; they deliberately deceive, because they have managed to anaesthetise their consciences, no doubt by means of their constant habit of deceit. This means that they do not believe their own ideology, but propagate it from the lowest motives. Hence we cannot agree with Spicq when he says that they have come eventually to believe their own propaganda.

3. **who forbid marriage and enjoin abstinence from foods**: any-

one who believes that Paul wrote these words, can only do as Spicq does and point to such phenomena as the Qumran sect, of whom both these statements could fairly be made. At least they practised celibacy in some of their settlements. But if the view taken in this Commentary is followed, we must see this teaching as an early form of Gnosticism, originating in Jewish dietary laws based on the Torah, but also operating with a strong prejudice against physical matter as the cause of evil, a prejudice which would be quite alien to authentic Judaism.

those who believe and know the truth: cf. 1 Tim. 2:4; 2 Tim. 2:27; 3:5; Tit. 1:1. The double phrase does not refer to two groups of people; it simply means baptised Christians. Brox denies any suggestion here that only Christians can appreciate God's gifts. But see our commentary on vv. 4–5, where rather more is read into this verse.

4–5. if it is received with thanksgiving: the word for **thanksgiving** in Greek is *eucharistias*. Only a few years after Pastorals were written we find Ignatius of Antioch using *eucharistia* for the Lord's Supper. Trummer (p. 167) claims that the author is answering the teaching of the heretics with an argument drawn from natural theology (God has created food for man's use) rather than from any specifically Christian source. If this is so, it is no discredit to the author, for his argument is perfectly valid, and does indeed go back to a sound Jewish tradition. But we may question whether his argument is as simple as this. The language, *eucharistia* and *hagiazetai* (**it is consecrated** in v. 5), as well as **those who believe and know the truth** in v. 3, recalls the sacramental practice of the early church. I have argued in *Studies* (ch. 8) that the author's language here is deliberately intended to recall the eucharist and perhaps baptism also. If one puts this passage together with 2 Tim. 1:10, one finds striking parallels with language used in the *Didache* in what is certainly a eucharistic context. This comes to a climax in v. 5 here, where the author says food is to be received with thanksgiving **for then it is consecrated by the word of God and prayer.** There has been much speculation as to what exactly **the word of God** refers to here. There are four theories. (a) It means the Word of God and is a reference to the Incarnate Word: he has blessed food for our use. But this is quite out of line with the author's christology. (b) It means the creative word of God, perhaps specifically in Gen. 1:31, 'And God saw everything that he had made, and, behold it was very good'. This is supported by Easton and Houlden. Presumably Trummer would follow this interpretation also. (c) It refers to grace over meat, the blessing which the pious Christian, like the pious Jew, uttered over the food he was about to eat. This exegesis has the backing of Jeremias, Kelly, Spicq, and Brox. (d) It refers to the bread and wine consecrated in the eucharist. The argument is that if Christ gave us the eucharist in which we consecrate bread and wine to be the means of his presence, they cannot be condemned as unclean in themselves; nor can any food, by extension. This interpretation is hinted at by D–C, who find in this phrase '*ein kultisches Motiv*'; it is also followed by Hasler, who links the phrase with the church's worship. In the chapter in *Studies* referred to above I have defended this interpretation, and, among other parallels, have pointed to Justin's description of the bread consecrated in the eucharist which he gives in *Apology* 66.2. He calls it 'the food over which thanks has been given by that word of prayer which comes from Christ'. The words translated 'that word of prayer' are in the Greek *di' euchēs logou*, which offers quite a good parallel to *dia logou theou kai enteuxeōs*, **by the word of God and prayer**, especially as Justin describes his word of prayer as coming from Christ. Holtz sees here (as almost everywhere in the Pastorals) a eucharistic reference, but takes the **word of God** in v. 5 as referring to grace over meat. We should not fail to notice the similarity between the false teaching described here and that which is attacked in Colossians. There is the same tendency to distinguish between clean and unclean foods and a hint of asceticism; see Col. 2:16–18 21–23. There is nothing in this incompatible with the dating of the Pastorals which we have suggested, as long as Colossians is regarded as deutero-Pauline rather than authentic. Perhaps it is significant that at the end of 4:10 we trace a parallel between a large section of 1 Tim. chapters 3–4 and Col. 1:24–29.

HOW A CHURCH LEADER SHOULD BEHAVE

4:6–16

6. before the brethren: this means of course the whole local church and is a very primitive term for Christians. **a good minister of Christ Jesus:** the word for **minister** is *diakonos*, used here in a general sense and not for a specific office, as in 3:8f. The author could not possibly mean that Timothy was a deacon, not a presbyter or a bishop. The author seems to be using in this verse and the next the vocabulary of Stoic educational theory: **nourished** (*entrephomenos*), **you have followed** (*parēkolouthēkas*) and (in v. 7) **Train yourself** (*gumnaze seauton*), are all technical terms in Stoic philosophy. The **words of the faith and of the good doctrine** must refer to written or oral catechesis in use in the church of the author's day. This was no innovation, since we have a very similar reference in Rom. 6:17. The difference between Paul's day and the author's was that in Paul's day this teaching could apparently be given by any competent person in the local church (see Rom. 12:7). In the author's day it was the prerogative of the ordained ministry.

7. **godless and silly myths**: editors are singularly reluctant to indicate what exactly they think these myths contained. The word translated **godless** (*bebēlois*) is literally 'profane, defiling'. The next epithet is feebly rendered by *RSV* with **silly**. *graōdeis* is literally 'suited to old women'. It is an epithet which was a commonplace in the philosophic abuse of the period. Both Jews and Christians prided themsleves that their religion had no element of **myth** in it, by which they meant that it had no stories of gods and goddesses, no immoral accounts of divine seductions or couplings. In the *Letter of Aristeas* 168, a Jewish apologetic work of perhaps the second or first century BC, the claim is made: 'Nothing absurd or mythical is related in our scripture.' We may therefore suggest that the sort of myths which the author has in mind are the accounts of the mutual relations of the aeons which we hear of in many Gnostic systems. Aeons are represented as mating with each other, producing litters of lesser aeons, wandering through the world, descending and ascending. Such fictions would be regarded as 'profane' because they associate God with quasi-human generation, and as 'suited to old women' because they demand boundless credulity on the part of those who accept them. Spicq gives a fair modern equivalent in the shape of 'encouraging the visions of pseudo-saints'.

Train yourself in godliness: for the Greek word see the note on v. 6. Brox comments that the author's emphasis on godly training is intended to counterbalance the false teachers' emphasis on extreme asceticism.

8. In this verse the author reaches the highest point in his praise for **godliness**, that favourite word *eusebeia*. It is this preference for *eusebeia* as a key-word, one which never occurs in the authentically Pauline writings, that distinguishes the author from Paul as much as any other single feature of his vocabulary or thought. In profane Greek usage *eusebeia* meant proper reverence for the gods, who themselves guaranteed the maintenance of society and public order. Both Spicq and A. Schlatter attempt to salvage the word for Pauline theology by interpreting it in terms of 'all for God's honour', but this requires a good deal of special pleading. D–C maintain that the central position of this concept in the author's thought indicates that in his day Christianity is coming to terms with the morality of the society in which it lives. Brox agrees that the idea is really incompatible with the message of Jesus or the theology of either Paul or the author of the Fourth Gospel. But he points out that *eusebeia* for the author has a definitely Christian connotation, it includes knowledge of the Christian mystery. In 1 Tim. 6:3, 5 it means not just

personal piety but ministerial piety, i.e. a piety needed for the service of the Christian community.

the life to come: not a Pauline phrase.

9–10. It is not at all easy to decide whether v. 9 refers to the preceding or the succeeding one. Is it to the statement that godliness is of great value, or to the claim that God is the saviour of all men? In fact we need not concern ourselves with this dilemma if we take the view advocated in this commentary that the 'faithful word' formula is not intended to underline any one particular statement in any context in which it occurs, but to give solemnity to the text as a whole when it seems to be growing too pedestrian. See the Note on the 'faithful sayings' at 2:17.

For to this end we toil and strive: we must not stress the word **for** to the extent of claiming that it shows the 'faithful word' formula must apply to the preceding verse, since the analogy of 2 Tim. 2:11 is against this. There the next sentence to the formula has **for**, but it is very probable that the formula is intended to refer to vv. 11*b*–13 and not to v. 10. In the phrase here in 1 Tim. 4:10 the author seems to be quoting Col. 1:29: 'For this I toil, striving with all the energy which (Christ) mightily inspires within me' (Holtz sees an echo of Col. 1:29 here). The two most significant words are in common to these two verses *kopiō* (**toil**) and *agōnizomai* (**strive**). Indeed, it is not fanciful to suggest that the whole of the preceding passage in 1 Timothy (right back to 3:14) could be regarded as an extended commentary on Col. 1:24–29. In that passage from Colossians we have the following elements (a) vv. 24–25: Paul is entrusted by God with the work of Christ's church; (b) vv. 26–27: the substance of the gospel expressed in terms of a mystery; (c) vv. 28–29: what it means to undertake this pastoral work. If we now review 1 Tim. 3:14–4:10, we can divide it as follows:

(a) 3:14–15: Timothy must learn how to carry out his work in the church. The author does not rise to the difficult Pauline concept of the church as the body of Christ, but he expresses the nature of the church in language which has messianic overtones. (b) 3:16: Here is the substance of the gospel expressed in a formula familiar to the author and no doubt to his correspondents. The content of the gospel is a **mystery**, in it Christ is **manifested**, and it includes **preaching** Christ – all elements common to the Colossians passage. (c) 4:1–10: What it means to undertake pastoral work, with particular reference to the need to refute heresy. The lofty purpose mentioned in Colossians of presenting every man perfect in Christ takes here the form of the requirement of godliness, supported by church teaching. He ends with a quotation of Col. 1:29 and a fine reference to hoping in the living God, which is the nearest he can get to the phrase in

Colossians 'Christ in you, the hope of glory'. If this comparison is valid, it is an excellent example of how the author transposes Pauline or deutero-Pauline material into his own key. See Introduction, section 5. There is an alternative reading to *agōnizometha* (**we strive**), which is *oneidizometha* (**we suffer reproach**), actually preferred by Easton. But the MS backing is feebler, and the parallel with Col. 1:29 seems to rule it out.

who is the Saviour of all men, especially of those who believe: commentators make valiant efforts to save this sentiment from the obvious charge of appalling ineptitude. In fact, however, a recent suggestion made by T. C. Skeat (*JTS* ns 30 [1979], pp. 173–7) absolves the author from this charge. He claims that the word translated **especially** (*malista* in Greek) is here better rendered as 'to be precise' or 'in other words'. Thus the author is not saying that God saves believers more than he saves others; he is simply modifying his general statement that God is the Saviour of all men by adding the limitation that you cannot be saved unless you believe. We may well admire this reiteration of God's universal will for salvation. But the author is not committed to Universalism in the modern sense. As Brox points out, he would still say *extra ecclesiam nulla salus*.

11. these things no doubt refers to what precedes, which is of more general application, whereas what follows applies to Timothy as the prototype of the church leader only. Spicq significantly decides that it refers to everything that has gone before from the beginning of ch. 4. The verse is one of those linking phrases whereby the author holds together his varied material. See Introduction, section 8.

12. Let no one despise your youth: in 1 C. 16:11 Paul writes to the Corinthians that they are not to despise Timothy. This verse here may well therefore be a genuine piece of historical tradition as well as an echo of 1 C. 16:11. Several editors, e.g. D–C and Brox, have seen this reference as a warning that local churches should not be contemptuous of young bishops (see Brox, *VC* 30 [1976], pp. 181–8; E. Stauffer, 'Eine Bemerkung', p. 35; D. Dornier, 'Les Épîtres Pastorales', in Delorme, p. 106). Ignatius certainly had this concern; see *Magnes.* 3.1.

set the believers an example: the church leader is held up as an example to Christians in Phil. 3:17; 2 Th. 3:9; 1 Pet. 5:3. The qualities here recommended, **love, faith, purity** do not seem to have any particular connection with each other. **purity** is *hagneia* in Greek. It is not actually used by Paul, but he uses its cognates quite frequently. In profane Greek the word had two distinct meanings, sexual purity and ritual purity. The first is probably in mind here. Compare this miscellaneous collection of points which a church leader should bear in mind with Paul's brilliant thumb-nail sketch of the Christian

character in Gal. 5:22–23. Brox well compares with v. 12*b* here 2
Tim. 2:22.

13. Till I come: this is to emphasise the abiding authority of Paul.
It does not mean that on Paul's arrival Timothy can cease these
activities. This verse is an interesting one because it gives us in the
words of J. H. Bernard, 'the three main departments of the public
duties of the pastor'. These are (a) *public reading of Scripture*. In the
Greek these four English words are represented by the one *anagnōsis*.
It could mean private study of Scripture (as in the Prologue to
Ecclesiasticus, vv. 10, 17). But no doubt the *RSV* interpretation is
correct. The skill would be not so much in the technique of public
reading as in the selection of the passages to be read. There were as
yet no lectionaries in use in the church as far as we know.

(b) *Preaching*: This is a somewhat over-interpretative translation of
the Greek word *paraklēsis*. It is used extensively by Paul. Its cognates
parakalein ('to appeal') and *paraklētos* ('comforter') have great theological significance in the *NT*. Paul in 2 C. 1:3 calls God 'the God of
all comfort' (*paraklēseōs*), and in Rom. 15:4 he writes of the encouragement (*paraklēsis*) of the Scriptures. In Ac. 13:15 a sermon
which Paul is about to give in Pisidian Antioch is called 'a word of
paraklēsis', and this is exactly how the author of Hebrews describes
his own letter in Heb. 13:22. Both these places refer to something
which is largely an exposition of Scripture. Indeed we can go farther
back than this and claim that the *paraklēsis* of Scripture was already
well known to the Jews. In 1 Mac. 12:9 Jonathan, writing to the
Spartans, says that the Jews have no need of alliance and friendship
'since we have as encouragement (*paraklēsis*) the holy books which
are in our hands'. And in 2 Mac. 15:9–11 Judas before battle encourages his men from the law and the prophets, and they are described as 'the inspiration (*paraklēsis*) of brave words'. So *paraklēsis*
here in 1 Tim. 4:13 must mean exposition of the Scriptures, probably
in public worship. C. K. Barrett notes that celebration of the eucharist
is apparently no part of the church leader's duties; but the author is
probably concentrating on those parts which need preparation, choice
of scripture passages and composition of the exhortation. The eucharistic prayer, though not at this period in the form of a fixed liturgy,
would probably not vary very much from one occasion to another.

(c) *Teaching*: Paul associates *didaskalia* (**teaching**) with *paraklēsis*
in Rom. 15:4. Probably in the author's day this activity had become
more formalised and could be described as formal catechesis. It would
not take place in a context of worship, but would (like *anagnōsis* and
paraklēsis) need preparation beforehand. Kelly agrees that these three
are the crucial activities indicated here. Nauck (p. 13) maintains that
all three activities are inherited from the synagogue.

14. David Daube (pp. 224–8) put forward a theory *à propos* this
verse that the phrase translated in *RSV* **when the elders laid their
hands upon you** should rather be rendered something like 'lawful
ordination to the presbyterate', appealing to a rite in rabbinic Judaism
called *simkat z^{e}qenîm*, literally 'leaning on of hands of elders',
whereby one rabbi commissioned another by laying hands on him.
He claimed that this rite had been taken over into Christianity. E.
Käsemann (*Essays*, pp. 86–7) also believes that the rite of ordination
as portrayed here has been taken over (since Paul's day) into the
church from Judaism.

The theory has appealed to some scholars, e.g. Bürki, Holtz, who
wish to correlate this reference to ordination with that made in 2
Tim. 1:6, regarding both as referring to an historical occasion on
which Paul (not the group of presbyters) ordained Timothy. Daube's
explanation is accepted by Kelly, Barrett, and Lemaire (*Les Ministères*, p. 130). But it is rejected by others, e.g. A. Sand (in Hainz, p.
227). The objections to it are that it is unnecessary to go to a Jewish
rite which may not have originated as early as the first century AD in
order to explain the word *presbuterion* (**the** [group of] **elders**), when
it is used perfectly straightforwardly by Ignatius only a few years
after the composition of the Pastorals to mean the body of presbyters
in a local church. And secondly the rite of one rabbi commissioning
another was quite different from the concept of ordination as we find
it in the Pastorals. See a valuable article by E. Lohse 'Die Ordination
im Spätjudentum und im Neuen Testament' (originally published in
1951), in Kertelge, pp. 501–23. Lohse argues that the actual rite of
laying on of hands was taken over from Judaism by the church, but
that ordination as described in the *NT* is not the act of commissioning
a disciple, but of authorisation. Ordination did not mean the ordainer
conveying some quality to the ordinand, as the example of Simon
Magus in Acts shows. On the other hand D–C maintain that in the
Pastorals ordination is a sacramental act whereby the grace (*charisma*)
of office is conveyed. A. Cousineau (*ScEsp* 28 [1976], pp. 160–1) also
rejects Daube's thesis. He points out that Timothy is never called a
presbyter, so he could hardly have been ordained to the presbyterate
as Daube's theory requires. G. Bornkamm (*TDNT* 6, pp. 651ff.) is
no doubt right in distinguishing between the purpose of this passage
and the purpose of 2 Tim. 1:6. This passage does refer to an ordination by the group of local presbyters. We conclude, therefore, that
the author is here describing an ordination as he knew it in his day.
The prophets had indicated who was the man of God's choice, the
group of local presbyters laid on hands in ordination (so Brox). We
have already discussed and rejected the theory that **by prophetic**

utterance in this verse refers to the actual ordination formula uttered by prophets. See Introduction, section 6.

15. Practise these duties: certainly the instructions given from v. 6 onwards, and possibly the advice given in the entire epistle. **devote yourself to them** is literally 'be in these things'. Spicq offers *'sois y tout entier'*. He well compares Lk. 2:49, where 'I must be in my Father's house' is literally 'I must be in the things of my Father', and could just as well be translated 'I must be about my Father's business'. We cannot help noticing the immense moral emphasis which runs all through the Pastorals, more than in Paul's works, no doubt because the author was more of a moralist and less of a mystic than Paul. **your progress:** the word for **progress**, *prokopē*, was an important one in the Stoic vocabulary.

16. Just as Timothy's moral conduct must conform to the Christian standard of morality, so his teaching must conform to the norm of Christian orthodoxy. **you will save both yourself and your hearers:** this contrasts markedly with Paul's reckless abandonment of himself to God's will. Paul was ready to be 'accursed and cut off from Christ' for the sake of his fellow-Jews (Rom. 9:3). What we have in the Pastorals is a prudential ethic. D–C well compare Jas 5:20: 'whoever brings back a sinner from the error of his way will save his soul from death and will cover a multitude of sins', where the meaning is no doubt that he will both save the sinner and atone for his own sins. The Pastorals and James have this in common that both are written pseudonymously and intended as general rather than as specific epistles. Both also seem to have elements of a prudential ethic that has more in common with the old dispensation than the new.

HOW TO BEHAVE TOWARDS VARIOUS GROUPS

5:1-2

1-2. an older man is *presbyteroi*, but it certainly does not mean a church officer here. Many examples could be cited from contemporary Greek literature for the requirement that one should treat elderly people as parents and contemporaries as siblings (see D–C for examples). Spicq well compares Rom. 16:13, where Paul writes: 'Greet Rufus . . . also his mother and mine', where Paul does not mean that his natural mother was in Rome! Dornier comments on the strong family feeling that runs through these two verses, a very primitive characteristic.

HOW TO DEAL WITH THE PROBLEM OF WIDOWS

5:3-16

3. Houlden points out that the author devotes more space to widows than to any other group in the community, no doubt because they were causing more trouble. This passage is however confused and obscure in some places, probably because the author is adapting an existing church order source. It is not immediately clear what is meant by **widows who are real widows**, and the author seems to be ambiguous on the question of the desirability of widows remarrying. There certainly was some sort of an order for widows in the church which the author knew. Those who joined the order were expected to perform certain duties in return for the support which the church gave them, notably intercessory prayer and assistance in the entertainment of the church's guests. The commentary on the passage that follows is based on the following assumptions: (a) There was an order to which widows could belong, but not any Christian widow was *ipso facto* eligible: a widow had to be really destitute, over the age of sixty, and not divorced and remarried in the past. (b) Any really destitute widow of any age would probably receive some help from the church. (c) The author does not disapprove of the remarriage of widows on principle, only of those who, having joined the order, are regarded as having consecrated themselves to Christ. (d) He has tried the experiment of letting younger widows join the order and it has not been a success. For a full discussion of the problems see J. Ernst, *ThG* 59 (1969), pp. 434-45, and Bartsch, pp. 113-38.

who are real widows we take to mean 'those who are genuinely destitute'. Some have suggested that a phrase from Ignatius (*Smyr.* 13) throws light on this, where he refers to 'the virgins who are called widows'. They have suggested that a widows' order may have been the seed-bed of the later witnessed order of consecrated virgins (see Ernst, *ThG* 59 [1969], p. 444). But there does not seem to be any trace of this in the Pastorals. On the contrary, the author emphatically affirms the ideal of the Christian married life.

Honour widows may mean 'pay them'; see our discussion on 5:17. But on the whole it seems more likely that the author means they are to be honoured in contrast to widows who behave in a profligate manner or, perhaps, who claim church support even though they have means of their own. Bartsch shows that in the later church widows began to claim the privileges of an ordained order, and had to be brought to heel. But this hardly seems to be the situation in the Pastorals.

4. let them first learn: it is more satisfactory to take **them** as the children. They are to **learn their religious duty** to their parents by

supporting their widowed mothers (so Spicq, D–C, Brox). Dornier
agrees with this interpretation but points out that the Vulgate applies
the verse to widows: 'she should teach her children their duty to the
family'. The phrase translated **their religious duty to their own
family** is an unusual one in Greek, *ton idion oikon eusebein*, literally
'to venerate their own house'. *eusebein* is often used of reverence
towards parents as a religious duty, but not often with any other
direct object except 'God', or 'the gods'. **in the sight of God:** literally
'before God', a Semitism according to Spicq. Brox notes that it is
characteristic of the author to enrol a natural duty among Christian
duties. Both he and Bartsch (p. 122) point out that the positive duty
is given in this verse and the negative of it in v. 8.

5. has set her hope on God: cf. 4:10; there the dative *theōi* is
used for God rather than the accusative, as here; it does not seem to
make any difference to the sense. See also 1 Tim. 6:17 (dative again).
The phrase is at most a technical term in the LXX for those who take
refuge in God as their last resource. Plainly only widows in desperate
need would join the order, but their dependent condition was made
easier for them by assigning them quasi-religious duties. Compare
Lk. 2:37, where Anna may be intended to be an example to Christian
widows. There does not seem to be any difference in meaning between
supplications and **prayers,** except that the latter (*proseuchais* in
Greek) could mean public prayer as well as private. **night and day:**
cf. 1 Th. 3:10. This also is a Hebraism, according to Spicq, for the
Jewish day began at sunset.

6. she who is self-indulgent: this can hardly apply to a destitute
widow, who would not have the means for self-indulgence. It must
refer to any widow, and it probably has a sexual overtone, though
the Greek word *spatalōsa* does not necessarily imply this. The strong
language of **dead even while she lives** must refer to something worse
than mere self-indulgence. Philo often uses the figure of someone
being physically alive but spiritually dead; cf. Rev. 3:1.

7. A rather feeble connecting sentence: commanding, instructing,
and expecting are prominent activities in the Pastorals.

8. The author reverts in a somewhat unordered way to the theme
he has already broached in v. 4, and to which he returns in v. 16.
This verse applies to anyone, including men who refuse to support
destitute relatives. **he has disowned the faith:** *pistis* (**faith**) here,
which can mean subjective trust, must be used in the sense of the
contents of the Christian faith; Rev. 2:13; 3:8. Spicq, anxious to
approximate the sentiment to within the range of Paul's theology,
takes it as 'fidelity and respect for obligations', but this is not plausible
in view of the use of **an unbeliever.**

9–10. Here we have very specifically the qualifications necessary for a widow who is to be admitted to the order, as **Let a widow be enrolled** indicates. We must bear in mind that not all destitute widows were eligible. The advantages of joining the order were regular support and status in the church. **having been the wife of one husband:** see the Note on 'Husband of one wife' at 3:7. **well attested for her good deeds;** presumably these good deeds will have been performed in the days of her prosperity while her husband was still alive. **one who has brought up children:** this does not necessarily imply that childless widows were ineligible; indeed the childless widow might be more likely to need the support of the church, as having no one to whom she could .turn; the word for **brought up children,** *eteknotrophēsen,* could mean looking after orphans. **washed the feet of the saints:** all commentators agree that foot-washing was essentially a servile task. Compare the example of the Lord himself in Jn 13:2–11. **the saints** means of course any Christians. In the *Didache* we have a picture of itinerant preachers or prophets going from one church to another. **relieved the afflicted:** does this mean 'comforted the bereaved' or 'assisted the destitute'? Both probably. D–C point out that Lucian (fl. between 115 and 200) represents Peregrinus, the pseudo-Christian who has got himself into prison, as being visited by widows and orphans from the local Christian congregation. But this was at a time when Christians were liable to persecution as they do not seem to be in the time of the author of the Pastorals.

11–12. The most satisfactory explanation of these verses is to assume that the author in the past has enrolled young widows in the order, but has found that too many of them have not really made up their minds to a celibate life. They have tried to get themselves married again (difficult for a destitute widow, since normally a father, or at least a male relative, was needed to arrange the marriage). This conduct has led to scandal. Thus **having violated their first pledge** does not refer merely to the fact that they have taken (or wanted to take) a second husband, but that they have broken the vow which they took on joining the order, whereby they became devoted to Christ instead of to a husband. Verse 14 makes is plain that the author has no objection to second marriages on principle. This is how Brox understands these verses (so also Holtz). In the church order book called the *Syrian Didascalia* (early third century) there are elaborate rules for the order of Widows: entry can be at the age of forty; but they prohibit remarriage altogether. The word for **younger** in v. 11 is *neōteras,* which rather militates against J. Elliott's theory (*CBQ* 32 [1970], pp. 367–91) that this word implies 'newly baptised'. A. Sand (*Bibel und Leben* [March 1971], p. 196) energetically rejects the suggestion that there could have been any requirement of a vow for those entering the order. It does not fit in with what we know of the period of the Pastorals, and in any case a vow of celibacy taken by a women of sixty could hardly be very meaningful. But suppose we are dealing with a situation where the experiment of admitting young widows has been tried and failed, would not the imposition of a sixty-year age limit be the obvious solution, letting the vow look after itself?

13. they learn to be idlers: something of a paradox, but the Greek is very strange, *argai manthanousin*, literally 'being idle they learn'. The nearest parallels are provided by Lock, *palaistes manthanei*, lit. 'being a wrestler he learns', i.e. he learns to be a wrestler; and similarly with the Greek word for doctor, not unlike the colloquialism: 'he learns school'. But these are specialised techniques and do not satisfactorily explain this passage. James Moffatt in his translation of the Bible, followed by Jeremias, actually assumes a corruption in the text, and emends it (without any MS support) to *lanthanousin*, which would mean 'they unconsciously slip into idleness'. **gadding about from house to house:** Brox points out that widows would be expected to visit others in the course of their duties anyway. **busybodies:** the Greek for this is *periergoi*. Barrett and D–C both point to 2 Th. 3:11: 'For we hear that some of you are living in idleness, mere busybodies, not doing any work'. 'mere busybodies' is *periergazomenous*: Barrett believes that the author is deliberately echoing this passage. In Ac. 19:19 we have a description of how 'a number of those who practised magic acts brought their books together and burned them'; 'magic acts' translates *ta perierga*, so several editors have suggested that the widows described here as *periergoi* engaged in some sort of superstitious practices. Spicq remarks that it is surprising how many charms and incantation formulae are found in Christian tombs in antiquity. So **saying what they should not** may mean not just silly gossip but uttering spells and incantations.

14. Here there does not seem to be any moral superiority attached to the unmarried state. The only question is, what is the best and most practical course for any given group in any given circumstances? (so Brox). D–C underline the absence of that expectation of the parousia which so much influenced Paul's views on the desirability or otherwise of marriage. **the enemy** is probably Satan rather than the pagan critic; see v. 15 and 3:6–7.

15. some have already strayed after Satan: this probably means they have become prostitutes rather than that they have been attracted by the false teachers. D–C are not sure which is meant. Spicq accepts that it does mean they have gone astray morally. Brox is inclined to think it refers to their having been beguiled by the heretics (and so also Bartsch, p. 134), but he describes it as a fictional situation. The author, in fact, is only trying to make our flesh creep. This seems unlikely; the unsuccessful experiment of admitting younger widows into the order is no fiction but painful experience, and it seems very likely that the sad fate of the erring widows is hard fact also.

16. If any believing woman has relatives who are widows: there is an interesting variation in the text here. Some MSS instead of **believing woman** (*pistē*) read *pistos* (**believing man**), and others offer both words. 'if any believer, man or woman. . .'. Bartsch (p. 137) suggests that the variation in the text indicates the presence behind the text of a document connected with church order which presumably early copyists would know. Moffatt, Easton, and the translators of *NEB* all accept the reading 'believing man or woman' as original. We must imagine a situation much more akin to the Hindu joint household than to anything we know in our largely nuclear families in the West. Aunts, sisters-in-law, nieces, daughters-in-law might all claim a place in the same household, any of whom might suffer widowhood. Either a man or a woman (the latter if she had inherited the family property) might find himself or herself liable for the support of a number of widows belonging to the family. The temptation to induce the church to be responsible for them must have been sometimes strong. Some scholars have connected this verse with the custom of *subintroductae* in the early church, virgins who lived in a state of continence with men. Spicq considers the theory that this whole verse is a later gloss 'discreetly authorising widows to put their virtue under the protection of a married Christian' (he reads *pistos* here). But he rightly rejects it. The conjecture is unnecessary, since the verse can be explained in more plausible ways.

HOW TO DEAL WITH PRESBYTERS

5:17–25

Dornier well says that three questions lie behind this section. (a) How to recompense those presbyters who have served well? (b) How to punish those who have deserved punishment? (c) How to get rid of those who have proved themselves unworthy of the ministry?

17. Let the elders who rule well be considered worthy of double honour: elders is of course *presbuteroi*. The word translated **rule well** is *proestōtes*. Paul uses the same word for those who exercise leadership in the local congregation; see 1 Th. 5:12; Rom. 12:8. Most scholars hold that this is what the verb means here; so J. P. Meier (*CBQ* 35]1973], p. 327), and A. Sand (in Hainz, p. 225). On the other hand this is the verb which Justin uses for the person who presides at the eucharist, so the phrase could mean 'those presbyters who preside well at the eucharist'. The author of Pastorals stands just

about midway between Paul and Justin. Perhaps the best solution is
to follow Barrett, who says that the term means leadership in general
but includes the duty of presiding at the eucharist. **double honour:**
the phrase in Greek could mean 'double reward, honorarium, or even
salary'. Most moderns agree that some sort of financial reward is
indicated here, e.g. all the commentators we refer to except Jeremias
and Holtz. These two prefer to translate it 'honour' in the interests
of Pauline authorship, since it is extremely unlikely that anyone was
paid for being a local church leader in Paul's time. J. Rohde (pp. 90–
1) would retain both meanings. We can also quote Bornkamm, Meier,
Sand, and Cousineau (p. 151) on the side of the view that financial
reward is meant. This seems the most natural conclusion, though we
should be prepared to accept Brox's suggestion that an honorarium
rather than a fixed salary is intended. See also J. A. Kirk (*Expt* 84
(1972–3], pp. 105–8), who comes to the same conclusion. **especially
those who labour in preaching and teaching:** it is not likely that the
author has two groups of presbyters in mind, a larger group who did
very little and an 'in-group' (who could also be called *episkopoi*)
referred to here. But it is quite reasonable to suggest that a very large
number of the respectable heads of Christian families might be regarded as presbyters, of whom only a relatively small number were
competent to preach and teach, or indeed to preside over the eucharist, since at this period that required the ability to frame a dignified
eucharistic prayer. Bartsch (p. 92), drawing his evidence from conditions that prevailed in the church of the third century, suggests
that presbyters were not at this period regarded as full-time clergy.
Only the deacon and the bishop were fully occupied in the ministry
of the church. Presbyters would either be men of independent means
or be making a living of their own. To give some sort of an honorarium to those among the presbyters who devoted more time to their
ministry would be quite appropriate. See on this G. Lohfink (*ThQ*
157 [1977], p. 101). Houlden also takes this view. We might suggest
that Skeat's translation, referred to at 4:10, might be relevant here.
If we translate *malista* not as **especially**, but as 'I mean', we get the
sense: 'Presbyters who preside well should be rewarded, I mean those
who labour in preaching and teaching'. This has the advantage that
it avoids any suggestion of two groups, a larger one who merely
presided, and a smaller who preached and taught.

   **18. 'You should not muzzle an ox when it is treading out the
grain':** This quotation from Dt. 25:4 is used by Paul in 1 C. 9:9 to
support his argument that those who preach the gospel have a right
to be supported by those whom they evangelise. It was a favourite
text with the rabbis, who, like Paul, did not hesitate to use it in an
allegorical sense. See my discussion of Paul's use of it in my *Studies*

in Paul's Technique and Theology (London, 1974), p. 166. By the time
the author of the Pastorals came to use it, it had become a stock
proof-text to show that the ordained ministry is entitled to some
financial reward. The author does not exactly quote Paul's version of
the text, but follows the LXX translation (using *phimōseis* for Paul's
kemōseis – both words mean **muzzle**). He quotes 1 C. 9:7, 10 in 2
Tim. 2:6, so he was well acquainted with this passage. Next comes
a logion from Jesus himself, which the author treats as being just as
authoritative as the scriptural quotation. It is to be found in Mt.
10:10 and Lk. 10:7. It is therefore from the source known as Q. This
is not to suggest that our author used this source, nor even that he
necessarily found this logion in Luke's Gospel, though he may have
done so, since he appears to know Acts. Spicq asks us to believe that
Paul is quoting Luke! In fact the author's version of the logion is
identical with Luke's version of it.

19. Another quotation follows here, this time from Dt. 17:6. Like
the previous one from Deuteronomy, it was widely used by the early
church, since it is quoted in several other places. Paul uses it in 2 C.
13:1 in his arguments with his unscrupulous opponents in Corinth.
We find it used to outline disciplinary practice in the church from
which Matthew's Gospel comes, Mt. 18:16, and it is used in Heb.
10:28 and Jn 8:17 in a much more theological sense. We may note
that the author here follows his master Paul's practice in using the
OT as *Halaka*: where the true Christian relationship of faith and love
had broken down, i.e. where Christians insist on behaving on a purely
legal basis, the Torah may be appealed to. Houlden points out that
the text is used by the Qumran sectaries in 1QS 8. Bartsch suggests
that the document which lies behind this passage about presbyters
originally proclaimed complete immunity from disciplinary action for
all presbyters, but that this proved impractical, hence the excepting
clause (see Bartsch, p. 100). We must understand the **two or three**
as church members, not necessarily fellow-presbyters. The author
assumes that someone (represented by Timothy) will have authority
to convene the disciplinary committee, summon the accused presbyter
and pronounce judgment (and probably execution of it is referred to
in v. 22). This looks like the beginnings of monepiscopacy.

20. those who persist in sin – a good translation of the present
tense in the Greek. The reference must be to presbyters, not to any
church member. The topic in this passage is the disciplining of
presbyters. D–C, Bartsch (p. 99), and Brox all agree that only presbyters are in mind here. But Brox disagrees with D–C, since he holds
that **the rest** means the whole congregation, whereas D–C thinks it
means the rest of the group of presbyters. On the whole D–C seem

to be in the right. It is with the discipline of the clergy, not of all church members, that the author is concerned here.

21. The line of thought seems to be: 'You are to judge others; remember that you are to be judged yourself'. The adjuration which the author uses is very remarkable. In the first place it is binitarian, not trinitarian (Collins, *LTP* 2 [1975], p. 163, notes this). In the second place **the elect angels** do not appear anywhere else in the *NT*. But cf. Rev. 14:10, where the damned are to be tortured 'in the presence of the holy angels and in the presence of the Lamb'. D–C think we have a liturgical formula here. Elect archangels are mentioned in *Odes of Solomon* 4.8, a book which some would date early in the first century. Houlden well compares Lk. 9:26, and points out that the angels are elect in contrast to the fallen angels. **from partiality**. The Greek is *kata prosklisin*. There is a variant reading *kata prosklēsin*. If this meant anything here, it would be a legal term for a challenge or offer made by one party in a suit to another, and would presumably mean that questions of presbyteral discipline are not to be settled out of court or compromised. But it is very unlikely to be original.

22. Do not be hasty in the laying on of hands: there are two alternative interpretations of this. It may refer to ordination. Timothy is to be circumspect about whom he ordains. If the ordinand turns out later to be a scoundrel, Timothy will be held responsible for his sins. This view is taken by Bernard, Higgins, Jeremias (with some hesitation), Käsemann (*Essays etc.* pp. 86–7), D–C, Kelly, Barrett, Dornier, and Brox. This is also the view of those who composed the Ordinal in the *Book of Common Prayer*. It could be called the obvious interpretation. The main objection to it is that, to judge by 4:14, ordination was carried out in the author's day by the group of presbyters, no doubt with the bishop, where there was one, presiding. It does not seem likely that a bishop would be in a position to ordain anyone hastily, even if he wished to. The alternative explanation, well set out by P. Galtier (*RSR* 39 [1951–2], pp. 317–20), is that this refers to the reconciliation of the excommunicated, which in the later church was effected by the bishop laying hands on the penitent sinner. This is accepted by Lock, Falconer, Easton, E. Schweizer (p. 207), H. von Campenhausen (p. 161), Bartsch (p. 101), Holtz, and Hasler. The objection to it is that the actual practice is not attested till more than a hundred years after the author's time. But it fits the context well; the statement that Timothy by hasty admission of sinners will **participate in another man's sins** follows on more naturally than if this were a warning against ordaining in haste; and it preserves the topic of this section, which is the discipline of presbyters. It seems to us more likely to be correct.

23. On the face of it, this verse seems to be an irrelevant intrusion into the text. Why should the author suddenly turn to giving advice on Timothy's diet? We can only follow the line of argument (*faute de mieux*) suggested by most modern editors, beginning with Bernard: 'Do not put yourself in a position where you may be held responsible for another man's sins. Keep yourself pure. By this I do not mean the pseudo-ascetic purity of the false teachers. On the contrary, use wine occasionally, since it is good for your health'. The reference to Timothy's frequent ailments is probably a piece of genuine historical tradition which the author is glad to work in here. For a discussion of Trummer's explanation of this verse, see Introduction, section 3.

24–25. The precise relevance of these two verses to the theme of this section depends on how we interpret v. 25. Does it refer to good and bad deeds, or to good deeds only? On the whole it seems better to take v. 24 of evil doers and v. 25 of well doers. This preserves the balance of the two verses and relates them to the topic of the disciplining of presbyters. But it must be confessed that the author had a positive talent for concealing his precise meaning behind relatively commonplace words. We take the two verses then, exactly as they are translated in *RSV*. The main point of the two verses is to show that it is not always possible to identify whether men are good or bad just by their deeds, but that God will make all plain at the last judgment. Presumably the purpose of the passage is to console Timothy in case he makes mistakes in disciplinary matters: it is not always possible to distinguish good from bad, but God will make all right at the end. The last clause **even when they are not they cannot remain hidden** refers to good deeds at the last judgment. This is no doubt what **pointing to judgment** means in the first clause, though Spicq takes it of the judicial sentence. There is a sentence from the *Epistle of Barnabas* (about AD 120–30) not unlike these verses: 'If he is good his righteousness will go before him; if he is evil, the reward of his iniquity is before him'; and compare Rev. 14:13*b*.

ADVICE FOR CHRISTIAN SLAVES

6:1–2

Obviously one of the problems of the early Church was the social position of slaves. Brox surmises that at this period slaves made up the majority of the Christian church. Bartsch actually believes that we can see the outlines of a document about the duties of Christian slaves and slave owners behind Colossians, Ephesians, the Pastorals, 1 Peter, Ignatius, *Didache* and *Barnabas*. If so, the author of Pastorals has used relatively little of it. Neither here nor in Tit. 2:9–10 is there any mention of the duties of masters (see Bartsch, pp. 146–7). Brox

criticises the author for his unimaginative attitude towards slaves; the
Christianity of the Pastorals is, he says, without paradox and without
scandal.

1. who are under the yoke of slavery: this probably means more
than just 'all slaves'. It suggests that slavery is a galling yoke (so
Spicq). This verse must apply to slaves who have non-Christian
masters (so Holtz, but Bartsch, p. 150, thinks the phrase means
'slaves under the yoke of Christ'). But the author would not be
addressing non-Christian slaves anyway, so there is no point in mentioning their Christianity. **so that the name of God and the teaching
may not be defamed**; this is a loose quotation from Isa. 52:5*b*. The
same citation appears in Rom. 2:24. But it is unlikely that the author
is consciously quoting Scripture: by the time Pastorals were written
the text had become a commonplace phrase to apply to scandalous
conduct on the part of Christians. Ignatius writing to Polycarp, says
that Christian slaves should not expect to be redeemed from slavery
by church funds. This suggests that some of them thought this ought
to happen. Hasler even conjectures that there may have been a group
of Christians who preached the duty to emancipate slaves. The classic
passage on slavery and the Christian in the *NT* is Paul's letter to
Philemon. We miss in the Pastorals Paul's magnificent assertion that
there is neither slave nor free in Christ. But it is possible that the
author is trying to express this in his own idiom in the next verse.

2. This verse certainly applies to slaves of Christian masters, but
there is a characteristic piece of obscurity at the end of the verse. The
clause translated in *RSV* as **since those who benefit by their service
are believers and beloved** is literally 'because those who share in the
good service are believers and beloved'. There are three possible ways
of understanding this clause. (a) As *RSV* takes it; the masters are
referred to; they benefit from the service given by the slaves. This
translation is accepted by Spicq, Dornier, *JB*, J. B. Phillips' translation, and *NEB*. The main objection to it is that in profane Greek
euergesia never means a service done by an inferior to a superior. But
the author might be using the word deliberately so as to stress the
ultimate equality of slaves and masters in God's eyes (b) 'The masters
are believers and beloved who devote themselves to the well-being of
their slaves'; so Bürki, D–C, Brox, Hasler, Holtz (indeed this seems
to be a purely German-speaking interpretation!). It may very well be
right, though it seems perhaps a little over-optimistic to assume that
all Christian slave-owners are as humane as this translation suggests
(c) I would myself suggest a third interpretation which combined (a)
and (b): 'since the masters, who share with slaves in Christian service,
are believers and beloved'. This is perfectly consonant with the Greek,
suits the rather generalised context, and reminds us of Mk 10:45:

'The Son of man also came not to be served but to serve'. Christian
life is service. The suggestion, supported by C. K. Barrett and Hasler,
that these two verses continue the theme of the presbyterate from
5:17–25, and are therefore intended to apply only to presbyters who
are slaves, does not seem very convincing. There is nothing in the
two verses that would not apply just as well to any slave who was a
Christian.

DENUNCIATION OF FALSE TEACHERS

6:2c–5

2c. Teach and urge these duties: primarily a device for moving
from one topic to the next. See Introduction, section 8.

3–5. The author now resumes a theme which he last dealt with at
4:1–5. **teaches otherwise** represents a word in Greek which the
author is the first to use in extant Greek literature. He may well have
coined it himself. **sound words;** cf. 1:10. He makes frequent references subsequently to the need for *sound* doctrine; see 2 Tim. 1:13;
4:3; Tit. 1:9, 13; 2:1, 2, 8. **words of our Lord Jesus Christ:** does
this mean the actual teaching of Jesus, preserved perhaps in one or
more of the Gospels? Spicq has no hesitation in concluding that here
Paul is referring to Luke's Gospel or to one of the other Gospels.
Others are much less positive: D–C compares 1 Th. 1:8 and suggest
that the author simply means the gospel, and so also Brox. Brox adds
that in the Pastorals the unity of the Christian message constitutes
the unity of the church – a surprisingly Lutheran conclusion for a
distinguished Roman Catholic commentator to make. Higgins thinks
that by **the sound words of our Lord Jesus Christ** the author just
means church tradition. **puffed up with conceit:** see on 3:6; 'blinded'
or 'beclouded' would be a more accurate rendering. **a morbid craving
for controversy:** literally 'he is sick concerning controversies'. Plutarch, a contemporary of the author of the Pastorals, writes of someone who has 'a morbid craving for glory'. **disputes about words:**
another Greek word apparently coined by the author. We must not
take the abuse directed at the heretics too much *au pied de la lettre*.
Accusations that their opponents were morbid quibblers were the
stock-in-trade of contemporary philosophical writers. Compare the
current atheist accusation in Soviet Russia that religion is an intellectual disease. **every dissension, slander. . . :** There seems to be a
certain echo here of Rom. 1:18–32. In that passage Paul issues a
general condemnation of the pagan world of his day, including no
doubt their philosophers. They have lost the knowledge of God which
could have been theirs and have consequently fallen into all sorts of
vices. The author similarly wants to accuse the false teachers of

culpable ignorance. They have gone wrong primarily for moral reasons. But if we compare the two passages we cannot help admitting Paul's huge superiority in both thought and style. At the end of v. 5 some MSS and 'avoid such people'. It is probably a gloss inspired by 2 Tim. 3:5. **wrangling among men:** the Greek word for **wrangling,** *diaparatribai,* is in fact unique. It may well be another coinage on the part of the author. It is strange that he coins so many new words in so short a passage. **imagining that godliness is a source of gain.** It is not easy to see how exactly the false teachers made money out of their teaching. It may be simply a general accusation of false motives which the author is always ready to attribute to his opponents. Kelly suggests that the teachers asked for fees in return for their religious and moral instruction. We must remember that they were still members of the local church; some of them may have been church officers who handled church funds and were thus open to the charge of embezzlement. Hasler points out that according to what we read in v. 9 some Christians (not necessarily heretics at all) were being led astray by filthy lucre. Perhaps, just as the conscientious presbyters might expect to receive honoraria from the flock, so the false teachers might have similar expectations from their adherents.

THE NEED FOR MODERATION IN LIFE-STYLE

6:6–10

Brox describes this section as 'a treatise on contentment'. Certainly the author concentrates into it more general maxims drawn from pagan philosophy than in any other passage in the three letters.

6. godliness with contentment: the word for contentment here is *autarkeia.* Paul uses it in 2 C. 9:8 in a midrash on Prov. 22:8, and the cognate adjective in Phil. 4:11 in a passage where he declares his independence of material affluence. Neither passage has the slightest philosophical overtone. It was a great word in Stoicism, expressing the essence of the Stoic ideal, which was to be independent of external circumstances. In view of the quasi-philosophical character of the verses which follow, we may be confident that the author is here using his stock of high school philosophy.

7. There is a problem about the correct reading in this verse: the major Greek uncials read the word *hoti* after **we brought nothing into the world.** The word means 'because' or 'that' or even 'as'. None of these meanings makes very good sense in this context. C. K. Barrett accepts the meaning 'because' and glosses as follows: 'The final nakedness of death demonstrates and underlines the initial nakedness of birth.' But this seems over-subtle for the author's mentality. Spicq thinks he can translate *hoti* with 'just as' or 'even as', but it seems doubtful, though Dornier follows him here. There are alternative readings of which perhaps the best is *dēlon hoti*, which would mean 'it is certain that' (as *RSV* margin). And this reading appears in Polycarp's text when he quotes this passage. Other MSS offer words for 'but' or 'and' (this is the reading in the *RSV* text). One early fragmentary Greek uncial omits the word altogether (see B. Reicke, *CN* 11 [1947], pp. 202–3). Some editors have suggested that *hoti* should be retained, but treated as the equivalent of quotation marks, since the author is consciously quoting a maxim from moral philosophy. On the whole the best solution seems to be to omit the word altogether, assuming, as some editors have speculated, that it was originally dittography for the last syllable of *kosmon* (**world**), which immediately precedes it in the Greek (so B. S. Easton). For the sentiment, cf. Job 1:21.

8. This verse also reproduces a Stoic commonplace. The word translated **food**, *diatrophas*, means 'one's keep'. There is an alternative reading *diatrophēn*, which would mean simply 'sustenance'; see Reicke, *CN* 11 (1947), p. 205. **clothing** translates *skepasmata*, a plural word. It could mean 'a roof over our heads', but D–C are no doubt right in preferring the sense followed by *RSV*. Spicq notes that the author has indicated 'the measure fixed by Jesus' (cf. Lk. 12:22; Mt. 6:25); but Brox believes the sentiment owes more to Stoic philosophy than to the teaching of Jesus.

9. temptation is *peirasmos*, and some have suggested that the author intends a pun with the word for **gain** in v. 6, which is *porismos*. One could give a rough parallel in English with 'gain' and 'pain'. Seneca (died AD 65), a Roman moral philosopher of the Stoic school, has a very close parallel to this sentiment: 'While we desire to achieve riches, we fall into many evils'. It is difficult to see why the author needed to use two words for the disaster which riches bring. Spicq, followed by Dornier, suggests that **ruin** (*olethron*) means material disaster, and **destruction** (*apōleian*) spiritual death. Certainly the latter word is regularly used in the *NT* for spiritual death. Holtz, who holds that both words refer to spiritual death, suggests that the author may have Judas Iscariot in mind.

10. the love of money is the root of all evils: a most un-Pauline sentiment. Paul would have said that human pride, striving to attain goodness independently of God, is **the root of all evils** (see Rom. 7). Spicq seeks to qualify the sentiment by pointing out that in the Greek all the author claims is that **love of money** is *a* root of all evils, but this hardly turns the author into a Paulinist. The word for **love of money**, *philarguria*, is never used by Paul. The adjective recurs in 2 Tim. 3:2 and the negative of the adjective has occurred in 1 Tim. 3:3. We meet it twice in 4 Maccabees and the adjective once, and we

have already noted the author's acquaintance with this book. Holtz
well points out that the Pauline word for the vice condemned here is
pleonexia, which we might paraphrase with 'ruthless self-interest'. It
is not at all difficult to parallel this sentiment among pagan moralists.
A 6th-century AD writer quotes one Bion the Sophist as having described **love of money** as 'the mother city of all inquity', and Di-
ogenes Laertius (possibly 3rd century AD) uses almost the same phrase
(reference in D–C). The words **it is through this craving** no doubt
give us the sense of what the author wishes to say. Strictly speaking,
he has written that **some have wandered away** because of their
craving for **the love of money**; but this is nothing more than an
infelicity of style. Despite his partiality for truisms in this passage,
one must admire the vividness of the metaphor whereby he describes
the rich as being self-torturers. As I write this comment I read in the
daily newspaper of a millionaire who has committed suicide. Hasler
actually suggests that the topic of presbyters has not yet been con-
cluded, since in the background, he believes, still lies the question of
what is a suitable income for a church officer. But this does not seem
likely. However adequately church officers might have been rewarded
at that period, they would never have approached the category of the
wealthy. For the significance of Polycarp's apparent knowledge of
this passage see Introduction, section 2.

A CHARGE TO THE NEWLY-ORDAINED

6:11–16

According to his characteristic technique, the author now changes
the subject, only to resume it in vv. 17–19. See Introduction, section
8.

11. But as for you, man of God, shun all this: a transitional
sentence, covering the change of subject. **man of God** is a rather
unexpected mode of addressing Timothy. In the *OT* the term is
applied primarily to prophets, but also to Moses (cf. 1 Chr. 23:14)
and to David (cf. Neh. 12:24, 36). Philo applies it to priests and
prophets. E. Käsemann (in Eltester, pp. 267–8) thinks the phrase
would recall the *theios anēr* of Hellenism. This was a class of 'supernaturally endowed men' in contemporary Hellenistic religion, into
which some circles in early Christianity may have wished to put Jesus.
He also sees a link with the *pneumatikos*, the 'spiritual man' whom
the Corinthian Christians of Paul's day so much admired. D–C maintain, rightly no doubt, that the phrase is meant to apply to any church
leader.
righteousness, godliness, faith, love, steadfastness, gentleness:
Paul would never couple **righteousness** (*dikaiosunē*) with **godliness**

(our old friend *eusebeia*). As Gealy well remarks, 'To aim at righteousness or faith is not Pauline language. To Paul these are God's gifts, not man's achievements'. It is true that we have something like Paul's trio in I C. 13:13, faith, hope, and love (**steadfastness**, *hupomonē*, could do duty for hope; it is a Pauline virtue), but they are anything but theological virtues here. The word for **gentleness** (*praüpatheia*) is not met elsewhere in the *NT*. It looks as if the author has thrown together a miscellaneous list of good qualities, most of which (he knows) Paul also commended. There has been considerable discussion among commentators as to what sort of a source the author is drawing on in this section. One view, defended by H. Windisch, Falconer, Jeremias, Spicq, Holtz, Pax (p. 228), and Kelly, is that it originally formed part of an (adult) baptism address. Another view is that it comes from an ordination address. This is supported by Käsemann (in Eltester), D–C, J. Roloff (p. 261), Barrett, Brox and Hasler. A third view is that it could be a personal confession by an individual Christian. Some have even suggested it was originally made before a pagan tribunal. J. Thurén (*ThZ* 26 [1970], pp. 241–53) defends this suggestion of an individual confession, but Käsemann dismisses the idea (in Eltester, p. 264). On the whole the most likely interpretation seems to be that we have here some parts of an ordination address; though this may include elements from a baptismal liturgy; the appellation **man of God**, the reference in v. 12 to making **the good confession in the presence of many witnesses**, and the liturgical-sounding language in vv. 15 and 16, all point in this direction.

12. Fight the good fight of the faith: the language here is not military, literally 'compete in the good competition'. Compare Phil. 3:12–14, a passage which the author of Pastorals may well have in mind here. The two have in common the figure of athletics, the notion of laying hold (of the prize), the hope of eternal life. Hasler notes the resemblance, but insists also on the difference between the two. Where Paul writes of fulfilling a vocation, the author thinks of growing in Christian devotion, moving on to a higher stage of holiness, and he points to 1 Tim. 4:15; 2 Tim. 4:7–8. **take hold of the eternal life: take hold** is *epilabou*, which recalls the verb used by Paul in Phil. 3:12 for 'I press on to make it my own', where 'make it my own' is *katalabō*. So the sentiment of **take hold of the eternal life to which you were called** is certainly Pauline, though perhaps Paul would have said: 'Take hold of that eternal life which has already taken hold of you'. **when you made the good confession in the presence of many witnesses**: Easton argues that there is a contradiction here. Timothy is being reminded of the confession which he made when he was baptised as an adult; but we are told in 2 Tim. 3:15 that Timothy was **from childhood acquainted with the sacred**

writings, so he must have been baptised as a child. In fact however no such conclusion follows. What is asserted in 2 Tim. 3:15 is that Timothy was from childhood acquainted with what we would call the *OT*. Every early Christian held that the *OT* (the only Scriptures he knew) could **instruct** one **to salvation**. All that is being asserted there then is that Timothy as a child was well instructed in the *OT*, which could be said of most devout Jews. In fact they did not **instruct** him to **salvation** until Paul came along and gave the Scriptures the Christian interpretation. 2 Tim. 3:15 is not therefore inconsistent with Timothy having been baptised as an adult. We conclude that 1 Tim. 6:12 is a reminder, in the context of an ordination address, of the confession of faith made by the candidate at the time of his baptism as an adult. The baptism was probably carried out in the context of the eucharist, hence the reference to **many witnesses**.

13. **In the presence of God who gives life to all things:** the verb **gives life**, *zōogonein*, is used only three times in the *NT*; eg. Lk. 17:33, where it is used of the disciple of Jesus 'saving' his life by losing it. It could therefore have an overtone of resurrection. There is a variant reading *zōopoiountos*, which is the regular word in the *NT* for God giving life to the dead. It is probably a correct gloss. The mention of **God** giving **life** strengthens the case, supported by Gealy, Kelly, and Brox, that vv. 13–16 come originally from a baptismal liturgy. **Jesus Christ who in his testimony before Pontius Pilate made the good confession:** an unexpected reference to the historical life of Jesus. D–C Houlden and Dornier all claim that *under* rather than *before* **Pontius Pilate** is meant. The Roman governor is only mentioned in order to date the incident. The clash with the Roman imperium is not emphasised.

There are two surprising omissions in this passage. The first is any mention of the cross, though Pax (p. 228) thinks the death is certainly implied here. The other omission is any reference to the Holy Spirit. Both in a quasi-baptismal context and in the case of an adjuration in the name of God, the Holy Spirit would seem to be impossible to ignore. It only goes to show how far the author is from a Trinitarian concept of God. What was the content of the **good confession**? If we are to be influenced by 2:6 (where **testimony** in Greek is cognate with **testimony** here), the witness was simply Christ's self-giving in death. We are reminded of Jn. 18:28–38, where the witness must refer to the entire career of Jesus including his teaching. Hasler actually maintains that Jesus' witness before Pontius Pilate as related in Jn. 18 is in mind here. The author wants to show that Timothy's confession was essentially the same as that of Jesus. The author sees God's salvation, he says, not as an offering made on behalf of men, but as the revelation of the divine will on earth at a particular time. This is interesting; but how far can we regard either 1 Tim. 2:6 or this verse as actually expressing the author's theology? If both passages are in origin credal or liturgical formulae, can we treat them as theological statements by the author?

14. keep the commandment unstained: what is **the commandment?** The obvious sense would seem to be the undertaking which the baptised Christian has given to believe the Christian faith and live the Christian life (so J. H. Bernard). But the word **unstained** seems to suggest more than that; it is the same word as is used in 3:2 and 5:7 of persons (rendered **above reproach** and **without reproach** respectively by *RSV*). It will probably therefore have an implication that something has to be kept intact, and that something can only be the deposit of faith, so Pax (p. 230), Holtz, Houlden and Brox. Others rather connect it with the commission which the newly ordained has just received (D–C, Spicq, Hasler), but this comes to very much the same thing, as he has been commissioned to preserve the faith. Roloff (p. 262) has a theory that it refers to the charisma which has been received at ordination, but this seems unlikely. **the appearing of our Lord Jesus Christ:** the word is *epiphaneia*, which the author uses both for the incarnation and for the parousia (see 2 Tim. 1:10; 4:1, 8; Tit. 2:13). The word was a familiar term in the imperial cult, and the author may well be using it here as an indirect refutation of that cult. Brox is certainly right in claiming that the phrase does not suggest a sense of the imminence of the parousia.

15. It is impossible not to recognise the liturgical element when we reach this verse. **at the proper time** suggests a certain rebuke for those who think the parousia is imminent or who think they can calculate when it will come (so Gealy). **the blessed and only Sovereign:** for **blessed** see on 1:11. The word translated **Sovereign** is *dunastēs*, from which we get the word 'dynast'. This is the only place in the *NT* where it is applied to God. But it is found in this sense in the intertestamental literature. The translator of the *Wisdom of Ben Sira* renders the Hebrew *'el 'elyôn* with *hupsistos dunastēs*, and the word is applied freely to God in the Maccabean literature. Kelly is therefore justified in describing the word as 'a gem from the devotional literature of the Hellenistic synagogue'.

the Kings of kings and Lord of lords: the original inspiration for this phrase comes from Dt. 10:17; but cf. also Rev. 17:14; 19:16. The phrase undoubtedly recalls and challenges the imperial cult. The title **King of kings** had been sadly debased by imperial times. Cleopatra and poor little Caesarion (her son by Julius Caesar) were officially styled 'Kings of kings'; see also 1:17. Spicq has persuaded himself that Paul carefully composed the seven phrases which make up vv. 15–16; to us they give the impression of being about as far from Paul's style and thought as anything in the Pastoral Epistles.

16. who alone has immortality: the word for **immortality** is *athanasia*, also used in 1 C. 15:53–54 for the state of the redeemed after the parousia. There is no corresponding word in Hebrew, but we have here a very Jewish concept. The soul is not naturally immortal, as Plato taught, but life beyond death is the gift of God. **and dwells in unapproachable light:** cf. Ps. 104:2. The notion that he who attempts to approach God runs the risk of being 'blinded by excess of light' is found in the rabbinic tradition. Strack-Billerbeck quote the Targum on Ezekiel's vision described in Ezek. 1; the prophet could not see God because of the dazzling light. Philo uses this word **unapproachable** of Mount Sinai at the law-giving and Josephus applies it to God. See also *Enoch* 12.15, where Enoch is unable to approach God because of the light in which he dwells. This language seems indeed to be drawn from the Hellenistic synagogue. Hasler suggests that here not only are we dealing with liturgical language but possibly even with a line or so that can be recognised as metrical. One could scan the Greek of **dwells in unapproachable light** thus: *phōs ōi/kōn ăprŏs/ītŏn* (spondee, dactyl, trochee); cf. Eph. 5:14.

whom no man has ever seen or can see: the invisibility of God is a topic that is common to Hebrew and Greek religious thought. In the *OT* some people are described as seeing God (cf. Gen. 32:30; Exod. 24:10), but it was a dangerous experience, and might result in death, because of the holiness and purity of the divine nature (cf. Jg. 13:22; Isa. 6:5). In Greek thought on the other hand, God cannot be seen because he is transcendent spirit and not a sensible particular. In the *NT*, as we might expect, both elements can be found; see Col. 1:15, where Christ is the image of the invisible God, and cf. Jn. 1:17–18. In both these passage Christ is the visibility of the naturally invisible God and in them the Greek element predominates. Here, however, we seem to be closer to the Hebrew element. There is no suggestion that God is naturally and essentially invisible. On the other other hand, at the parousia the *epiphaneia* (**appearing**) is to be of Christ, not of God the Father. Brox's suggestion that the author is here deliberately using Gnostic vocabulary does not seem justified. It does not accord with what we know of the author's untheoretical approach to false teaching. But certainly the language could be understood in a Gnostic sense. **To him be honour and eternal dominion:** perhaps the ending of a eucharistic prayer. The word for **dominion** is *kratos*; Spicq suggests that this is deliberately used to counter the emperor's claim to be *pantokratōr*, 'the Omnipotent', a term which the later Greek church applied to Christ.

THEME OF LIFE-STYLE RESUMED

6:17–19

Certain editors (Harnack, Falconer, Easton) have wished to extrude these verses as a later interpolation because they seem to interrupt the theme, which is the need to guard the deposit of faith. But our study of the author's technique of composition should make us wary of using an abrupt change of subject as a reason for suspecting an interpolation.

17. not to be haughty: the Greek verb rendered by these words, *hupsēlophronein*, seems to be a coinage of the author's; but in Rom. 11:20 Paul uses the two elements in the verb, writing *mē hupsēla phronei*, 'do not become proud'. **the rich in this world:** the phrase **in this world** corresponds to Paul's phrase used in Rom. 12:2; 1 C. 1:20; 2:8; 2 C. 4:4; Gal. 1:4. The *RSV* tends to translate Paul's phrase with 'in this world' as in 1 Tim. 6:17, except that in 1 C. 1:20; 2:8; Gal. 1:4 it uses 'age' instead of 'world'. But in fact Paul's phrase is not identical with that of the Pastorals; cf. 2 Tim. 4:10; Tit. 2:12. **nor to set their hopes:** a good rendering of the Greek perfect infinitive, which conveys the sense of action completed. **who richly furnishes us with everything to enjoy:** this is in line with 4:3–5, and is directed against Gnostic asceticism. Brox comments that in this passage we are in direct contact with the author's own sentiments, to some extent in contrast (we may add) with the preceding verses. Hasler notes that there is no suggestion that the rich should share their wealth because all Christians are brothers in Christ.

18–19. These verses are reminiscent of two other passages, one in Paul and one in the Apocrypha. The Pauline passage is Rom. 12:13–16, where we have 'contribute to the needs of the saints' ('contribute' is *koinōnountes*, cognate with *koinōnikous* which is rendered **generous** here), and 'do not be haughty' in 12:16, which is *mē ta hupsēla phronountes* (see on v. 17). It is quite possible that the author had the Romans passage in mind. The verse from the *Apoc.* occurs in Tob. 4:9: 'So you will be laying up a good treasure for yourself in the day of necessity'. This is in the context of an exhortation to almsgiving, and the language is very similar, though not identical, to what is used here. Some editors have gone so far as to alter the text of 1 Tim. 6:19 so as to read *thema lian kalon*, 'a very good basis', instead of *themelion kalon* (**a good foundation**), in order to make this an explicit citation of Tobit. Of these is James Moffatt, but he had a penchant for striking though unsupported conjectures, and we are not justified in altering the text on the strength of no MS evidence whatever. We can however rightly conclude that the author was thinking of this passage in Tobit when he wrote these words.

Dornier says that the difference between **liberal** and **generous** here
is that the first refers to the external act and the second to the internal
disposition. There is more than a suggestion here that it is possible
to store up a treasury of merit with God by doing **good** deeds; for
other references to good works see Tit. 2:7, 14; 3:8, 14. Spicq is
perfectly justified in pointing to Jesus' own teaching as illustrated by
such passages as Mt. 6:20; Lk. 16:9; but Holtz's cross-reference to
Rom. 2:9 does not constitute a very powerful argument that this
passage is compatible with Paul's thought. Dornier more relevantly
cites 2 Tim. 1:9 as proof that the author had no thought that anyone
could be saved by works. That is however a liturgical passage and
cannot be relied on as giving us the author's own belief in the same
way that this one does. **life which is life indeed** is a fine phrase; see
5:3, where **real** represents the same word as is rendered **indeed** here.
There is an alternative reading here for that word (*ontōs*); it is
aiōniou, 'eternal'. It is quite well supported in the MSS, but looks
very like a gloss which crept into the text.

RENEWED WARNING AGAINST FALSE TEACHING

6:20–21a

A last heart-felt plea that Timothy should preserve orthodoxy and
avoid heresy. It is not at all Pauline but rings completely true to the
author's intention.

20. G. Lohfink (p. 96) justly remarks that this verse sums up
everything the author has to say in this letter. **what has been entrusted to you:** D–C well comment that the author is interested in
tradition rather than succession. Barrett believes that the author uses
this one word *parathēkē* (represented by six in *RSV!*) rather than
paradosis ('the tradition') because the latter is too suggestive of purely
human traditions; cf. Jude 3. K. Wegenast makes the illuminating
suggestion that in the author's time the word *paradosis* had acquired
a Gnostic association which he wishes to avoid. K. Wegenast (pp.
133, 140, 157) adds that the *parathēkē* is to be handed on rather
than interpreted or criticised. **Avoid:** Timothy and Titus are constantly urged to take avoiding action; see 1:4; 4:7; 2 Tim. 2:16; 3:5;
Tit. 3:9. This is partly no doubt because the author himself preferred
to avoid arguing with the heretics; he prefers the method of denun-
ciation and abuse. **godless chatter:** the second word is *kenophōnias*
literally 'empty noise'. The Vulgate renders this with *novitates*, which
suggests that it had in its Greek version the word *kainophōnias*; this
would mean literally 'new noises', i.e. innovations in doctrine. The
first word *kenophōnia* actually occurs in Dioscorides, a writer of
about the end of the first century AD. The second is most unlikely to

have been a word in use in the author's time and cannot be original. **contradictions:** in about AD 140, Marcion, a heretical teacher in Rome, published a book called *Antitheseis*, which is the word used here. B. S. Easton suggested on the basis of this that this whole verse was interpolated some time after 140 in order to condemn Marcion. But it has now been shown that the accusation of teaching nothing but specious paradoxes was one common among the polemic philosophical writers of the age. Lucian for example accuses the sophists of his day of uttering meaningless paradoxes (see Karris, p. 559).

what is falsely called knowledge: here is *gnōsis* (the word for **knowledge** in this phrase) out in the open. The author cannot afford to repudiate *gnōsis* altogether both because Paul wrote about a true Christian *gnōsis*, and because some perfectly orthodox Christians highly praised *gnōsis*. A hundred years later we find Clement of Alexandria claiming to be a Christian gnostic.

21a. for by professing it: D–C argue that this shows that the author was facing a rival system which could be consciously adapted. Hasler remarks on the note of authority and official teaching that runs through these two verses, characteristic of the author's work as a whole.

FINAL GREETING

6:21b

21b. Grace be with you: You is plural, thus suggesting that the letter was intended for a community not merely an individual. Paul's only genuine letter to an individual ends with: 'The grace of the Lord Jesus Christ be with your (plural) spirit' (Phm. 25), but he is writing to a house church. Some MSS actually read 'with thee' here but this is no doubt an attempt by a later scribe to preserve the character of a personal letter more faithfully.

.

THE SECOND EPISTLE TO TIMOTHY

THE CONTENTS OF 2 TIMOTHY

OPENING GREETING

1:1–2

This greeting is closely parallel to that in 1 Tim. 1:1. 'by command of God our Saviour' there corresponds to **by the will of God** here. 'Christ Jesus our hope' there corresponds to **according to the promise of life which is in Christ Jesus** here. In 1 Tim. 1:1 Timothy is 'my true child', and here he is **my beloved child**. Otherwise the two greetings are identical. The parallel is too close to be anything but constructed.

1. **by the will of God** is a wholly Pauline phrase: see 1 C. 1:1; 2 C. 1:1; Col. 1:1; Eph. 1:1. What exactly does **according to the promise of the life which is in Christ Jesus** mean? Does it mean

Paul is an apostle commissioned to announce God's promise, as Dornier, Houlden, and Brox believe? Perhaps a better interpretation is that followed by Spicq and Hasler: 'an apostle by God's appointment in accordance with the whole divine scheme which comprises God's promise of life'. Holtz has a third suggestion: 'Paul appointed an apostle in order to fulfil the promise', but this seems less likely.

2. Note the markedly binitarian nature of the greeting here. This is a feature common to the greetings of all three letters. Though the author believed in the Holy Spirit, it did not occur to him to associate the Spirit with the Godhead. Hasler remarks of the greeting as a whole: 'The warm feeling in the greeting indicates not a sentimental reconstruction, but the canonical legitimation of the leader's office.'

PERSONAL EXHORTATION TO TIMOTHY

1:3–8

3. I thank God: a thanksgiving at this point was the correct thing in a letter. Paul nearly always observes this custom; the author only here. **whom I serve with a clear conscience:** the authentic Paul was capable of claiming to be conscious of complete sincerity in his behaviour; see 2 C. 1:12. But the actual phrase **a clear conscience** is characteristic of the Pastorals; see 1 Tim. 3:9; also 1:5, 19 for 'a good conscience'. We seem therefore to be closer in this passage to the Paul of Ac. 23.1; 24:16, in both of which passages Paul is represented as serving the God of the Jews with a clear conscience. **as did my fathers:** why should the author mention Paul's Jewish ancestry here? Unlike Paul, he is not at all interested in the problem of the relation of Christianity to its parent Judaism. It may be because he is about to remind Tomothy of his Jewish ancestry. Both D–C and Brox believe that the author has modelled vv. 3–5 on Rom. 1:8–11. Certainly the parallel is remarkable, though Holtz thinks Phil. 1:3 is equally in mind. **when I remember you constantly in my prayers: when** is probably the best translation of the Greek word *hōs* here. Paul gives thanks upon every remembrance of Timothy; cf. Phil. 1:3. Otherwise, if *hōs* is translated as 'that' or 'how', it is not clear what exactly Paul is represented as giving thanks for. Brox believes he is giving thanks for Timothy's faith. Hasler suggests we have a picture here of Paul the martyr pleading day and night before the throne of God for the infant church.

4. As I remember your tears: this has naturally occasioned considerable discussion among commentators. On what occasion did Timothy shed these **tears?** Most editors suggest it was at their last parting. We could not possibly hope to escape without at least one British scholar writing of 'the uninhibited emotion natural in the

East', an emotion most often remarked by those who have never been there. Certainly an impressive list of commentators agree that it is tears at parting that are meant; so Bernard, Barrett, Dornier, Holtz, Hasler, Brox. Spicq crowns the scene by suggesting that Timothy burst into tears when the imperial police arrested Paul! Houlden believes the author knew Ac. 20:37 and is recalling the tears of the company present then. Compare the solution of de Lestapis (p. 102) that Timothy was present at the incident described in Ac. 20:37–38, and shared in the tears shed then. Brox suggests that we may very well have authentic historical tradition here, which is by no means unlikely. **I long day and night to see you:** cf. Rom. 1:11; Phil. 1:8 2:26; 1 Th. 3:6.

5. I am reminded of your sincere faith: this must be Christian, not merely Jewish, faith. **a faith that dwelt first in your grandmother Lois and your mother Eunice:** it is at Ac. 16:1–3 that we first encounter Timothy, where we are told that 'he was the son of a Jewish woman, but his father was Greek'. This should dispose once and for all of the beautiful picture so many commentators have painted of Timothy's upbringing in a pious Jewish home. His mother had excommunicated herself from the fellowship of devout Jews by marrying a Gentile, and her mother had presumably permitted this. Eunice did not have her son circumcised on the eighth day after birth as the law required. Of course we do not know the pressures which these women experienced. As mere women they may have had no say in the matter at all. But it was not a pious Jewish home. At Ac. 16:1 some MSS insert the word 'a widow' after 'son of a Jewish woman', and Lake and Cadbury suggest that the word 'for his father was a Greek' in Ac. 16:3 (*hupērchen*, not *ēn*) implies that he was dead at the time of Paul's visit. We may, therefore, if we like, picture the mother and grandmother reverting to Judaism after the death of Timothy's father, and subsequently being converted to Christianity. The author does not make anything of the ambiguity of the word **faith** in this verse. Brox (Introd., p. 57) remarks that such an unthinking passage from Judaism to Christianity would have been impossible if the real Paul had been writing. He concludes from this passage and 3:15 that the author himself was born and brought up a Christian; but this seems an unjustified conclusion. It is absurdly sceptical of Hasler to doubt the authenticity of the names of these two ladies; it is a part of the author's authentic historical tradition. He knew the names of Timothy's mother and grandmother, and that they had been converted from Judaism to Christianity. We need not assume any further historical knowledge than this.

6. rekindle the gift of God that is within you through the laying on of my hands: gift is *charisma*. There is a contrast between the view of *charisma* we find in Paul and what we meet here. In Paul, God through the Holy Spirit gives various spiritual gifts (*charismata*) to various members of the church to enable them to contribute to the building up of the church as a whole. There is no correlation between *charismata* and ordained ministry, because there was nothing one could call an ordained ministry in Paul's day (see A. Ehrhardt, *The Apostolic Succession* [London, 1953], p. 100). Käsemann (*Essays*, pp. 86–7) maintains that the ordination rite referred to here must have been introduced (he thinks from Judaism) between Paul's time and the time of the author of the Pastorals. This seems a little too specific. What we can say is that this period witnessed a gradual institutionalisation of the ministry and with it no doubt the birth of a doctrine of ordination. This leads in the author's time to the doctrine that at ordination the *charisma* is conferred that enables the ordinand to perform the function for which he is ordained. It did not follow in the author's day that all *charismata* were thought of as conferred by some quasi-sacramental act. As Ehrhardt says, prophets, virgins, confessors, martyrs, gnostics were thought of as possessing their own *charismata* right up until a period long after the Pastorals were written. But no doubt R. F. Collins (p. 162) is right in saying that we have here the genesis of the Catholic doctrine of ordination. Spicq points out that the Council of Trent quoted this verse as proof that orders are a sacrament. If this understanding of the verse is correct, it follows that there is no real contradiction between this passage and 1 Tim. 4:14. In the first passage, the author reproduces the ordination custom with which he was familiar. In the second, he assumes that Paul must have ordained Timothy himself. Whether Paul actually did so or not, we have no means of knowing. Ordination by the local group of presbyters was not incompatible with one person presiding over the ordination, and thus being able to have laid hands personally on the ordinand. Compare the custom followed at the ordination of a priest by a bishop today.

7. For a detailed comparison of this verse with Rom. 8:12–17 see Introduction, section 5. Houlden's dismissal of this verse as showing 'a hazy recollection' of Rom. 8:15, is most unfair; it is a careful transposition of that passage in Romans. Dornier well compares 1 Jn. 4:18. **a spirit of timidity**: as we have observed in the Introduction, there is a play on words here. Paul had written *douleias* ('slavery'); the author substitutes *deilias*. **power and love** are certainly qualities that Paul would describe as gifts of the Spirit. Whether he would have added **self-control** is doubtful. In Gal. 5:23 *enkrateia* (also translated 'self-control') is among the virtues that go to produce the fruit of the Spirit, but the word the author uses here, *sōphronismos*, has

a slight element of prudential ethic in it that is foreign to Paul's way
of thinking.

8. Do not be ashamed then of testifying to our Lord: Houlden,
probably rightly, sees here a reference to Rom. 1:16. He suggests
that the author's context is more specific than was Paul's since he has
in mind testifying in court. Houlden may be right, but if so it is only
in view of Paul's known experience of testifying frequently in court
and of ultimate martyrdom. The author does not seem to envisage
that church leaders in his day may have to testify in court. According
to Heb. 13:23, Timothy did suffer the experience of imprisonment.
1 Clem. 5.4–7 emphasises that both Peter and Paul witnessed before
the authorities on their road to martyrdom; cf. also 1 Tim. 6:13.

take your share of suffering for the gospel: the first five words in
this phrase correspond to one word in Greek, *synkakopathēson*, also
used in 2:3. The word seems to have been coined by the author. It
means 'to suffer hardship in company with others'. Holtz maintains
that it means 'suffer in company with Christ', but we do not find this
Pauline concept in the Pastorals, so we must accept the meaning **take
your share of suffering** with other Christian leaders. Spicq well
renders it *'prends part avec moi aux souffrances de l'Évangile'*. See the
remarks on the author's theology of suffering in Introduction, section
7.

LITURGICAL PIECE INTRODUCED

1:9–10

Most editors believe that these two verses constitute a liturgical fragment introduced by the author into his text at this point, though
there is wide disagreement as to the original nature of the fragment.
Easton, followed by Holtz, believes it was a hymn; Gealy says either
a hymn or a baptismal confession (or one made at ordination); D–C
call it 'a kerygmatic formula'; Dornier says it is a confession of faith;
Hasler suggests a baptismal hymn.

9. who saved us and called us with a holy calling: the sentiments
are entirely Pauline, though the language seems to be more reminiscent of Eph. 2:8–9. Indeed Brox believes that this passage is
modelled on Eph. 2:8f. **a holy calling** (Greek *klēsei hagiai*), not a
Pauline phrase, though Paul frequently addressed his correspondents
as people 'called to be saints', *klētoi hagioi*. Spicq points out that in
LXX Israel in the wilderness is *klētē hagia*, a people called to be holy.
**in virtue of his own purpose and the grace which he gave us in
Christ Jesus ages ago:** once again this language recalls Ephesians:
cf. Eph. 1:11; 2:5–10; 3:11. Compare also Rom. 16:25–26, probably
a deutero-Pauline passage. It is a characteristic of the deutero-Pauline

literature to be concerned about the relation of God's salvation in Christ to the cosmos as a whole and the whole of human history. Pax (p. 232) and Holtz claim that the language here implies a doctrine of the pre-existence of Christ. As far as the original source goes, this is no doubt true (the author of Ephesians certainly believed in the pre-existence of Christ), but we cannot be confident that the author of the Pastorals always understood the theological implications of the source material which he used.

10. There is strange language in this verse. Nowhere else in the *NT* is it suggested that Jesus Christ **brought life and immortality to light**, as if **life** and **immortality** had been lying hid, waiting to be discovered. But some sort of a parallel can be found in *Didache* 9 and 10. Thus in *Didache* 10 there is a prayer which gives thanks 'for the knowledge of faith and immortality which thou hast made known to us through Jesus Christ thy Servant'; and in *Didache* 9 the writer gives thanks for 'the life and knowledge which thou hast made known to us'. I have argued in *Studies* (Ch. 8) that 1 Tim. 4:3–5 and 2 Tim. 1:10 are in fact extracts from the eucharistic prayer with which the author was familiar, and in particular that here **life** refers to new life in baptism and and **immortality** to the eucharist. Ignatius describes the eucharist as 'the medicine of immortality, the antidote against dying' (*Eph.* 20). One might therefore legitimately conclude that in this whole passage 1:9–10 the author is using material from his own tradition of eucharistic prayer. There is some reason to believe that Clement does the same thing in his letter to the Corinthians. **the appearance of our Saviour Christ Jesus:** this is the only place in the Pastorals where *epiphaneia* (**appearance**) is used of the incarnation instead of the parousia; but cf. 1 Tim. 3:16; Tit. 2:11, in both of which places 'appearance' or 'manifestation' language is used of the incarnation. Spicq suggests that the reference is to the appearance of the risen Lord to his disciples, but this seems unlikely. The use of the two terms *epiphaneia* and *sōtēr* (**Saviour**) in this passage has led a number of editors to conclude that the author is here consciously opposing the imperial cult, since both these terms figure prominently in that cult. So Dornier, though Pax (p. 232) in his study of the use of the word *epiphaneia* rather minimises the importance of this con- nection. Both D–C and Brox in their discussion of the author's use of *sōtēr* conclude that his choice of the word is probably influenced by contemporary pagan religion rather than by Hellenistic Judaism. If so, the obvious rival is the imperial cult and we must concede that the author has some notion of putting forward Christ as a rival to the emperor. Not very many years earlier St John the Divine had done exactly this (using a very different literary technique) in the book of Revelation.

PAUL'S COMMISSION TO GUARD THE DEPOSIT OF FAITH

I:11–14

11. I was appointed: Holtz suggests that the passive, with no indication as to who appointed Paul, is characteristic of a Jewish-type reluctance to refer to God by name. The three titles given to Paul here are intended to enhance his sole authority in the churches which he founded. Brox believes that Paul is presented here not as *a* **herald,** etc., but as *the* **herald,** *the* **apostle,** *the* **teacher.** Brox also points out that Paul in his authentic writings does not call himself **teacher.** Hasler rightly adds that this very authoritative office necessarily involves suffering and martyrdom. There are two interesting variant readings in this verse: for *didaskalos* ('**teacher**') some MSS have *diakonos* ('deacon, minister'), and some MSS have *ethnōn* ('of the Gentiles') after *didaskalos.* Lemaire (*Les Ministères,* p. 137) thinks *diakonos* is original, but it is weaker than *didaskalos* and looks more like a copyist's error or alteration. Pax (p. 233) judges that *ethnōn* is secondary here, no doubt correctly.

12. but I am not ashamed: in the light of v. 16, we should follow D–C and Spicq in concluding that he is not ashamed of being a prisoner for the gospel. **until that Day:** no doubt the parousia; it is not a Pauline phrase; but in the context of the author's time he is reminding us that Paul did keep what had been entrusted to him intact until the day of his martyrdom. We must bear in mind that the English phrase **what has been entrusted to me** represents *tēn parathēkēn mou* in Greek, literally 'my deposit'; hence the rendering in *RSV* margin: 'what I have entrusted to him'. There are only two reasonable interpretations of this phrase: the first is that it is Paul's own self or soul; so Bengel, followed by Bernard and Dornier. We think of Wesley's hymn, 'A charge to keep I have'. The other interpretation, followed by the great majority of modern editors, is that 'my deposit' is the faith; see I Tim. 6:20. If so, we can see the purpose of this charge. It is to encourage church leaders in the author's day to do as Paul did, keep the faith intact until death. The reference to the parousia thus becomes little more than decorative detail. The author has no sense of its imminence. Brox follows Spicq in the belief that the figure is taken from Roman law concerning trusteeship. The day for rendering up the deposit is formally the parousia but actually the day of one's death.

13. Follow the pattern of the sound words which you have heard from me: note that the Greek has no word for **the** before **pattern.** There are two possible translations here: that which *RSV* gives here, which means in effect 'take the oral teaching I have given you as a satisfactory outline of the gospel'. The other is 'hold on to the pattern of sound words which you have heard from me', i.e. do not abandon the creed which I have taught you. But this encounters the difficulty that there is no word for **the**. Also **pattern** here (*hupotupōsis*) does not mean a finished product, but a rough sketch. Timothy is therefore being urged not to stray from the outline of faith which he has learned. So this verse does not refer to credal formulae, but to a general outline of teaching. A third interpretation is that given by James Moffatt in his translation of the *NT*: 'Model yourself on the sound instruction you have heard from me.' But the author seems to be preoccupied here with doctrinal orthodoxy rather than with right behaviour; cf. Rom. 6:17. Schlier (in Kertelge, p. 478) and Dornier agree that an oral tradition rather than a written credal formula is in mind here. We could compare the eucharistic prayer, which at this period would be an outline rather than a fixed liturgical formula. It is interesting that, though doctrinal orthodoxy is so very much emphasised in the Pastorals, it does not yet seem to have taken a fixed credal form. **in the faith and love which are in Christ Jesus:** both D–C and Brox characterise this phrase as *'formelhaften'*, no doubt rightly.

14. guard the truth that has been entrusted to you: a paraphrase rather than a translation. The Greek means literally 'guard the good deposit', and it refers of course to the true Christian teaching which Timothy has received from Paul, exactly the same behest as we met in 1 Tim. 6:20. Holtz however here and at v. 12 above interprets the deposit as 'your soul, your self'. Those who believe that Paul wrote these words are naturally inclined to this interpretation, since the authentic Paul does not refer to a 'deposit of faith' in the way that the author does. **by the help of the Holy Spirit who dwells within me:** a truly Pauline concept, and one of the few references to the Holy Spirit in the Pastorals; cf. Rom. 8:11; 2 Cor. 6:16f. Compare also Jas 4:5, where the same verb (*katoikein*) is used as we have here. The author has taken the Pauline concept of the indwelling Spirit and used it of the inspiration which ordination affords to enable those ordained to guard the deposit of faith (so Spicq, Kelly, Brox). We have thus another instance of the process whereby what Paul predicates of all Christians the author attributes to the members of the ordained ministry.

DETAILS ABOUT PAUL'S SITUATION IN ROME

1:15–18

15. all who are in Asia turned away from me: this is a strange phrase if it is meant to convey that all who were in Rome from Asia turned away from Paul when he was in prison in Rome. Spicq solves the problem by saying that *pantes hoi en tē Asiai* is a Hebraism for *pantes hoi ek tēs Asias*, 'all from Asia'. But this seems a little facile. The labelling of this detail as legendary does not solve the problem, for we still have to ask what the author wished to convey. The simplest solution is to conclude that it means Paul was deserted by all his Christian friends in Asia at the time of his arrest in Asia. If so, it may well be historically true, as C. K. Barrett suggests (see our Introduction, section 3). It is unlikely that the phrase means that the Asian Christians abandoned Christianity, as Houlden believes. **Phygelus and Hermogenes** are probably historical characters known by oral tradition to have abandoned Paul in his need. It is very unlikely that they were contemporaries of the author whose unorthodoxy the author wishes to besmear by associating them with false friendship towards Paul. Such a charge could have been too easily refuted. Hasler takes a third view: they are names invented by the author in order to pile on the agony in his presentation of Paul's sufferings. He even suggests that the name **Phygelus** could be taken to mean 'skulker'. But this does not seem in accordance with the author's rather straightforward mentality, and **Hermogenes** cannot be allegorised in this way.

16. May the Lord grant mercy to the household of Onesiphorus: many commentators (e.g. D–C) conclude that Onesiphorus is represented as having died between the time of his kind service to Paul and the time when 2 Timothy is supposed to have been written, hence the reference to his **household** and to the parousia in v. 18. Spicq even conjectures that Onesiphorus had suffered imprisonment for his pains. Brox (*JAC* 13 [1970], p. 74) is another scholar who believes that Onesiphorus is represented as having died.

17. when he arrived in Rome: this is literally 'being in Rome'; but Spicq points out that in *koinē* Greek this construction could perfectly well convey the sense of 'having arrived'. However, strenuous efforts have been made by scholars to give a different sense to this phrase in the interests of providing a reconstruction of the apparently historical details in the Pastorals that will harmonise with what we know of Paul's movements from his authentic letters and from Acts. One such ingenious suggestion is that this phrase, which is in Greek *genomenos en Rōmē/i*, should be rendered 'when he had recovered strength', taking *rōmē* as a Greek word for 'strength', not the name of a city. This avoids the necessity of locating this incident in Rome. D–C are surely justified in labelling this suggestion as *unwahrscheinlich*. Another such suggestion is made by B. Reicke, (*ThL* 101 [1976], p. 90) who wishes to bring this whole episode to Caesarea, and therefore glosses the verse thus **when he arrived in**

Rome he searched for me eagerly and found me (in Caesarea). This
is scarcely a plausible conjecture.

**18. may the Lord grant him to find mercy from the Lord on that
day:** D–C suspect, and Spicq emphatically asserts, that there is a play
on the word **find** in vv. 17 and 18. As Onesiphorus *found* Paul in his
prison, so may he **find mercy** at the parousia. The double use of **the
Lord** is strange. It is also, strictly speaking, a mistranslation, since
the definite article is missing from the word rendered **from the Lord.**
D–C, followed by Houlden, believe that it is because two formulae
have been run into one here. This still leaves us with the question as
to who are referred to by the two occurrences of **the Lord.** There are
obviously four possibilities: (a) The first refers to God and the second
to Christ. Though I took this view in my smaller commentary, I do
not hold it now. As Spicq points out, **the Lord** should refer to Christ,
and the second **Lord**, anarthrous in the Greek, as being the LXX
rendering of the Tetragrammaton, to God. (b) The first refers to
Christ and the second to God. This is the view of Spicq, Dornier
(who well compares 1 Tim. 6:14–15) and also of Brox. (c) Both refer
to God the Father. This seems most unlikely, and indeed pointless.
(d) Both refer to Christ. This view is taken by most of the ancient
commentators, according to Dornier. It is possible, but not the most
likely solution. The best seems to be (b): It is, as Spicq says, a prayer
to Christ to intercede with the Father that Onesiphorus should receive
mercy at the parousia. In that case we have clear scriptural support
for prayer for the dead. Spicq mentions the astonishment and indig-
nation of those whom he calls 'non-catholic commentators' at this
conclusion. In fact, however, the moderns who are not Roman Catho-
lics seem to accept this with remarkable equanimity: see Bernard,
Easton, Holtz. But it is perhaps an indication that this passage was
written by someone who did not have a very keen sense of the
imminence of the parousia. **you well know:** the Greek is literally 'you
know better (than I do)' but no doubt *RSV* has rendered the correct
sense.

EXHORTATION TO GUARD THE FAITH, WITH A HINT THAT CLERGY
SHOULD BE ADEQUATELY REMUNERATED

2:1–7

Brox claims that the main exhortatory section of the epistle begins
here and lasts till 4:8. This is formally true, but, faithful to his
eclectic method, the author manages to get plenty of other material
into his exhortation, including a midrash on a Pauline passage (2:20–
21) and a note on the use of Scripture (3:16–17). D–C claim that 2:1f.
has the nature of a testament made by a dying man. Hasler maintains

that the author is trying to assert Paul's authority in opposition to somebody else's authority, and he wonders whether some contemporaries of the author were claiming to be the heirs of Peter or John. It seems however a sufficient explanation of this passage to say that the author is trying to counteract the authority claimed by the heretics.

1. This verse itself is one of those transition pieces which the author uses in stitching his materials together. See Introduction, section 8. **be strong in the grace that is in Christ Jesus**: the verb for **be strong**, *endunamou*, is used by Paul in Rom. 4:20; Phil. 4:30; cf. Eph. 6:20. Houlden believes that in this section the author is looking back in peaceful times to the period of heroic suffering represented by Paul's career.

2. **before many witnesses**: naturally commentators speculate as to what precise event is alluded to here. A general reference to the various stalwart Christians whom Timothy has encountered (as Holtz and Hasler suggest) is not sufficiently specific. The only alternatives are that it refers either to baptism or to ordination (D–C suggest both) with a slight probability in favour of the latter in view of 1:6 (so Spicq, Brox). Barrett well remarks that the **many witnesses** are meant to contrast with the secret, esoteric teaching of the Gnostics. **entrust to faithful men who will be able to teach others also**: Holtz compares 1:11, and points out that only Paul can be **apostle** and **herald**, but that others can be teachers. We certainly have here a doctrine of succession, but it is succession in teaching rather than succession in authorised office. We might well compare with this what Clement says on the same subject in chs. 42 and 44 of his letter to the Corinthian church. He is writing of the apostles:

> Having therefore made proclamation in country and town, they appointed their firstfruits, having tested them by the Spirit, to be *episkopoi* and *diakonoi* of those who should believe. And this was no novel expedient, for ages ago it had been written about *episkopoi* and *diakonoi*, since this is what the Scripture somewhere says: 'I will appoint their *episkopoi* in righteousness and their *diakonoi* in faith'. . . And our apostles knew through our Lord Jesus Christ that there would be strife concerning the office of oversight (*episkopē*). For this very reason, since they had received complete foreknowledge, they appointed those whom I have mentioned above, and in the mean time they arranged for a continuity [or 'an ordinance' or 'an additional structure' – there are at least two alternative readings] in order that, if they should fall asleep, other approved men should receive their office in succession. We do not therefore think it right to expel from their office those who were

appointed by the apostles, or subsequently by other respectable men, with the consent of the whole church, especially when they had already served the flock of Christ blamelessly and modestly, in no ostentatious or mercenary spirit, and had earned a good reputation from all for many years (my tr.).

We take the view that Clement is writing some years after the composition of the Pastorals (perhaps fifteen or twenty years). It is interesting to observe how the concept of ministerial succession has developed in the interval. Clement traces succession in ordination back to the apostles, whom he regards as men supernaturally endowed with foresight into the future. He seems to believe in an 'apostolic succession' of office, though not necessarily a tactual succession. He provides a proof from Scripture for the ordinance of *episkopoi* and *diakonoi* (Isa. 60:17b, quoted in a version different from LXX). The author of the Pastorals is content to trace his succession back to Paul; he is much more concerned with a succession of orthodox teaching than of ministerial office, and he does not attempt a scriptural proof. Note the equivalence of the **faithful men** in this verse with the 'approved' and 'respectable' men in *1 Clem.* 44.2-3.

3. **Take your share of suffering:** one word in Greek, the same as occurs in 1:8 (q.v.). It looks very much as if in vv. 3-7 the author has in mind a number of passages from 1 C. 9. Note particularly 1 C. 9:7a, where Paul uses the military metaphor; 9:7b, where he uses the metaphor of a vine-grower; and 9:24-27, where he draws his illustration from various sorts of athletics. We can even add that the author has 1 C. 9:12 in mind also, since there Paul writes that all considerations of remuneration must be subordinated to the overriding need to proclaim the gospel of God. In the same way the author is urging perseverance and self-discipline on church leaders in order that they may be able to defend and propagate true orthodox teaching.

4. **in civilian pursuits:** this is a possible rendering, but in the context it is more likely to mean 'in making his livelihood', i.e. he must not take up trading on the side. Here first appears the motif that is probably the main point of vv. 4-7: the full-time church official should be content with the support given him by the church and not try to make money by some worldly occupation. Thus, as D-C point out, the author is using Pauline figures in order to say exactly the opposite to what Paul said. Paul insists that he and his fellow-workers have a right to support themselves by the labour of their hands if they choose. The author is hinting that this should not be required of the clergy. **the one who enlisted him:** probably Christ (so Spicq). Dornier well compares Ignatius, *Pol.* 6: 'Satisfy him for whom you fight: it is from him that you receive your wages also.'

Brox points out that the work of ministry involves hardship, but not apparently martyrdom.

5. unless he competes according to the rules: this may not be as far from Paul's use of the illustration of the athlete as may appear at first sight. Bernard brings evidence to show that at Olympia the athletes had to swear that they had kept in training for ten months. Holtz's explanation is more elaborate and less probable: the ancient games required that competitors should compete naked; so the Christian athlete must strip himself of worldly encumbrances. Barnett (p. 267) agrees, against Hasler, that the author is deliberately echoing 1 C. 9 here.

6. This seems to be a generalisation of what Paul says in 1 C. 9:7. Those who treat the Pastorals as Pauline tend to jib at the idea that Paul is urging Timothy to expect full-time support, though Spicq admits that **the first share of the crops** may include the idea of remuneration as well as of the joy of ministry and eternal reward. Holtz and Dornier repudiate the idea of salary altogether. But the salary (or at least remuneration) motif grows clearer and clearer as one reads through vv. 4–7. **hard-working** renders the Greek verb *kopian*, which is frequently used by Paul of pastoral work. If all the author meant was that the church worker ought to experience the joy of ministry, he would not have spoken of the farmer having the first share of the crops, but of the farmer enjoying his work.

7. think over what I say: almost *verb. sap.* The author wishes to convey his instructions to church leaders that they have a right to expect financial support from the church. But, as the letter is probably going to be read out at the worship meeting of the local church, he does not wish to say so quite explicitly. He is therefore content to drop a broad hint, and does so in this verse. Spicq quotes Thomas Aquinas' commentary on this verse, to the effect that it does certainly refer to the support Timothy may reasonably expect from the church, but he suggests, very reasonably, that Timothy is to exercise his discretion as to how and when to make his request and how much to ask for.

THE CONTENTS OF THE FAITH RECALLED AND A HYMN OF HOPE AND
WARNING QUOTED

2:8–13

8. Many scholars believe that the author is quoting a theological or credal formula here. So Jeremias, D–C, Spicq, Kelly, Houlden, Brox. It contains a reference to Christ's resurrection, which is very rare in the Pastorals. It recalls the formula in Rom. 1:3–4, but it does not contain two very important features that are present there, the

title 'Son of God' and a reference to the Holy Spirit. It is mysterious
that the resurrection should be mentioned first and then the Davidic
lineage. Spicq believes the formula is of Jewish Christian origin: first,
one believes in the risen Lord, then one identifies him with the
Davidic messiah. But the formula has already named him as *Christ
Jesus*! Dornier claims that the formula is meant to inspire Timothy
with courage to face suffering and death. But it does not mention the
crucifixion! Brox sees a double-birth scheme here: born on earth as
son of David, reborn in the spiritual sphere by the resurrection. But
if so, the events are mentioned in the wrong order. No doubt the
formula is introduced by the author in order to add a note of solemnity, but it still remains a very peculiar formula. **as preached in
my gospel:** almost a Pauline tag; see Rom. 2:16; 16:25, though the
latter is probably not by Paul.

9. the gospel for which I am suffering: the Greek is literally 'in
which I suffer'. No doubt *RSV* has rendered the meaning correctly.
Holtz wants to make it refer to 'Jesus Christ, in whom I suffer'. But
this is to introduce a Pauline concept which the author does not
reproduce elsewhere. Barnett (p. 268) believes that the author is
modelling himself on Phil. 1:12–14. This may well be right, though
the only point in common in this verse is that Paul is bound while
the gospel is not. **wearing fetters like a criminal**; cf. Ac. 28:20. In
fact Luke does not represent Paul as having had any criminal charge
framed against him before a Roman magistrate. This is one of the
reasons why there is reason to believe that the author has in mind
here a second, later trial which Paul underwent, at which he was
accused of treasonable activity.

10. Most commentators regard this verse as based on Col. 1:24.
But there are no signs elsewhere in the Pastorals that the author holds
the difficult concept mentioned there of Paul 'completing what is
lacking in Christ's afflictions'. It is more likely that we are still in
touch with Phil. 1:12–28. That passage is full of the thought of Paul
suffering, dying, and rising with Christ, and of his Philippian converts
following his example in this. After all that is precisely the theme of
vv. 8–13 here. So we may conclude that what Paul expressed in his
fervid, inspiring language in Phil. 1:12–28 the author is briefly re-
capitulating in his much more pedestrian style here. And the answer
to the question as to how Paul helps the **elect** by **enduring everything**
is given us in the passage in Philippians. He encourages them by his
example to live the life of Christ (Paul would say), to live the life of
godliness (the author would say). **Therefore** must not be pressed; it
is more in the nature of a link-word than a part of a carefully reasoned
argument. **the elect:** probably a fairly conventional phrase for believing Christians, without any strong overtone of predestination. **which**

goes with eternal glory: the Greek has only 'with eternal glory'. Something very like the phrase occurs in 2 C. 4:17, but there it is closely integrated into Paul's argument. Here it is thrown in as a makeweight.

11–13. This is the fourth of the 'faithful words'; see the Note at 1 Tim. 1:15. As far as context is concerned, it could refer either to what precedes or to what follows, though, in view of the hymn-like structure of what follows, it is probably to be associated with vv. 11–13. But we should beware of trying to attach this formula too closely to its context. The author uses it primarily as an indication that he is now dealing with solemn and important material. It is more like the bell that is rung at the consecration in the mass. It is intended to make the readers give special attention to the material in the midst of which it occurs. The four lines that follow in vv. 11*b*–13*a* are undoubtedly a quotation from an early Christian hymn. The theology implied in the hymn is thoroughly Pauline, indeed more Pauline than is the theology of the author of the Pastorals himself. It is therefore probably a hymn composed in the Pauline churches, perhaps after Paul's death in the same milieu as that from which Colossians and Ephesians come. **If we have died with him:** the obvious reference in this is to the Pauline doctrine at baptism; cf. Rom. 6:1–11. The aorist tense of *sunapethanomen* (**if we have died with him**) points to a definite event in the past, which can only be baptism. But several commentators, in view of the next line **if we endure, we shall also reign with him**, wish to associate the thought of martyrdom with the mention of baptism here; so Holtz, Brox, Hasler. If we do allow the thought of martyrdom to be relevant here, we must regard it more as a looking back at Paul's martyrdom (and that of the victims of the Neronian persecution), rather than as an exhortation to be steadfast under the threat of present martyrdom. In any case, there are plenty of passages in Paul's letters which could be compared with v. 12*a*; e.g. Rom. 8:17; 1 C. 4:8 6:2. D–C point to a passage in Polycarp's letter to the Philippian church (5.2) which seems to be quoting the same hymn: 'If we behave worthily of him, we will also reign together with him – as long as we believe'. **If we deny him, he also will deny us:** the reference must be to the parousia; cf. Mt. 25:41–46. **if we are faithless, he remains faithful:** Knight (p. 127) believes this means 'if we are unfaithful' rather than 'if we do not believe'. Spicq also comments that the verb does not suggest apostasy, only weak faith. Editors are divided as to whether v. 13*a* contains a threat or a promise. J. H. Bernard and Lock regard it as a threat, but most moderns, including Jeremias, Spicq, Kelly, and Brox, take it as a promise. In view of the author's admirable emphasis on the universal scope of God's love in Christ, we should surely regard it as a promise.

for he cannot deny himself: this is probably the author's own comment rather than part of the hymn (so Dornier, Houlden). The comment enforces the author's emphasis on God's nature manifested in Christ, as being essentially loving towards all mankind; cf. 1 Tim. 1:16; 2:4; Tit. 2:11; 3:4. Though this hymn is a triumphant assertion of the love of God, it does have its reference in v. 12*b* to the obverse of this, that refusal of God's love brings judgment. Hasler well remarks, à propos the hymn, that the author is writing in a situation in which church leaders are in process of deserting the great church for heretical sects – they must be warned.

HOW TO DEAL WITH FALSE TEACHERS: INCLUDING A MIDRASH ON TWO
SCRIPTURAL PASSAGES AND A MIDRASH ON A PAULINE PASSAGE

2:14–26

14. Remind them of this: one of these transitional phrases which are part of the author's technique. See Introduction, section 8. **before the Lord:** there is a well-attested alternative reading 'before God', which is actually preferred by the editors of the United Bible Societies' *Greek New Testament*. But it makes very little difference to the meaning. **to avoid disputing about words:** five words in English to render two in Greek, *mē logomachein*. The verb is unique, perhaps invented by the author. But Varro, a Roman writer of the first century BC, called one of his satires (now lost) *Logomachia*. In the context here it means merely quibbling, disputing about words without regard to the meaning they convey. The verb could mean 'to fight with words' (instead of with blows), but that would not make sense here. One suspects that the author uses this sort of language in order to avoid disputes that would take him (philosophically) out of his depths. He has already used the noun *logomachia* in 1 Tim. 6:4. There is an alternative reading *mē logomachei*, which would mean 'do not dispute about words'. But it gives a harsh asyndeton with what follows. **but only ruins the hearers:** *RSV* has rendered a noun in the Greek with a verb in English. The literal translation would be: 'Tell them not to dispute about words (it is useless) only for the catastrophe of the hearers.' We have translated the Greek noun with its English equivalent. It must be confessed that in any reading the style is rather staccato here. Some editors wish to take *katastrophē* in the sense of 'subjugation'. The hearers are subjugated to the heretics; but this is not necessary. Brox well points out that the mention of **the hearers** shows that the heretics already are carrying out a regular teaching activity. Hasler says the question is, how must a church leader tackle the defence of the faith? It is plain that discussion and debate are taking place inside the church. Heretics are to be answered (but by monologue, not dialogue, says Brox) by means of the authority of the church's ministry.

15. a workman who has no need to be ashamed: some editors (e.g. Bernard, Lock) take this as meaning that he will not make God or Christ ashamed of him, but it is more likely to mean what *RSV* implies, he will have no need to be ashamed of his work. Brox well remarks that it is to be explained in terms of Mk 8:38*a* rather than 38*b*: **workman** is quite a normal word in the *NT* for any Christian worker. **rightly handling the word of truth:** this represents an obscure phrase in the Greek, *orthotomounta ton logon tēs alētheias:* D–C remark that it is so far not satisfactorily explained; the verb means literally 'rightly cutting', so that editors have suggested all sorts of cutting figures to explain the meaning; wood-cutting (Bernard); squaring stones rightly (Spicq). Others have suggested ploughing a straight furrow or driving a straight road (no one has yet come up with 'keeping a straight bat'!). But on the analogy of a very similar word *kainotomein*, we may suggest that such recourse to various cutting activities is unnecessary. The word *kainotomein* originally meant 'to open a new vein in a rock', but in *koinē* Greek came to mean simply 'to innovate'. So *orthotomein* which originally meant 'to cut rightly', came in *koinē* to mean simply 'to do rightly', hence the *RSV* rendering **rightly handling the word of truth** is correct. The church leader is to oppose the heretical teaching by giving the correct teaching. Spicq points out that Quadratus (a Christian apologist of *c* AD 124) uses the phrase *apostolikē orthotomia* to mean 'the strict orthodoxy of the apostles'. But both Brox and Hasler offer a different interpretation; they take it to be a reference to the church leader's behaviour rather than his doctrine. Brox suggests 'handling the truth in a straightforward manner' as contrasted with the quibbling, ambiguous methods of the heretics. He refers to Sophocles (*Antigone* 1195): *orthon alēthei' aei*, 'the truth is always straightforward'. Hasler claims that the word in later usage had reference to one's conduct, and offers a quotation from Hermas in which the leaders of the church are urged to 'straighten their ways' (*Visions* 5.II.2.6; III.5.3). But there the word in question is not used, only the verb *katorthein*, 'correct', which is quite a common one. He concludes therefore that Timothy is being urged to oppose heretical teaching with pious conduct rather than with correct doctrine. It is true that this sort of advice does occur later on in vv. 23–26; but the context here seems to suggest that the church leader is facing a false teaching which is upsetting the faith of many. It seems much more appropriate that in these circumstances he should be urged to counter this with correct teaching rather than merely with right behaviour.

16. This verse is very similar to 1 Tim. 6:20–21; exactly the same

phrase, **godless chatter**, is found in both places, and the same verb
astoichein is used in both, though *RSV* translates it 'swerved from
the truth' in v. 18 and by 'missed the mark as regards the faith' in
1 Tim. 6:21. D–C interpret the second half of this verse somewhat
differently from *RSV*. They take the heretics as the subject of **lead
people into more and more ungodliness**. In the Greek there is no
word corresponding to **people**, so D–C can translate it: 'they (the
heretics) progress into greater and greater ungodliness'. They suggest
that *prokopsousin*, 'progress', is used sarcastically: these progressives
only make progress in ungodliness. This may well be right: cf. 2 Jn.
9, where the 'progressive' is the man who has not remained in the
teaching of Christ. When we put together all the features of the false
doctrine, a recognisable picture seems to emerge: we have disputes
about words, impious nonsense, a dialectic of spurious knowledge,
and the assertion that the resurrection has already taken place. We
could easily reconstruct a Gnostic system containing an elaborate
hierarchy of aeons (**godless chatter**), nice distinctions between *sigē*
(silence) and *bythos* (depth), or between Jesus and the Christ (**disputes
about words**), a pairing of male and female entities (**contradictions
of what is falsely called knowledge**), and a declaration that the elect
could not possibly be lost and had already transcended the limits of
the body (**the resurrection is past already**, v. 18).

17a. and their talk will eat its way like a gangrene: *JB*'s translation 'corrodes like gangrene' is exactly right. Barclay's 'spread like
a cancerous ulcer' is sensational but inaccurate, since the Greek *gan-
graina* does not mean an ulcer. D–C point out that Plutarch uses
exactly the same figure of a man maligning his friends, so this cannot
be used in favour of the theory that the author had any special medical
knowledge.

17b–18: Among them are Hymenaeus and Philetus: see 1 Tim.
1:20 for **Hymenaeus**. Those who believe that the Pastorals are written
by Paul usually claim that by the time 2 Tim. 2:17 was written Paul
had carried out his threat and excommunicated Hymenaeus. But
there is no indication of that there. We conclude that these were the
names of genuine opponents of Paul, who may have had followers
claiming to be their successors in the author's day. The other two
alternatives are that they were the names of the author's contemporaries, or that they are purely fictional names, both of which suggestions seem less probable. D–C draw the interesting conclusion that
the author could not have been as remote as Rome from the Ephesian
situation, a good point.

by holding that the resurrection is past already: there is an important variant reading here actually preferred by Holtz; it consists in
omitting **the** before **resurrection**: 'a resurrection has taken place

already'. But this is important, because it is very close to what Paul taught (see Rom. 6:1–14), and practically indistinguishable from what is taught in Ephesians (see Eph. 2:4–6). Hasler associates these heretics with charismatic enthusiasts, and actually sees traces of such teaching in Colossians, Ephesians, and the Fourth Gospel. However, it is more likely that **the resurrection** is the original reading and that Barrett is right in defining this teaching as 'gnostic denial of eschatology'. D–C point out that something like this teaching is attributed to the heretic Menander by Justin. Spicq finds traces of it in the *Gospel of Philip*. It seems that the Corinthian church was troubled with something like this teaching at some time in the first half of the second century, for the document called *2 Clement* has in 9:1: 'and let none of you say that the flesh itself is not judged and does not rise'. If K. P. Donfried's argument is right that *2 Clement* is the Corinthian church's answer to *1 Clement*, then this reference comes quite close in time to the Pastorals (see K. P. Donfried, *The Setting of Second Clement in Early Christianity*, Leiden, 1974). The conclusion of W. L. Lane (*NTS* 11 [1965], p. 166) that we have here not a mistaking of baptism for the resurrection but an anticipation of the parousia does not carry much conviction.

19–21: I have very fully expounded these three verses in *Studies*, ch. 3, and must refer the reader there for detailed exposition. In fact the author of the Pastorals is in these three verses trying to solve the theological problem which the appearance of false teachers in the bosom of the church presented: how can it be that baptised and apparently committed Christians can turn into enemies of the faith? He answers it by drawing on two traditions, the tradition of Scripture (which for him meant what we would call the *OT*), and the tradition of Paul's teaching on predestination as set out in Rom. 9. In v. 19 he deploys his scriptural argument, and in vv. 20–21 carries out his Pauline transposition.

19. But God's firm foundation stands: this 'foundation' language goes back to Isa. 28:16, which was a favourite proof-text in early Christianity. It runs:

> Behold I am laying in Zion for a foundation
> a stone, a tested stone,
> a precious cornerstone of a sure foundation:
> 'He who believes will not be in haste'.

The original meaning was that quiet reliance on Yahweh would be the means by which Israel would escape from its contemporary predicament, but early Christians took it as a prophecy of Christ (and not only early Christians were interested in it; the Qumran sectaries applied it to their community). We therefore find Paul quoting it in

Rom. 9:33 (conflated with Isa. 8:14, another messianic 'stone' passage), the very chapter that the author handles in vv. 20–21. Isa. 28:16 also lies behind Eph. 2:20–21, where the apostles and prophets are the **foundation**, *themelios*, the same word as here, and Christ is the cornerstone. We must probably understand 'cornerstone' in Eph. 2:20 as referring not, as we might imagine, to a keystone of an arch, but to a plugstone in the foundation. See R. J. McKelvey, *NTS* 8 (1962), pp. 352f.; and also his book, *The New Temple* (Oxford, 1969). Hence we should probably understand the foundation in v. 19 to refer primarily to Christ. This conclusion is not in accord with what most scholars maintain; D–C, Spicq, Holtz, Brox, and Hasler all think that the church is indicated here, but they have not explored the scriptural background very far (Dornier thinks the **foundation** is faith).

bearing this seal: this is a strange metaphor. The foundation of a building does not usually bear a **seal**, and a seal is not usually thought of as consisting of quotations. No doubt Holtz and Hasler are right in seeing in the **seal** a reference to baptism (I had already suggested this in the chapter referred to above). In Ephesians, which certainly lies behind this verse, the verb 'to be sealed' (*sphragizō*), cognate with *sphragis* (**seal**) here, is very probably twice used of baptism (1:13; 4:30).

So far, then, what the author says is that, despite the threat posed by the false teachers, Christ, into whom Christians have been baptised, will not fail. But now he has to face the problem that the false teachers are themselves baptised Christians, so he brings forth his first quotation from Scripture: **The Lord knows those who are his**. It comes from Num. 16:5 and is a rather loose version of LXX, perhaps because it has been extensively used in Christian circles apart from its original context. But its original context is significant for all that. It comes from the story of the revolt of Dathan and Abiram against the authority of Moses and Aaron. The quotation is actually Moses' answer to the challenge of the rebels. We can hardly fail to see its appropriateness to the author's situation, for the false teachers were certainly challenging the authority of the official ministry. Notice that Moses calls on the faithful remnant in the congregation of Israel to 'separate themselves' from the rest (Num. 16:27). But the first quotation is followed by a second: **Let everyone who names the name of the Lord depart from iniquity**. It seems to be a composite quotation from Isa. 52:11:

Depart, depart, go out thence,
touch no unclean thing;
go out from the midst of her, purify yourselves,
you who bear the vessels of the LORD.

Originally a call to the exiled Israelites to come out from doomed
Babylon, it is echoed here (for we cannot say it is quoted) to remind
the heretics of the responsibilities of baptism. It is combined apparently with a tag from Lev. 24:16: 'He who names the name of the
LORD shall surely die'. But the text is recalled only to bring home to
Christians the difference between their situation and that of the Jews
of old. Whereas the Jews were forbidden to utter the sacred name,
Christians, who know God revealed in Christ, are privileged to name
the name of the Lord Christ. We do not suggest that the author of
the Pastorals put these two quotations together himself, but he does
use them to provide a theological answer to the problem of heresy
arising in the bosom of the church. No doubt v. 19 originally stood
in a baptismal context. The two quotations would fit the theology of
adult baptism very well. The first, **The Lord knows those who are
his**, reminds us of the divine initiative. The second could well refer
to the promises in baptism and the confession of the name of Jesus
Christ. Thus the author of the Pastorals has advanced some way
towards answering the question that faced him. Despite the alarming
phenomenon of heresy among baptised Christians, Christ will not
allow the church to collapse. The calling which baptism implies still
stands. There is even a hint that the heretics, or at least their adherents, may yet become conscious of their lapse and return – a hint
which becomes explicit in the next two verses.

20–21: For a reference to this passage see Introduction, section 5,
and for a much fuller exposition of it see my *Studies*, pp. 29–35. The
author is here consciously rehandling a Pauline passage, Rom. 9:19–
24. He has in fact chosen one of the most difficult and obscure of
Paul's meditations on God's design in Christ, the passage in which
Paul comes closest to a theory of double predestination. The argument
of Rom. 9:19–24 is that men have no right to question God's election.
God has chosen certain people to be 'vessels of wrath' and uses them
to carry out his own purpose. But that purpose is that ultimately he
should have mercy on both Jews and Gentiles. Paul is therefore
wrestling with the problem of God's dealing with his chosen people
the Jews and trying to see how they fit into God's plan now that it
has become plain that Gentiles also are to become members of his
chosen people. The author of the Pastorals uses this passage for a
different purpose. He is puzzled how it is that some Christians seem
to have become 'vessels of wrath'. But he has no notion of Paul's
concept of the divine predestination, so he is able to introduce into
his argument the idea that **what is ignoble** can become **a vessel for
noble use**. We might paraphrase his argument thus: 'There are some
Christians who have become apostate, but the faithful remnant stands
firm by virtue of their relation to Christ and by baptism. We must

not be dismayed that inside the church itself some should prove to
be reprobate. The important thing is that you should free yourself
from any association with the apostates (**If anyone purifies himself
from what is ignoble**), and thus become a useful servant.' Obviously
the author has some hope of gaining back some of the adherents of
the false teachers, though not probably the leaders themselves. He
has in fact taken Paul's arduous, dark, and far-reaching theology and
domesticated it to the dimensions of his own thought. Looking at his
solution to the problem in the light of the *NT* as a whole, we can say
that he has effected an uneasy compromise between the Pauline
conception of a mixed church, some of whose members may ultimately leave it, and the Johannine conception of an indefectible
church, of which we can say that apparent members who have fallen
away were never really members at all. According to the author of
the Pastorals, some of the heretics are reprobate and doomed to
destruction, but some may yet be reclaimed. Practically all commentators see the link with Rom. 9:19–24. Dornier cautiously remarks
that one must not press the metaphor – a wise piece of advice, seeing
that the author has transformed Paul's 'vessels of wrath' (even perhaps
'instruments of wrath') into domestic furniture. Holtz well remarks
that these verses are opposed to a Donatist view of the church. But
in fact the first quotation in v. 19, **The Lord knows those who are
his**, points in a Donatist direction. The author moves uneasily between the two ecclesiologies.

Note on the use of the Old Testament in the Pastorals
Commentators have often remarked on the absence of interest in the
OT in the Pastorals, and have even cited this as an indication of
non-Pauline authorship. It is certainly true that the author uses the
OT in a way very different from the way Paul uses it. He rarely
employs it as a tool in argument, and does not often go direct to the
text of Scripture as Paul does. But it is not accurate to say that he
hardly ever uses the *OT*. On the contrary, it is possible to detect a
number of references throughout the Pastorals, some of them playing
an important part in his message. We will proceed to look briefly at
twelve, or possibly thirteen, places where he has referred to the *OT*
(thereby differing from Barnett, p. 251, who finds only six), and end
with some comments on his technique.

We begin with a reference to Exod. 34:6 which we detected in 1
Tim. 1:14–17. The wording seems to have been composed by the
author himself, unless the liturgical element in v. 17 indicates that it
came to him from a liturgical source. It shows quite a mature theology
of God's love revealed in Christ, a subject which appealed to the
author of the Pastorals; in expounding it he is at his finest. Then in

1 Tim. 2:4-5 I suggested that the liturgical material may have originally formed a Christian midrash on Isa. 45:21-22; but I expressed
doubts as to whether this midrash was of the author's own composition. This passage does nevertheless owe its theological content
partly to the Isaiah passage; one can hardly count the echo of Job
9:32-33 in this category, since the formula was certainly not derived
from Job by the author of the Pastorals. In 1 Tim. 2:13-15 the author
elaborates Paul's treatment of the fall story, drawing certain anthropological conclusions. We may be sure that this is his own work. The
scriptural background to 1 Tim. 3:15 we have explored thoroughly.
It is unlikely that the author himself composed this midrash on 1 Kg.
8:13, but he had the perspicacity to use it in an effective way. In 1
Tim. 5:18 and 19 he quotes Scripture twice, on each occasion in a
fairly conventional way. He was aware of course that he was quoting
Scripture (he says so in v. 18), but both texts were no doubt in
common use in the church. Next come the two passages we have just
been discussing. Here, as in the case of 1 Tim. 3:15, we must give
the author the credit of having used Scripture to good effect, even
though he was not in all probability the person who composed the
liturgical fragment in which the quotations occur. At 2 Tim. 3:8 we
have a reference to a piece of *haggada* based originally on Exod. 8:18–
19. The author of Pastorals had accepted the *haggada* as part of his
tradition, but does not develop it, or even refer back to the text of
Scripture. Some editors see an echo of Ps. 34:19 in 2 Tim. 3:11, and
perhaps we should allow for that possibility. Several scholars have
suggested that 2 Tim. 4:16-18 is based on Ps. 22. This seems quite
a reasonable conjecture. If so, we see here the author using Scripture
in a remarkably subtle fashion. If there is a scriptural background
(and I am inclined to think there is), the author is comparing Paul
with the suffering servant of the Psalms. The link with Christ's
suffering must exist in the author's mind, though, in accordance with
his extraordinary practice of never mentioning the cross, it is not
made explicit. Finally, in Tit. 2:14 there are two echoes of Scripture:
'to redeem us from all iniquity' echoes Ps. 130:8; and 'a people of his
own' echoes Dt. 4:20. Theologically these echoes of Scripture are
very significant, but it is most unlikely that the author found them
for himself. As we shall be seeing, he is using a liturgical piece here,
and may not even have been aware that there were scriptural citations
embedded in it.

All in all, the Pastorals may well be acquitted on the charge of
ignoring the *OT*. The *OT* features much more prominently in them
than it does in some other parts of the *NT*, e.g. I John. It is true that
the author rarely goes to the *OT* directly for his material, though he
is capable of doing this, and of using it in quite a subtle and effective

way. But on the whole he prefers to use material from his sources that had already, so to speak, digested the *OT*. However, he is usually aware of the significance of Scripture in such passages, and uses it quite deliberately. Our verdict at the end of this review must be that the author was no ignoramus or tiro when it came to the use of Scripture (what he says in 2 Tim. 3:16–17 should convince us of that). He does not have Paul's brilliance, originality, or creative vision, but he does know how to handle Scripture effectively for his own purposes.

22 D–C claim that the personal exhortation from v. 15, interrupted by the section on heretics, is now resumed. R. M. Grant (*Historical Introduction*, p. 214) rightly observes that the sentiments expressed in this verse offer a particularly flagrant example of un-Pauline thought. Commentators are divided as to what is the nature of the **youthful passions** which Timothy is to shun. The obvious meaning would seem to be wine and women, but Dornier (following Kelly and Higgins) thinks they are tendentiousness and extreme party zeal, and Brox believes it is a warning against arbitrary and headstrong treatment of the false teachers. **aim at righteousness, faith, love, and peace:** in Pauline thought **righteousness** was not a virtue to be aimed at along with other virtues. **those who call upon the Lord:** almost a technical term for Christians; cf. Rom. 10:13. Hasler says that to **call upon the Lord** simply means to pray. He comments: 'Liturgical practice and moral qualification belong together'. **from a pure heart:** this means 'conscience', according to Jeremias, who well compares 1 Jn. 3:19. It is a Hebraism, for Hebrew had no specific word for 'conscience'. There are a number of variant readings for the phrase **with those who call upon the Lord;** the most remarkable is *meta ton kaloumenon*, which would mean 'after him who calls', and *meta tōn agapontōn*, 'with those who love the Lord'. But all the variants seem to be secondary.

23. With this verse compare 1 Tim. 6:4. **stupid,** in the sense of 'pointless' rather than 'half-witted', according to Holtz. **senseless:** not a very accurate rendering of the Greek *apaideutous*, which bears the meaning of lack of discipline of education, perhaps 'illiterate', which is something like Brox's translation, would be better. D–C point out that in Epictetus the word is used of someone who has not learned how to think.

24–25a. **the Lord's servant:** strangely enough, this phrase does not occur anywhere else in the *NT*, although Paul often calls himself 'a servant of Jesus Christ'. No doubt it is meant to indicate the clergy in contrast to the laity. **an apt teacher:** this renders *didaktikos*, a rare word, which in Philo means 'teachable'. The author of the Pastorals lays more stress on the teaching office of the ministry than on any other feature of it. **correcting his opponents:** cf. 1 Tim. 1:10. **with gentleness:** the Greek is *praütēs*, a quality of Christ (cf. 2 C. 10:1), as Dornier remarks.

25b–26: God may perhaps grant that they will repent: *RSV* has followed the text which reads the optative *dōē/i* (**may perhaps grant**). Except in certain set phrases, the optative had almost dropped out of use in *koinē* Greek. It would sound archaic; Blass-Debrunner insist we ought to read the subjunctive *dō*, which would give the sense 'God may grant'. **come to know the truth:** elsewhere in the *NT* this phrase, *epignōsis tēs alētheias*, is used of being converted to Christianity; see Heb. 10:26. It is used in that sense indeed in 1 Tim. 2:4; Tit. 1:1. But here it must mean 'return to orthodox belief', as in 3:7 below. **that they may escape:** the Greek is literally 'become sober', properly used of returning to one's senses after a drinking bout; so the author has produced a mixed metaphor, a thing, it must be said, which his master Paul was quite capable of doing. In 1 C. 15:34 Paul uses the same verb when he wants the Corinthians to 'come to their right mind' from a state of sin. **after being captured by him to do his will:** in this phrase the author has managed by careless writing to obscure his meaning. The difficulty lies in the fact that the two words for **his** in Greek are different; the first **his** renders *autou* and the second *ekeinou*. In Classical Greek the two words are clearly distinguished as 'he' and 'that one' respectively, corresponding to the Latin *hic* and *ille*. The distinction grows blurred in *koinē* Greek, but it is very rare indeed for the two to be used referring to the same person in the same sentence (not to mention in the same clause, as here). Consequently editors have attempted to avoid this by taking them to refer to different persons. This gives us two alternatives:

(a) 'they may escape from the snare of the devil, being captured by God's servant to do God's will'. This is supported by Bengel, Lock, and Falconer. But it makes very difficult Greek indeed; that the two pronouns should refer not to the nearest noun (**devil**), but to two nouns so remote from the clause in which the pronouns occur, is almost incredible.

(b) 'that they may escape from the snare of the devil, after being captured by him, to do God's will'. So Bernard, Jeremias, Barrett (without great conviction), and *RSV* margin. But the word **God** is very remote from the pronoun which is supposed to refer to it. It makes difficult syntax.

(c) That which we have in *RSV* text, which is followed by Easton, Kelly, Spicq, D–C, Gealy, Holtz, Dornier, Brox, and Hasler. We think it is the most satisfactory solution. But we might perhaps suggest some reason why the author makes use of this almost unpar-

alleled phrase. In fact Grimm-Thayer quote only four examples in all
Greek literature. We shall consider two of them (the other two are
Thucydides 1.132.6(5); and 4.29.3). The first is Xenophon, *Cyropae-
deia* 4.5.20: 'he is not deserted now, when his friends are annihilating
his enemies', *hēnika hoi philoi autou tous ekeinou echthrous apolluasin*.
This is closest to our example, because both *autou* and *ekeinou* occur
in the same clause. The only possible reason for this usage can be the
desire to avoid repeating the word *autou* twice in the same clause.
This does not seem a very likely motive for our author, who is not
very careful about his style. He can use *autos* and *ekeinos* quite
correctly for two different subjects in the same sentence; e.g. 3:9
below. The second example may give us the true reason. It comes
from Wis. 1:16. The author is speaking of the connection between
the ungodly and death, and he writes:

> and they made a covenant with him (*autou*),
> because they are fit to belong to his (*ekeinou*) party.

Now here the author of Wisdom may have used *ekeinos* in the sense
of 'that one', 'we-know-who', 'the dreaded one', which is a possible
use of *ekeinos* according to Liddell and Scott. May it not be therefore
that there is a nuance of this meaning here? 'being captured by him
so as to do the will of that (dread) one'. This would make good sense.
Alternatively, *ekeinos* could be used so as to give a slight emphasis,
as is probably the case in Thucydides 4.29.3. This would give the
rendering: 'being captured by him so as to do *his* will (not God's)'.

RENEWED DESCRIPTION OF HERETICS AND OPPONENTS, INCLUDING A
LIST OF SINFUL CHARACTERS BASED ON PAUL, AND A PIECE OF
HAGGADA ABOUT JAMES AND JAMBRES

3:1–9

1. **But understand this:** a transitional phrase: the author is about
to introduce new material. **in the last days there will come times of
stress:** the use in the same clause of **last days** (*hēmerais*) and **times**
(*kairoi*) **of stress** is unusual. In the *NT* generally *kairos* is used of
some particular decisive time. But **the last days** are a decisive time
anyway. The truth is that the author is not really concerned about
the last days, as is for example the author of Mk. 13. When we reach
v. 6 below, we find that the deceivers who are to be a phenomenon
of **the last days** are already present. So that the author is repeating
what he did in 1 Tim. 4:1, putting into the mouth of Paul a prophecy
which he wishes us to understand is being fulfilled in his own day;
for the same technique see Ac. 20:29; 2 Pet. 3:3. In 1 Jn. 2:18 the
appearance of heretics is taken as an indication that the last hour has

arrived; cf. Mk. 13:6. Some commentators have suggested that the author has a different group of people in mind from those whom he stigmatised in 1 Tim. 4:1f.; but D–C dismiss this as unlikely, no doubt rightly. To the author's simple mind, heretics are sinners. Hasler points out that a warning as to what is to happen after one's death is a feature of Jewish religious testaments, a literary form into which 2 Timothy as a whole falls.

2–4. The author now gives us a list of vicious characters. There does not seem to be any obvious reason why this list should come here, but it was probably part of the author's source material. Holtz suggests that the list is based on Hellenistic models, and that it may originally have been used in catechisms. It is impossible to find any particular arrangement of vices running through it, though editors have made valiant attempts to do so. Spicq, followed by N. J. McEleney (*CBQ* 36 (1974) 215), says that the only element common to all the vices listed is self-centredness. Dornier claims that spiritual rather than sensual sins are stigmatised, though even this is questionable in view of **profligates** in v. 3 and **lovers of pleasure** in v. 4. What we can say with confidence is that this list is modelled on Rom. 1:29–31. In that passage Paul utters a general indictment of the pagan world. If we begin at the last word of Rom. 1:29, 'gossip', we can trace quite a close parallel with the list here in 2 Tim. 3:2–4, down to the end of Rom. 1:31; most of the vices in the author's list have an exact or fairly close parallel in Paul's list.

It is possible that the author's list here is in effect Paul's list smartened up by the author's acquaintance with Philo, because there is a very close parallel in Philo to one phrase in the author's list: **lovers of pleasure rather than lovers of God** (*philhēdonoi mallon ē philotheoi*). Philo has 'lovers of themselves rather than lovers of God' (*philautoi mallon ē philotheoi*; *De Fuga et Inventione* 81), Spicq believes that our author has in fact adapted this phrase from Philo, whereas there is no evidence that the authentic Paul ever read Philo's works. There are other links with Philo as well in the list. Both D–C and Brox suggest this list is based on that of Rom. 1:29–31. One important difference between Paul's list and the list here is that Paul's list refers to pagan society, whereas the author's list refers to members of the church. This is made clear by v. 5.

proud, arrogant: this is not the absurd vanity of Sir Andrew Aguecheek, but the self-conscious superiority of the imposter. **implacable:** this translates *aspondoi*, literally 'those who do not make (or keep) truces', so it could mean 'truce-breakers'; but *RSV* translation is the more likely. **treacherous**, literally 'traitors'. It does not mean Christians who betray their fellows to the Roman authorities, says Dornier. It is not very clear who or what they are traitors to. A feature of this list, as of Paul's list also, is a preference for jingles: two vices are linked together by a resemblance of sound. Thus we find *philautoi, philarguroi* (**lovers of self, lovers of money**), *prodotai, propeteis* (**treacherous, reckless**), *philhēdonoi mallon ē philotheoi* (**lovers of pleasure rather than lovers of God**). This rather points towards a catechetical origin, since the jingles would serve as mnemonics.

5. It is rather surprising, after this horrific list of evil characters, to find that they are apparently respectable members of the church. If one took this seriously one would have to conclude that the church in the author's day was rather like the Western Church in the fifteenth century, with people in the highest offices of the church who are devoid of all moral principle. But in fact we do not need to take it *au pied de la lettre*. The author has copied this list from Paul, modified it himself by the help of Philo, and decided that this is an appropriate point at which to introduce it. It will help to denigrate the heretics. Spicq seizes the opportunity to apply this damaging description to the heretics of his day, who, he claims, are reinterpreting tradition in order to accommodate it to the fashion of the day. Brox points out that the heretics have not yet been excommunicated, and thinks that **Avoid such people** is an indication that they are about to be excommunicated. In fact, however, this phrase is a sort of refrain that runs all through the three letters and does not necessarily imply that any formal action was to be taken.

6-7. The description of the tactics of the heretics in these verses would seem to suggest that the author had in mind a fairly well-to-do type of household. Slaves or petty tradesmen would not have leisure or means to provide the sort of women's quarters that are envisaged here. Partly because of this, some scholars (e.g. Spicq, Hasler) believe that the author has pagan households in mind. But this does not fit in with the rest of the letter; what the author is concerned about is the deleterious effect of the false teaching on Christians. The Greek habit of keeping their women secluded and not very well educated would naturally foster credulity in the seraglio. At the same time it must be acknowledged that this description is not inapt for a certain type of woman today, educated only sufficiently to be the natural prey of those who are exploiting fancy religions, e.g. the quasi-oriental teachers who haunt the shadowy world of theosophy. There is some evidence that Gnostic teachers were sometimes accompanied by female initiates. Houlden compares Ptolemaeus' *Letter to Flora* (a Gnostic teacher in Rome of the mid-second century). Marcus, of about the same date, is described by Irenaeus as making a practice of courting rich women by telling them that they had the gift of prophecy, seducing them, and making off with their money. In the phrase **burdened with sins** there is a hint of sexual as well as doctrinal error.

Compare 1 C. 14:35, which may not be by Paul and may even conceivably be from the school of the author of the Pastorals, and 1 Tim. 2:11–12. The author may have been troubled by women seeking authority in the church. **make their way into**; perhaps better 'creep into'. The author assumes that no right-thinking man would have anything to do with these repulsive egg-heads. The heretics therefore have to adopt underhand methods.

capture weak women: the word is *gunaikaria*, a contemptuous diminutive of *gunē*, 'woman'. Holtz points out that *gunaikaria* could mean 'women's quarters'; but this will not fit with the next clause, which grammatically belongs to *gunaikaria*. After **various impulses** there is a variant reading which adds *hēdonais*, giving the sense 'swayed by lusts and various pleasures'. But the addition looks very like a gloss. **who will listen to anybody** is a paraphrase rather than a literal translation, which would be 'always learning but never able to come to a full knowledge of the truth'. Holtz observes that the Stoics, especially Epictetus, made fun of people who were always learning but never acquiring any knowledge. **a knowledge of the truth**; see on 2:25 above. It must mean 'orthodox belief' here. Brox well comments that by this point the author has dropped all pretence that he is describing what is to happen in the future. He is coping with a situation which confronts him as he writes.

There is quite a remarkable parallel between this passage and the brief Epistle of Jude in the *NT*. Indeed one could draw out the parallel further to cover the Pastorals as a whole. Both documents use the method of abuse rather than argument in dealing with heretics; both have the concept of a deposit of faith (Jude 3). Both accuse the false teachers of creeping surreptitiously in (Jude 4). Both imply there is an element of profligacy in the teachers' methods (Jude 4 mentions 'licentiousness'). In both documents the heretical teachers reject the authority of the church's ordained ministry. Both claim that the rise of evil men in the last times has been prophesied by apostolic authority (Jude 17–18); both show an interest in inter-testamental writings; compare 2 Tim. 3:8 with Jude 6f., 9. Both use the example of the rebellion of Korah and his companions (Jude 11); both authors use liturgical fragments (Jude 24–25). Both suggest that there is some hope of repentance among some of the adherents of the false teaching (Jude 22–23). Both are not averse to using a reference to pagan literature; see Tit. 1:12; and see on Jude 13, J. P. Oleson, 'An Echo of Hesiod's Theogony vv. 190–2 in Jude 13', *NTS* 25 (1979), pp. 492–503. These remarkable resemblances may well suggest to us a similarity of historical conditions, and even membership of the same school of writers. But we must not speculate about any identity of authorship. The author of the Pastorals does not have

Jude's inflated style. In Jude's situation the false teachers have already separated themselves from the church (see Jude 19), and in his brief twenty-five verses the author of Jude shows a markedly greater interest in the *OT* and inter-testamental literature than does the author of the Pastorals in his thirteen chapters.

8. As Jannes and Jambres opposed Moses: this is a reference to a piece of *haggada* based originally on Exod. 8:18–19, where Pharaoh's magicians try unsuccessfully to rival the plague of gnats, and are forced to admit that it is God's action that has produced it. A need being felt in Judaism to identify Moses' opponents here more specifically, first the name Johana was evolved, and then his brother Jambres. **Jannes** is a grecised form of Johana. **Jambres** is a jingling modification of 'Mambres' (which is actually read by one Greek MS); this in its turn is a grecised form of the Hebrew *mamrey*, which originally meant 'the apostate' or 'the opponent' and applied to Johana, but soon became personified into his brother. There was a luxuriant growth of Jewish legend about this pair, most of it later than the time of the Pastorals. Those who wish to pursue it can consult H. Odeberg, '*Iannēs* and *Iambrēs*', *TDNT* 3, pp. 192f.; also R. Bloch, *RSR 43* (1955), pp. 213–24; H. McNamara, pp. 85–6 gives the point of development which the legend had reached in approximately the time of the author of the Pastorals. For more recent studies, see K. Koch, *ZNW* 57 (1966), pp. 79–93; and C. Burchard, *ZNW* 57 (1966, pp. 219–28), though these two articles more or less cancel each other out. In my *Studies* (pp. 25–8), I attempted to trace the course of the legend up to the time of the Pastorals, and suggested some link with Wis. 15:18–16:1. A couple of hundred years before the Pastorals the legend appears in the *Zadokite Document* of the Qumran sect (5.17–19); there Belial is represented as 'setting up Johana and his brother' against Moses.

these men also oppose the truth: it is interesting that it is **the truth** which they are described as opposing, not the religious authorities. **men of corrupt mind and counterfeit faith:** a clear echo of Rom. 1:28, where Paul says of the pagan world generally, 'since they did not see fit to acknowledge God, God gave them up to a base mind'. The phrase 'to a base mind' is *eis adokimon noun*; Here **corrupt mind** is *katephtharmenoi ton noun* and **counterfeit faith** is *adokimoi peri tēn pistin*; so the author has reproduced two of Paul's key words, *nous* and *adokimos*. The word *adokimos* means 'disreputable, reprobate', hence the translation **counterfeit** where it is applied to **faith**. Dornier claims that they are called **counterfeit** because they pretended to be converted by Moses and joined Israel in the wilderness, but later showed their treachery by siding with Balaam in attempting to seduce Israel. But there is no evidence for this development of the legend as early as the end of the first century AD. Brox suggests that this comparison with the Egyptian magicians is intended to imply that the heretics practised magic. But the evidence for this is lacking.

9. but they will not get very far: contrast 2:17 and 3:13, in both of which places no end seems to be envisaged to the heretics' progress. Hasler explains this by saying that their progress only leads to their own destruction, not that of the church. **their folly will be plain to all:** presumably the reference is to the Egyptian magicians' folly in opposing Moses. It became **plain** because they were unable to reproduce the plague of gnats. Dornier points out that according to the legend Jannes and Jambres perished miserably after the incident of the golden calf, but there is no hint of this in the text and the mode of their death belongs, it seems, to a later version of the legend. The author shows a robust confidence in the ability of the orthodox faith to survive the onset of heresy.

PAUL'S LAST WILL AND TESTAMENT, INCLUDING A NOTE IN THE USE
OF SCRIPTURE AND PAUL'S OWN EXPECTATION OF MARTYRDOM

3:10–4:8

10. We are now presented with a list of references to Paul's life, all under the general rubric that Timothy is acquainted with them. In the Greek this takes the form of a string of nouns in the dative case which continues into v. 11 and only ends with **my sufferings.** But the type of thing referred to changes as the list goes on. The first three nouns refer to Paul's guidance and instruction of Timothy, the next four to Paul's personal characteristics, and the last two to the events of Paul's life. This rather indiscriminate stringing together of disparate things is characteristic of the author. **my aim in life:** Lock maintains that this should be translated 'manner of life', but this meaning does not seem to be supported by the lexicons. The word *prothesis* could mean 'method', but Paul is not saying 'You know my methods, Watson'. **my faith:** the theological virtue, not the creed believed, as Dornier rightly maintains. *NEB* add the words 'my son' to this verse quite gratuitously as far as I can see. Brox suggests that the reason why Timothy is treated both as a tiro in need of elementary instruction and as one who has had a lot of shared experience with Paul is that the author is in fact writing a manual of instruction for church leaders, and wishes to provide for leaders at all stages.

11. my persecutions, my sufferings, what befell me at Antioch, at Iconium, and at Lystra: the references are to Ac. 13:50; 14:5–6; 14:19. The astonishing thing is that all these events took place before Paul met Timothy (Antioch is of course Pisidian Antioch, not the Antioch in Syria). The whole verse reads like a general review of the events narrated in Ac. 13 and 14, quite unlike what one might expect the central character in these events to write. He makes no reference to the many experiences which Paul must have shared with Timothy. If we want to gain an idea of how the real Paul wrote about such experiences we can read 2 C. 6:4–10; 11:22–33. It is (for me, at least) impossible to believe that the man who wrote those passages in 2 Corinthians also wrote 2 Tim. 3:10–17. This means that the author of the Pastorals had read Acts; indeed, the Pastorals are therefore the earliest witness we have to Acts. Houlden's suggestion that it is the other way round, and the author of Acts copies the Pastorals, seems to have little to commend it. See the discussion of the theory that Luke wrote the Pastorals, in the Introduction, section 1. **yet from all these the Lord rescued me:** Dornier and Hasler detect an echo here of Ps. 34:19:

> Many are the afflictions of the righteous;
> but the LORD delivers him out of them all.

The word for *afflictions* in Ps. 34:19 LXX is not the same as the word for **persecutions** here; but Ps. 34:19*b* is verbally very like 2 Tim. 3:11*b*. If there is an echo here, then the author is doing what he probably does in 4:6–8, 17, applying to Paul's life the experiences of the suffering servant in the Psalms. This is not a Pauline technique. Paul would only apply them to himself in Christ, because they had already happened to Christ. Both Brox and Hasler write of a *Leidenstheologie* in this and the ensuing verses. But it is not a theology of martyrdom, and above all it lacks that central element in Paul's theology, the cross. It does, however, form something of a bridge between Paul and Ignatius of Antioch. Ignatius has a very marked theology of martyrdom, to which the cross is absolutely integral; but it may be that the theology of suffering of the Pastorals to some extent made possible Ignatius' very remarkable theology of martyrdom. See Introduction, section 7.

12. **to live a godly life in Christ Jesus:** at first sight this looks like Paul's doctrine of the life 'in Christ', but a phrase that comes just after a passage where the cross is conspicuous by its absence, and a coupling of living **in Christ** with leading **a godly life** does not look like Paul. The author uses the phrase **in Christ Jesus** because he knows it is Pauline, but not because he understands the full Pauline sense of the phrase. Holtz's attempt to explain the use of *eusebōs* (godly), while retaining Pauline authorship, on the ground that it comes from the language of eucharistic devotion, has no evidence to support it. There is no hint of imperial persecution here. The righteous will be harassed by wicked men but not by Roman magistrates.

13. evil men and imposters: the word for **imposters** is *goētes*, which could mean 'magicians', and some commentators have suggested that the author is accusing the heretics of magical practices. The reference above to the Egyptian magicians might seem to support this. But Karris (*JBL* 92 [1973], p. 560) thinks that it is a general charge of insincerity, one which was common in the philosophical polemic of the day. At any rate they do not seem to be conscious **imposters**, because they are deceivers and deceived. But it is quite possible that the author wishes to have it both ways: the heretics are both deliberate frauds and self deceived. Brox comments that this general charge of evil men growing worse is all part of the vague prognostications about evil growing worse in the last days which we find running all through the Pastorals. This means therefore that the attempt to bring this sort of language within the orbit of Pauline thought by calling it apocalyptic, as Spicq and Holtz do, is unconvincing.

14. knowing from whom you have learned it: this is certainly a reference to the *parathēkē*, the deposit of faith. D–C and Brox believe that the specious reference is to Lois and Eunice (see 1:5), but it is hardly likely that the author means us to understand that it was they who instructed Timothy in the right tradition of Christian doctrine. It is more likely that Paul is supposed to be referring to himself. The difficulty with this interpretation is that **whom** is in the plural, *tinōn*. This no doubt indicates the true state of affairs, which is that the author wishes to remind the church leaders of his day that they have received the deposit from their predecessors. There is in fact a well-supported alternative reading *para tinos* (singular), 'from what person'. Spicq says the singular is more conformable to the context, but the plural is better supported. The plural is no doubt original, the singular was perhaps inserted by a scribe who took the Pauline authorship seriously. Holtz actually suggests that **what you have learned** refers to baptismal instruction. Brox well points out that a similar anomaly occurs when we compare 1 Tim. 4:14 with 2 Tim. 1:6. We are already in a second-century situation, he says, in which appeal is made to the succession of teachers going back to the apostles against the Gnostic heretics. But we must also give the author credit, as Brox does not, for realising that the deposit of faith must be based on Scripture; see the ensuing verses. This question is more fully discussed in the Introduction, section 9.

15. from childhood you have been acquainted with the sacred writings: Timothy was born in a household where the mother had broken the rules of orthodox Judaism by marrying a Gentile. If this detail is historical at all, we must imagine Timothy's mother and grandmother as overruled by the ambitious marriage schemes of the

father of the household (presumably a non-practising Jew). Lois and
Eunice secretly plan together to bring up little Timothy in the knowledge of the true God – or else only find themselves free to do so
when Timothy's father dies while the child is still young. We must
also presume that both Lois and Eunice were sufficiently literate to
read the LXX – a beautiful but rather romantic picture. **the sacred
writings**: there is a well-attested alternative reading which omits **the**,
thus allowing one scholar to describe Timothy as instructed in 'sacred
letters' (Lock), as if he had taken a degree in theology! The phrase,
whether with or without the article, means the *OT*, and nothing else.
which are able to instruct you for salvation: only, of course, when
interpreted by a Christian, and Houlden is right to insist that this is
what **through faith in Christ Jesus** means. In any case Timothy could
not have been 'instructed for salvation' till Christianity in the person
of Paul arrived in Lystra, by which time Timothy must have been at
least a teenager. That Lois and Eunice were devout Jewesses and
afterward believing Christians we need not doubt. On the basis of
this verse Brox believes that the author had been born and brought
up a Christian (see his Introduction, p. 57), but it is not clear why
this should be so. Hasler says that the author assumes the *OT* can be
christianised by means of allegory, and that like Clement he sees it
'not as a document of messianic promises, but as a handbook of
Christian piety'. This is unfair to the author. Our study of his use of
the *OT* shows that he is more inclined to a Pauline typology than to
allegory, and on the whole he does not use the *OT*, as Clement does,
as a handbook of ethics. On the contrary, he tends too much to take
his ethics from contemporary popular philosophy.

16. This verse is a very important one for understanding the author's view of Scripture; it also plays an important part in his cam-
paign against the false teachers. We can distinguish a triple purpose
behind this verse and the next one. (a) He uses it to bring Rom.
15:3–4 up to date; it is a midrash on Paul. (b) He uses it to urge
church leaders to study the Scriptures, in which the author himself
has a sincere belief. (c) He uses it to insist that the Scriptures are on
the side of orthodoxy. I have explained the author's use of Rom.
15:3–4 in the Introduction, section 5. It is a classic example of the
author's use of transposition. See also ch. 4 of *Studies*, where I place
these verses in the context of other references to the inspiration of
Scripture in the *NT*. **All scripture is inspired by God and profitable:**
we have a double problem of translation here. First of all we must
challenge the *RSV* rendering **All scripture**. The Greek is *pasa graphē*:
in the *NT graphē* by itself can mean only one of two things when it
is a question of Scripture: either 'the Bible as a whole' or 'a passage
in the Bible'. But the translation **all scripture** would require *pasa hē*

graphē in Greek. The article is absent, hence we must choose the only possible alternative: 'every passage of Scripture'. Next, there is a problem about the relation of the ensuing adjectives **inspired by God** (*theopneustos*, only one word in Greek) and **profitable**. There are two possible translations: (a) 'Every scripture inspired by God is profitable also for teaching, etc.' (roughly *RSV* margin reading). This translation is followed by Bernard, D–C, Spicq, C. K. Barrett, Brox, Hasler, and *NEB*. J. W. Roberts (*ExpT* 76 [1964–5], p. 359) asks us to believe, not only that Paul wrote this passage, but also that under **scripture** he included most of the *NT*! The great objection to this rendering is that it implies that you could have a passage of Scripture which was not inspired by God. This is probably one of the tenets against which the author is arguing. Some of the Gnostics were eclectic about their use of the *OT*. We turn therefore to the second alternative. (b) 'Every passage of scripture is inspired by God and also profitable for teacher, etc.' This interpretation, at least as far as the two adjectives are concerned, is followed by Lock, Jeremias, Gealy, Kelly, Dornier, and Holtz. It is also followed by *JB* and *RSV* as far as relates to the two adjectives. C. K. Barrett protests that *graphē* by itself does not necessarily mean 'Scripture' at all, and therefore wishes to take *theopneustos* as an adjective qualifying *graphē* and not as a predicate. But in the context it is clear enough that *graphē* must refer to Scripture. We have had *hiera grammata* ('sacred writings') in the previous verse, and the author is reinterpreting Paul's *hosa proegraphē* ('whatever was written in former days') in Rom. 15:4 anyway. The author is therefore saying that *every* passage in Scripture is inspired (not only *some*, as the heretics suggested) and therefore may be used for teaching and polemic. Houlden objects that the author would hardly claim every word in Scripture as being suitable for teaching and polemic; but this is a doubtful argument. The author himself may not have been a great expert in handling Scripture (unlike his master Paul), but he would probably have held that any passage in sacred Scripture is capable of yielding edification for the Christian if properly understood. After all, the author of 2 Peter, whose outlook on Scripture seems to be identical with that of the author of Pastorals, makes great spiritual capital out of the incident of Balaam's ass. See 2 Pet. 2:15–16, and my *Studies*, pp. 50–52.

for correction (*epanorthōsis*), **and for training in righteousness:** Epictetus describes the Eleusinian mysteries as having been instituted 'for the purpose of training and correction of life', where 'training' is *paideia* and 'correction' is *epanorthōsis*. It looks very much as if the author was seasoning his Pauline studies with what he had learned in school from Epictetus (see D–C for references). It is hard to imagine a more un-Pauline phrase than **training in righteousness**.

17. the man of God: probably he means primarily the church leader, and therefore at this period the ordained cleric. Houlden detects here 'early signs of clericalism'. This is hardly fair; as Brox points out, v. 12 applies to all Christians, and the author shows no signs of wanting to exclude the laity from the teaching office. But Hasler is right in his observation that the Pastorals are not addressed to the church at large; they are intended for church leaders. **complete:** C. K. Barrett well renders the Greek word behind this, *artios*, as 'efficient'.

4:1. Despite his seeming diversion to speak about Scripture, the author has never lost sight of the fact that Paul is writing his last will and testament, and this element comes to the fore now. Spicq points out that there was in pagan usage an accepted form of adjuration (*diamarturia*; the Greek word for **I charge** here is *diamarturomai*) whereby one could solemnly and legally hand on a heritage or office. This adjuration language has already occurred in 1 Tim. 5:21 and 2 Tim. 2:14. **in the presence of God and of Christ Jesus:** once more we notice the markedly binitarian theology; the author has less idea of God as being three-in-one than Paul had, and Paul certainly had no developed doctrine of God as Trinity. **who is to judge the living and the dead;** cf. Ac. 10:42; 1 Pet. 4:5, 'a confessional formula', according to Brox. **and by his appearing and his kingdom: appearing** is *epiphaneia*, almost certainly the parousia rather than the incarnation (see Pax, pp. 236–8). Hasler claims that the genuine Paul writes only of God's kingdom; he must therefore relegate Col. 1:13 and Eph. 5:5 to the category of deutero-Paulines. The Pastorals, he adds, do not regard the kingdom in a dynamic light, as Paul does, but simply as an event that will be revealed at the end of history.

2. be urgent: perhaps a better translation would be 'be at your post': Houlden offers 'be on your guard' and Holtz '*sei zur Stelle*'. **in season and out of season:** this could be taken in either a subjective or an objective sense, either 'when you feel like it and when you don't' or 'whether those you are dealing with desire it or not'. Probably the latter is intended. Several editors (e.g. Lock, Dornier) point to the example of Paul's dealings with the Corinthians. He certainly appeared on at least one occasion when he was anything but welcome at Corinth! Similarly **convince, rebuke, and exhort** applies very accurately to Paul's dealings with any of the churches which he founded. **be unfailing in patience and in teaching:** a loose phrase linking together two things which belong to different dimensions; cf. Lewis Carroll's line 'they revived him with forks and hope'. The author wishes to give a place both to *makrothumia* (literally 'longsuffering'), a quality commended by Paul Rom. 2:4; 9:22; 2 C. 6:6; Gal.

5:22, and to **teaching**, which was so essential to counter the heretics; he simply throws the two together.

3. For the time is coming: once again the author projects into what is future from Paul's point of view events that are plainly contemporary with the time of writing. **having itching ears they will accumulate for themselves teachers to suit their own likings:** the metaphor of itching ears is a common one in ancient philosophical polemic. Cicero accuses the Greeks of discussing ideas, not in order to make a judgment about them, but 'to please their ears' (quoted by Dornier). Spicq describes the errant Christians as 'making the round of the professors'. the **itching** may indicate either that they always want something new or that they only want what will please them; perhaps both. But if we translate with **itching** we are thinking of the first meaning, whereas the second meaning would be better conveyed by 'hoping for their ears to be tickled'. Jeremias is no doubt right in his suggestion that the author has in mind the various Gnostic systems, which, whatever their demerits from the point of view of sense and reality, were often ingenious and original. We can easily find a modern parallel: no book has a good chance of being published unless it can be called 'radical, provocative, novel'.

4. wander into myths: if we are right in understanding this false teaching primarily in terms of Gnosticism, then **myths** will refer to the various Gnostic systems with their hierarchies of aeons and accompanying histories of how the aeons related to each other. We must not fail to notice that in Tit. 1:14 we have the phrase 'Jewish myths'. Does this mean that there is a special Jewish element in the false teaching encountered in Crete? There was a strong Jewish colony there. It is more likely that the author in both passages is thinking of false teaching as a whole, any false teaching, and that he adds the epithet 'Jewish' at Tit. 1:14 because of the well-known strength of the Jews in Crete.

5. be steady: Kelly takes this in the sense of 'steer clear of the heady wine of heretical doctrine'; but this seems a little too specific. Spicq claims the verb (*nēphein*) is a technical term in oratory: it means not allowing oneself to be carried away by one's emotions. D–C well compare 1 Th. 5:6. **endure suffering:** cf. 2:9; it probably means 'endure hardship' rather than suffering, since there is no suggestion that Timothy is likely to face martyrdom. Hence Spicq's claim that it only means 'work conscientiously' is not convincing. He quotes examples of the word being used of conscientious magistrates. **do the work of an evangelist:** the word **evangelist** recurs elsewhere in the *NT* only at Ac. 21:8 and Eph. 4:11. In none of these places does it seem to indicate an office rather than a function (in Acts Philip is perhaps called 'the evangelist' to identify him with the figure of

Ac. 8). It is certainly not an office here. Brox well compares Phil.
2:22, where the authentic Timothy is described by the authentic Paul
as having 'served with me in the gospel'. **fulfil your ministry:** often
used in the papyri of paying back a debt, says Spicq. Brox points out
the parallel with Jesus' ministry. Certainly the author here presents
a fine and Christ-like picture of the Christian minister as a servant.
In his strange way, however, he fails to make the comparison explicit.

6. For I am already on the point of being sacrificed: the word
for **sacrificed** (*spendomai*) is literally 'poured out as a libation'. The
author is here modelling himself on Phil. 2:17: 'Even if I am to be
poured as a libation upon the sacrificial offering of your faith . . .'.
The words 'poured as a libation' are *spendomai* in Greek. Indeed the
author has modelled much of the language of 4:5–22 on Phil. 2:12–
30. The two passages have in common the figure of a libation, instructions about the sending and arrival of assistants; a complaint of
being deserted; a reference to Timothy working for the gospel; a
reference to the race that Paul has run (Phil. 1:16 and 2 Tim. 4:7),
and a reference to a coming judicial decision about Paul. We could
say of 2 Tim. 4:5–18 that it is Phil. 2:12–30 rewritten in the light of
Paul's death as a martyr. **the time of my departure:** the word for
departure is *analusis*, cognate with the word Paul uses in Phil. 1:23,
'My desire is to depart'. Holtz interprets it to mean merely 'release
from bonds, not death', but this is hardly likely. Spicq felicitously
points out that one offered a libation before slipping anchor, and
analusis can be used of a ship loosing from the quay and setting sail.

7. I have fought the good fight: the word for **fight** is *agōn*, a
competition in the games, whether running or boxing, not a serious
military encounter. Paul uses this sort of language, as we have seen
in 1 C. 9:24–27, where both the footrace and the boxing match are
in mind. He also implies it in Phil. 3:13–14. But this last passage
shows us how the author's sentiments differ from those of Paul:
there, Paul is not certain of ultimate salvation; here, he speaks with
a confidence born no doubt of hindsight. **I have finished the race:**
see Phil. 2:16. There Paul only hopes to be proud that he has not
run in vain 'in the day of Christ', i.e. at the parousia; cf. Ac. 20:24,
which uses identical language. We suggested in the Introduction that
the author of the Pastorals knew Acts. **I have kept the faith:** this
translation is on the whole the more likely. It means that Paul has
successfully guarded the deposit of faith, and, presumably handed it
on to his successors such as Timothy. But most modern editors,
including D–C, Spicq, and Brox prefer the alternative rendering 'I
have kept faith'. It is difficult to identify the one with whom he has
kept faith, God or Christ, or even, as Spicq suggests, his baptismal
confession or his apostolic commission. The author's anxiety about

preserving the deposit of faith intact seems to incline the balance of probability in favour of the first alternative translation.

8. there is laid up for me the crown of righteousness: D–C point out that *apokeisthai*, the verb which lies behind **is laid up** here, was a technical term for the credit in which oriental monarchs held those who had served them well. Paul does use the language of **the crown** and of a prize at the end of one's life: see 1 C. 9:25; Phil. 3:14. But **the crown** consists in eternal life and the prize *is* the high calling of God in Christ. Certainly the notion that one gains the crown of eternal life as a reward for one's righteous life on earth is in total opposition to Paul's thought; and yet this seems to be what the phrase means here. Barnett (p. 269) believes that this verse is an echo of Phil. 3:12–14. If so, the contrast is as striking as the resemblance. It is worth noting that in Phil. 3:12 some MSS read: 'Not that I have already obtained this or am already justified' (*dedikaiōmai*, cognate with *dikaiosunēs*, **righteousness**, here; and in Phil. 3:13 for 'I do not consider' some MSS have 'I do not yet consider'. If our author had a MS of Philippians with these readings, he may have been writing this verse to indicate that what Paul in Philippians believed to be still in the future has now taken place: by his martyr's death Paul has been justified. Both D–C and Brox maintain that this confident expectation of reward for service rendered is not characteristic of the authentic Paul. **to all those who have loved his appearing:** some MSS omit **all**, but it makes little difference to the sense. Presumably the **appearing**, *epiphaneia*, means the parousia, in which case we must interpret **loved** in the sense of 'longed for', a perfectly legitimate meaning for the verb *agapan*, but not one which the authentic Paul uses. The verb here is in the perfect, which should imply an action in the past with continuing effects in the present. If so, presumably it means 'those who have shown their love by the Christian life they live'. These three verses, 6–8, represent the author at his finest. He has a noble conception of Paul the martyr, one, we may be sure, entirely true to the way in which the historical Paul did meet his death. There is nothing exaggerated or sentimental, but it does not strike us as the sort of way in which Paul would in fact have expressed himself.

INFORMATION AND INSTRUCTIONS ABOUT THE MOVEMENTS OF PAUL'S
COLLEAGUES

4:9–15

For a discussion of whether any historical information is to be culled from these verses, see Introduction, section 3. We go on the assumption that the author is acquainted with the fact and circumstances of Paul's martyrdom; he knows something about Paul's final trial; he knows that Paul was deserted (and perhaps betrayed) by those who should have supported him (see *1 Clem.* 5.5–7); he has some information about the movements and names of Paul's associates. All this does not add up to very much as far as concerns reconstructing the last days of St Paul, but we are not justified in ruling out of court any possibility of genuine historical information to be gained from these verses, as R. Jewett (p. 45) does, for example.

9–10. Do your best to come to me soon: if the letter is ostensibly written from Rome to anywhere in Asia Minor, this is a strange request. It would take weeks for the letter to travel to Timothy and further weeks for Timothy to obey. Yet Paul seems to expect death very soon. Perhaps it is not meant to be taken very seriously. **For Demas . . . has deserted me and gone to Thessalonica:** Demas is mentioned in Phm. 24. He is therefore a genuine colleague of Paul. He also appears in Col. 4:14. I personally find it impossible to believe that Col. 4:10–18 is not by the historical Paul, whatever judgment may be made about the rest of Colossians. We are therefore left with the choice either to assume that the author of Pastorals invented a desertion of Paul by Demas, or that he had genuine information that this had taken place. This latter view seems more probable. **in love with this present world:** Spicq, no doubt rightly, helds that this only meant that Demas grew discouraged and returned home, not that he turned apostate. **gone to Thessalonica:** probably because it was his native soil. **Crescens has gone to Galatia:** this character is mentioned nowhere else in the *NT*. There is an interesting variant reading *Gallian* for *Galatian*. This would mean Gaul. Spicq maintains that even *Galatian* could mean Gaul also. Those who believe Paul did visit Spain will find here a faint confirmation of their belief. The second alternative reading *Galilaian* ('to Galilee') is very improbable. **Titus to Dalmatia:** Dalmatia was an area in northern Greece. Brox believes that here we may have a piece of genuine historical information, in the sense that Titus, he thinks, was a native of Dalmatia. In Tit. 3:12 Titus is summoned to join Paul in Nicopolis. The most likely of the many towns called Nicopolis in the Roman empire could be described as being in Dalmatia. The authentic Paul had visited Illyricum, which is in the same area (Rom. 15:19). But all these fragments of information do not add up to anything that can be reasonably formulated into a coherent theory about Paul's movements before or after AD 62.

11–12. Two of the characters mentioned in these verses also appear in Colossians and Philemon, and **Tychicus**, the third, appears in Colossians. Following the methodology outlined in the Introduction, section 3, we do not regard these verses as offering any new historical material. It is very likely that by the time of the Neronian persecution (AD 64) **Mark** was in Rome. Probably the author of the Pastorals knew this. It would be rash to assume that the **Luke** mentioned here has any connection with the Gospel of Luke or with Acts. **Get Mark:** this is a somewhat stark translation of the Greek *analabou*, which means 'pick him up'. The idea is that Timothy picks him up *en route* for Rome. **he is very useful in serving me.** Holtz thinks this should be rendered 'in the service of the gospel', a possible translation. Since the Greek is literally 'useful for ministry', this is probably an echo of Phm. 11: 'Formerly he was useless to you, but now indeed he is useful to you and to me.' In that passage Paul puns neatly on Onesimus' name, which means 'useful'. The word which Paul uses for 'useful' is *euchrēstos*, the same as is rendered by **useful** here. **Tychicus** must have been a much travelled man, since he appears in Eph. 6:21 as heading for Ephesus; in Col. 4:7 as making for Colossae, and in Tit. 3:12 as about to be sent to Crete. Those who hold to the Pauline provenance of this letter often pick on Tychicus as the bearer of it (e.g. Jeremias). But if this were the case it would be quite unnecessary to tell Timothy that Tychicus had been sent to Ephesus. The arrival of the letter would have informed him of that. Whatever be the historical value of the references in these verses, they have a certain value in that they represent the earliest references to Philemon and to Colossians.

13. For a discussion of Trummer's attempt to discredit the historical character of this verse, see Introduction, section 3. Others besides Trummer have attempted to do the same. Hasler suggests that the **cloak** is the symbol of Paul's apostolic office, which he hereby bequeaths to Timothy, on the analogy of Elijah's cloak which was bequeathed to Elisha in 2 Kg. 2:8. The **parchments** indicate that a collection of Paul's letters is now being made. This sort of speculation discredits itself. In any case if the author had intended to recall the Elijah-Elisha episode, he would have used the word for cloak which we meet in the LXX of 2 Kg. 2:8, *mēlōtēs*. In fact he uses a Latin word *phailonē*. Some scholars believe that *phailonē* should be translated 'portfolio' or 'book-holder'. Chrysostom knew of this alternative, and the Peshitta, the official translation of the NT into Syriac, has it. But it does not seem very likely. Most editors conclude that **the parchments** contained the OT in Greek, or parts of it.

But there have been other suggestions. Some think Paul is sending for his certificate of Roman citizenship, written on parchment. Others again believe Paul wanted blank parchment sheets for writing on (in goal? in Rome? expecting a death sentence soon?). D-C protest that Paul could not be sending for a **cloak** which he left three years ago in Troas. But the belief that this is a piece of authentic information about Paul does not necessarily imply that the author of the Pastorals has put it in its correct context. We regard it as a piece of oral tradition which the author acquired, perhaps from **Carpus** himself (he is mentioned nowhere else), or from his family. The same point holds for Brox's arguments against the authenticity of this verse. What Brox rightly objects to is the syllogism: 'This detail cannot be inauthentic, therefore the whole chapter (or the whole letter, or all three Pastorals) must be authentic.' However, T. C. Skeat (*JTS* ns 30 [1979], pp. 173–7) has recently used just this argument on the basis of what he, with a great deal of convincing evidence, claims is the correct rendering of *malista*, which *RSV*, slightly inaccurately, here translates **and above all**. Skeat says it should be, 'I mean the parchments'; i.e. *malista*, instead of emphasising one element out of several, identifies the meaning of the previous word: **the books** are defined as being **the parchments**. (See Introduction, section 3, for a reference to his article.) Skeat (p. 177) maintains that this usage is colloquial and epistolatory, and that this proves that the Pastorals are genuine, not pseudonymous, letters: 'The Epistles in which [this usage] occurs, whatever their authorship, are, in origin at least, genuine letters and not deliberate forgeries or pastiches, since composition of these would not be likely to provide opportunity for the locution here discussed'. He also concludes that **the parchments** are 'certainly not literary works of any kind . . . but probably notes or memoranda such as lists of Christians in various communities'.

We must be grateful to Skeat for his illuminating translation. Indeed we have applied it ourselves at 1 Tim. 5:17, which he does not refer to in his article. But he is certainly not justified in vindicating the authenticity of the Pastorals as genuine letters on the basis of this detail alone. In the first place, his suggestion that Paul needed the parchments because they contained notes or lists of Christians is not very convincing. Why should Paul write notes on expensive parchment when he could use papyrus or wax tablets? Secondly, his theory would rule out the secretary hypothesis. This is a usage which marks the authentic letter-writer, but here the letter-writer, if authentic, can only be Paul. 2 Timothy is, however, as we have seen, the letter which lends itself least easily to a theory of direct composition by Paul. Thirdly, this usage is not confined to letters. One of his examples (pp. 175–6) is from a government edict of AD 260. We conclude therefore that Skeat's translation is an improvement on the traditional one, but that the details in this verse, though probably authentic, do not justify us in vindicating the authenticity of the chapter, or the letter, as a whole. We simply do not know for what purpose Paul needed the **parchments**, as Dornier very sensibly concludes. Skeat has however one more useful suggestion to make. He points out that a few MSS read *malista de tas membranas*, 'and especially the parchments' (which is what *RSV* translates, though it is not clear whether it follows this reading). This, he suggests, is an attempt to ease the meaning of *malista* as 'especially' instead of the true sense of 'I mean', and is a gloss. This seems most probable.

14–15. Alexander the coppersmith: editors have been uncertain whether to connect him with the heretical Alexander of 1 Tim. 1:20, or with the Alexander of Ac. 19:33, who played an ambiguous part in the Ephesian riot according to Luke's account. It is unlikely that he has any connection with the heretic of 1 Tim. 1:20; some editors (e.g. Dornier) think he is designated **the coppersmith** so as to distinguish him from the heretic. It is not at all clear from Luke's narrative in Ac. 19 what part Alexander did play. He seems to have no connection with Demetrius and his guild of silversmiths. Some editors (e.g. C. S. C. Williams, R. P. C. Hanson) suggest that he may have been trying to convince the Ephesian mob that Jews were to be distinguished from Christians. On the other hand there is some reason to suspect that Luke's account may be covering up, or glossing over, an actual imprisonment of Paul in Ephesus, to which Paul refers in 1 C. 15:32. In that case it would not be at all surprising that someone should have accused Paul and succeeded in getting him into trouble. Spicq points out that the Greek behind **did me great harm,** *polla moi kaka enedeixato*, may imply that Alexander laid a successful (or temporarily successful) information against Paul, since the verb *endeiknumai* could mean 'to give information' in this sense. If so, the author is actually preserving a relic of a more historical version of what happened in Ephesus than that which Luke presents. This is by no means improbable (see R. Jewett, p. 19). **Beware of him yourself:** this is hardly likely to be authentic. The danger would have passed away long before the author's time. Hasler's suggestion that the author is indicating a heretic contemporary with himself is most unlikely. Everyone would know that Paul had died forty years earlier. **for he strongly opposed our message:** the Greek is literally 'our words', but *RSV* has probably given the correct sense. Brox agrees that the phrase refers to Christian teaching generally. Spicq believes the phrase is a Latinism and refers to Paul's formal defence in court.

A REFERENCE TO PAUL'S LATEST TRIAL

4:16–18

16. At my first defence: there seems general agreement that this refers to the *prima actio* in Roman legal procedure, at which the aim was to clarify the details of the charge. Bernard and Kelly think a verdict of *'non liquet'* ('the matter is not clear') was returned. If this is historical (and it well may be), it must refer to the beginning of the proceedings that ended in Paul's condemnation and execution, not to

a trial after the two years mentioned in Ac. 28:30, as a result of which
he was released. Timothy would know all about that already. **all
deserted me:** Brox believes this may be historical; cf. *1 Clem.* 5.2,
5. **May it not be charged against them:** Dornier enlarges on Paul's
forgiving spirit, so like that of his master Christ. But we may compare
v. 14, where a different sentiment is expressed. In any case, if there
is authentic history here, it does not occur in the form of Paul's
ipsissima verba, but of correct oral tradition. The words are the author's, not Paul's.

17. Brox points out that the author wishes (quite legitimately) to
use all the details of Paul's final trial in order to enhance his status
as a martyr and hence the progress of the gospel. So a note of triumph
runs through his language, perfectly justifiable when later Christians
are reflecting on the event, but not in accordance with the way in
which the historical Paul probably viewed his death. Hence the phrase
that all the Gentiles might hear it probably means that Paul's heroic
death helped to spread the gospel throughout the pagan world rather
than that it is a reference to any feature of his trial. **I was rescued
from the lion's mouth:** probably an echo of Ps. 22:21. The imperial
power could be described in these terms. Josephus tells us that the
death of Tiberius was announced by the words 'The lion is dead'.
Herod Agrippa's freedman heard the news while in Capri, hastened
to Rome, where he found his master just emerging from the bath.
He conveyed the news by uttering the words in Aramaic. Even so it
may have been a reference to Ec. 9:4 (see Josephus, *Antiq.* 18.228).
See below on v. 18. Ignatius of Antioch describes the guards that
were conveying him from Syria to Rome as 'ten leopards' (Ign., *Rom.*
5.1). In 1 Pet. 5:8 the devil is compared to a lion. Certainly, in
slightly later Christian martyrology, there was a tendency to associate
Satan's activity with the action of Roman magistrates in condemning
Christians. The phrase must refer to some respite or relief gained in
the course of the trial. It could not be merely a super-triumphal way
of saying that Paul was condemned to death.

18. This verse on the other hand reads like a pious termination to
Paul's message about his martyrdom composed by the author to
round off the reference. **will rescue me from every evil:** this sounds
like an echo of the Lord's Prayer; cf. Mt. 6:13. If it is, the author
knew it in the Matthean rather than the Lucan version, and understood *apo tou ponērou* to mean 'from evil' not 'from the evil one'.
There is no reason why this should not be so. Hasler, on the strength
of the curious argument that the whole verse has a liturgical ring
about it, denies any connection with the Lord's Prayer. **save me for
his heavenly kingdom:** this is in line with the teaching on the subject
of the kingdom we find in the Pastorals, that it is an event which

only takes place at the parousia. This is not Paul's conception. It does however recall the ending to the Lord's Prayer which occurs in some MSS of Mt. 6:13, but which is very unlikely to be original to Matthew: 'for thine is the kingdom and the power and the glory for ever. Amen'. Holtz well compares 2 C. 5:1. **To him be the glory:** this must mean 'to Christ'. Prayer then was being directed to Christ as to God by this time. Perhaps Pastorals in this respect represent a stage between the Pauline avoidance of the word *theos* ('God') for Christ and Ignatius' bold use of the word. See Introduction, section 7. **for ever and ever. Amen.** This sounds liturgical, and where the author uses **Amen** elsewhere in the Pastorals it indicates the presence of a liturgical fragment; see 1 Tim. 1:17; 6:16. Perhaps it came in because he is consciously quoting the Lord's Prayer. Or it may be merely part of his pious ending to the last will and testament of Paul. Several scholars have claimed that behind parts of this chapter lies Psalm 22, or some verses from it. There is a certain parallel, though it is not very obvious. It can be best expressed by the following comparison:

Psalm 22 (LXX *trans.*)		*2 Tim. 4:16–18*	
12	do not desert me . . .	17a	but the Lord stood by me
	because there is none to help	16	all deserted me
17b	a congregation of evil men have surrounded me	18	the Lord will rescue me from every evil
22a	save me from the lion's mouth	17a	I was rescued from the lion's mouth
28	all the ends of the earth shall turn to the Lord, and all the families of the Gentiles shall worship before him	17c	that all the Gentiles might hear it

The parallel is not self-evident. The suggestion that the passage is inspired by Ps. 22 was originally made by Lock, and is commended by Spicq. There may well be something in it. If so, the author does not use the *OT* as Paul does; Paul would certainly have applied Ps. 22 first to Christ and only then to himself. If it is valid, it must be the author's own composition, perhaps he felt that so heroic an event as Paul's martyrdom could best be described in the words of Scripture.

GREETINGS AND FURTHER INFORMATION

4:19–21

19. It is curious that, having reached an edifying climax in v. 18, the author now tacks on a number of other personal greetings. Is it perhaps that he wishes to end in proper epistolary style, having tended in recent verses towards writing what is more a last testament? **Priscilla and Aquila**; in Ac. 18:1–3 Paul meets these two, who had recently been expelled from Rome by a decree of Claudius; he travels with them to Ephesus and leaves them there. In 1 C. 16:19 they send their greetings to the church at Corinth, and in Rom. 16:3 Paul greets them as his fellow-workers. The author certainly imagines them as being in Ephesus when Paul writes at the very end of his life. Does he ignore Rom. 16:3? Hasler thinks so. But there is some evidence to suggest that Rom. 16 was originally a letter, or part of a letter, intended for Ephesus not Rome. The author may have known it in this form. This is Houlden's view. **the household of Onesiphorus:** this seems to imply, as does 1:16–17, that Onesiphorus himself was dead. The apocryphal *Acts of Paul* represent him as very much alive and present in Iconium with his family. But that is a scene which is meant to take place well before Paul's death.

20. Erastus: in Ac. 19:22 an Erastus is sent with Timothy by Paul to Macedonia. In Rom. 16:23 he sends his greetings from Corinth, and is described as 'the city treasurer'. Some modern scholars have doubted whether the Pauline emissary could be the same as the important city official and have conjectured that two different people are meant here. (So D–C, Brox). It was certainly a common name among Greeks. In 1929 an inscription was found in Corinth mentioning an Erastus, described apparently as *procurator aedile*, who had laid down a pavement at his own expense. It dates from the second half of the first century. The author of the Pastorals at least would have no hesitation in identifying the two Erastuses. Brox (Introd., p. 94f.) believes this reference to the Ephesian Erastus may be historical. **Trophimus I left ill at Miletus: Trophimus** is named in Ac. 20:4 as an Asian who accompanied Paul from Macedonia at least as far as Asia Minor. Later in Ac. 21:29 he is found as a companion of Paul in Jerusalem, is described as 'the Ephesian', and is the Gentile whom the Jews wrongly accused Paul of introducing into the part of the temple reserved for Jews. It is hard to imagine why the author should have invented an illness for him, so this detail may well be historical, though we do not know what part of Paul's life it belongs to.

21. Do your best to come before winter: perhaps a little less urgent in tone than v. 9, but still difficult to harmonise with the expectation of imminent martyrdom of vv. 6–8. It is probably part of the author's epistolary trappings. **Eubulus, Pudens, Linus,** and **Claudia** are all unique in the *NT*. Subsequent legend got busy with some of them. The name of **Linus** occurs in Irenaeus' succession list of the bishops of Rome. He writes: 'The blessed apostles, having founded and built the church, committed the ministry of the episcopate to Linus . . . and his successor is Anencletus; and after him, in the third place from the apostles, the bishopric is allotted to Clement.' This is unhistorical anyway in that it assumes that the church in Rome had monepiscopacy in the first century, which it certainly had not. Even in Clement's day (whom we place in the AD 120s) there is no sign of monepiscopacy. It is also probably quite unhistorical to envisage either Paul or Peter or both as entrusting to anyone the leadership of a church which neither of them had founded. But there may be a faint echo of history in the name. Are we to imagine the author of the Pastorals as freely inventing all these names? It does not seem likely. They are probably part of his oral tradition. We have tried to adhere to our plan in dealing with the plethora of personal references in these verses, which is to judge each reference on its merits. It would be easier if we could accept all as conveying historical information, or dismiss them all as historically worthless, as do Hasler and Jewett. But the best results in historical research are not gained by applying *a priori* assumptions. The ensuing picture is very far from clear and we cannot claim that we can make any coherent reconstruction of Paul's movements on the basis of what we have judged to be historically credible in this chapter. But it does not look as if the author of the Pastorals had any clear scheme of Pauline history in his mind either. He had a certain amount of genuine historical tradition, and he used that in order to give his letter an impression of authenticity, not in order to support any particular historical theory.

FINAL BLESSINGS

4:22

22. The Lord be with your spirit: this is a Pauline phrase, Gal. 6:18; Phil. 4:23; Phm. 25. It is second person singular in Greek and therefore refers to Timothy. Dornier points out that the question of what 'and with thy spirit' means has recently been raised in connection with translating the liturgy. Most experts conclude that it is a Hebraism for 'you'; but some maintain it refers to the Holy Spirit in those who have received Holy Orders, and should not be used in addressing anyone under the rank of deacon – a distressingly clericalist conclusion. Do the laity not possess the Holy Spirit? In any case it is unlikely that any such thoughts troubled the author of the

Pastorals. **Grace be with you:** as in the case of 1 Tim. 6:22, this **you** is plural and some MSS offer the singular instead, no doubt in order to preserve the epistolary form. Hasler says that the second greeting is intended for all who read the letter, which is certainly a probable conclusion.

THE EPISTLE TO
TITUS

THE CONTENTS OF TITUS

OPENING GREETING

1:1–4

The author has prefixed a more elaborate greeting than meets us in the other two letters. Houlden points out that 'Titus is richer for its size in doctrinal passages than its companion pieces', so the introduction may be setting the tone for the rest.

1. a servant of God: the word is *doulos*, literally 'slave'. The authentic Paul never describes himself in these terms. The nearest self-description to this in the *NT* is Jas 1:1: 'James, a servant of God and of the Lord Jesus Christ'. But the faithful are called servants of God in Lk. 2:29; Ac. 2:18 (in an *OT* citation); 4:29; 17:17; 1 Pet. 2:16; Rev. 1:1 (of Christian prophets). R. E. Collins (*LTP* 2 [1975],

p. 149) believes that by using this title the author ranks Paul with Moses, David, and the prophets. **to further the faith of God's elect:** this is a rendering of the vague Greek construction *kata pistin*, literally 'according to the faith'. In all three introductions the author uses this vague *kata* construction to amplify the opening self-designation: 1 Tim. 1:1, *kat' epitagēn*, literally 'according to the command'; 2 Tim. 1:1, *kat' epangelian zoēs*, 'according to the promise of life'. Paul does not permit himself such vague language. Naturally commentators have differed considerably as to the exact meaning here: 'the sphere in which Paul exercises his apostleship' (Kelly); 'if measured by the faith' (A. R. C. Leaney); 'marked as such by faith' (*NEB*, followed by Houlden); '*au service de la foi*' (Dornier); and Holtz offers the same interpretation. Brox says the apostleship corresponds to and serves the faith of the elect; and Hasler comments: 'The servant of God is the bearer of revelation'. If we think there is an exact sense, we may conclude that both **servant** and **apostle** do duty for a verb and the meaning is 'acting as servant and apostle in accordance with the faith which he shares with the elect'. But must we conclude that there is an exact meaning here? It may be that *kata* here is like *kathōs* in 1 Tim. 1:3, a vague prepositional phrase intended to establish a loose connection between Paul's office and Christian orthodoxy. **God's elect** only means all Christians without any particular emphasis on predestination. **and their knowledge of the truth which accords with godliness:** the whole phrase means orthodox Christian faith. D–C well point out that Christianity is here described as a faith, a knowledge, and a hope, profound enough we may well admit. Spicq and Dornier believe that **faith** is subjective here. This may be questioned, especially if the 'exact' interpretation is correct. If however the 'vague' interpretation is right, **faith** may well have both meanings. Brox comments: 'Paul is recognised as the organ, norm, and guarantee of the orthodox teaching of the church.' Hasler distinguishes the authentic Pauline usage of 'servant of Jesus Christ', which means that Paul is Christ's own property, from the **servant of God** usage here, which means that Paul is the 'authorised revealer of God'.

2. in hope of eternal life: this phrase includes the two elements found in the greetings in the other two letters. 1 Tim. 1:1 has 'Christ Jesus our hope', and 2 Tim. 1:1 has 'according to the promise of life which is in Christ Jesus.'

which God, who never lies, promised ages ago: the phrase **who never lies** represents two words in Greek, *ho apseudēs*, literally 'the unerring [God]'. This epithet is applied to God nowhere else in the *NT*; but cf. Heb. 6:18. D–C compare Ignatius, *Rom.* 8.2, where Jesus Christ is characterised as 'the unerring (*apseudēs*) mouth by which the Father spoke'; but that is far more specific than this passage. The phrase **ages ago** is reminiscent of Rom. 16:25, which, as we have already noted, is probably deutero-Pauline. Some editors take the whole verse as referring to the course of salvation history (so Brox), in which case we must understand **ages ago** as bringing us back no farther than Abraham, or at the remotest Noah, to whom the first promises were made. But others, e.g. Hasler, think that there is a Platonic element here (Plato did say 'the divine cannot lie', *apseudes to theion*): salvation belongs to the timeless eternal world; only revelation belongs to time. On the whole this seems more likely.

3. **and at the proper time manifested in his word**: *RSV* has smoothed out the slightly disjointed syntax of the Greek, which runs literally: 'eternal life, which God promised . . . and manifested his word'. Thus **his word** is the direct object of **manifested**. On the face of it the phrase might almost accord with Jn. 1:1–18. But no editor suggests that we should really render it 'manifested his Word'. The phrase seems to be based on Col. 1:25–26: 'the word of God . . . the mystery hidden for ages . . . but now made manifest (the Greek is *ephanerōthē*, the same verb as is used in Tit. 1:3) to his saints'. This is all the more likely since in that Colossians passage Paul (or his disciple) is speaking of his apostolic commission. This verb *phaneroun* is certainly a Pauline one, and Paul uses it in connection with the manifestation of God's design in Christ; see Rom. 3:21; 2 C. 2:14; 4:10–11. Holtz compares Ignatius, *Mag.* 8.2, where he describes Christ as 'the Word proceeding from silence'; but we are here in a Johannine atmosphere. It is interesting that twice in this opening passage of Titus we have been led to compare the Pastorals with a text in Ignatius, and in each case Ignatius' theology is more developed. It suggests that in some respects Pastorals represent a half-way stage between Paul and Ignatius. So the **word** here is the preached word by means of which God in Christ is made known. The emphasis we find here on the mystery hidden from all ages but now revealed seems typical of the immediately post Pauline period, as evidenced in Colossians, Ephesians, and Rom. 16:25–27. The authentic Paul certainly spoke about a hidden mystery revealed in Christ, but what hid it was the foolishness of the cross, not the fact that God chose not to reveal it; see 1 C. 1:18–31; 2:6–16. **God our Saviour**: as we have noted already, the author applies *sōtēr* indiscriminately to God and Christ; cf. 1 Tim. 1:1.

4. **To Titus, my true child in a common faith**: many editors believe that this phrase implies that Titus had been converted to Christianity (or at least ordained: Brox) by Paul; so Schlatter, Jeremias, H. Maehlum (p. 57), Dornier. This is at least what the author wishes us to understand, whether it was actually the case or not. **in a common faith**: common to Paul the Jew and Titus the Gentile, says

Barrett, and I accepted this in my commentary of 1966; cf. Jude 3.
But in the author's time the Jewish-Gentile issue was not a burning
one, so it is more likely that it means either 'common to both of us'
or 'common to all (orthodox) Christians'. Spicq even suggests it
means something like 'catholic'. He thinks it also implies that the
faith has been handed down from Paul to Titus, which may well be
right. **Grace and peace:** note the number of textual alternatives here,
playing on the combinations of **grace, peace,** and **mercy.** It indicates
how relatively little difference it makes what exactly the author puts
into his greetings. **Christ Jesus our Saviour:** see note on v. 3, where
God has been called **Saviour.** This indiscriminate use of *sōtēr* undoubtedly implies a rather muddled soteriology on the part of the
author of the Pastorals. It may also indicate a desire to counteract the
imperial cult, which applied this title to Caesar. See the detached
Note on the imperial cult at 2:14. We can certainly sympathise with
the author here, but in, so to speak, making a take-over bid for the
imperial titles, he did run some risk of reducing Christ to the status
of a deified Caesar. The author has certainly deployed an impressive
theology in these first four verses; he can legitimately claim to stand
in the true theological succession of the church's teachers. But
whether we compare him with Paul, with the author of the Fourth
Gospel, or with John, we must admit that at times he seems to be
out of his depths in the theological vocabulary which he employs.
When we compare the three introductory verses to the three letters
respectively we can see a strong structural resemblance between them.
The author appears to have planned them carefully according to the
same scheme. It is remarkable that the shortest letter should have the
longest introduction.

QUALITIES NECESSARY FOR A BISHOP

1:5–9

5. This is why I left you in Crete: for a discussion of the question
'Why Crete?' see Introduction, section 3. We conclude that Paul had
sent a mission to Crete and that Titus had had a part in this. The
author gives us more details about Crete than he does about Ephesus:
there is a strong Jewish element; the Cretans are liars by their own
testimony. We know nothing of the history of Crete about the end of
the first century AD. Dio Cassius, a third-century Greek historian,
tells us that in about AD 117 there were anti-Roman riots instigated
by the Jews in Egypt, in Cyprus, and in Cyrene (*Roman History*,
68.32). They had to be repressed with considerable slaughter. Crete
would be a natural staging post for anyone travelling from Asia Minor
or Palestine to Cyrene, and even perhaps for the traveller by sea from

Egypt to Cyrene. Notice how in Ac. 27:17 the voyagers try to hug the coast of Crete in case by venturing into the open sea they might run into the sandbanks of the Syrtes on the north coast of Africa opposite. It may be therefore that in the time of the author the Jews in Crete were being affected by a nationalist movement which a few years later manifested itself in the riots related by Dio Cassius. This movement might react on Cretan Christians in the shape of increased aggressiveness on the part of Jewish neighbours, or even in restiveness among Jews who had been converted to Christianity. But it must be confessed that all this is very speculative. We may however assert with confidence that the author of the Pastorals was concerned about the condition of the church in Crete in his day.

For *apelipon*, **I left you**, some MSS read *katelipon*, which might be translated 'I left you behind', and would imply that Paul had visited Crete. H. Binder (in Müller, p. 77) chooses another reading, *apeleipon* (imperfect), which might mean 'I let you remain in Crete'; but this is in the interest of preserving Pauline authorship of the Pastorals. **that you might amend what was defective**: Liddell and Scott refer to this passage and say it must mean 'complete unfinished reforms'. It therefore implies that the church in Crete, far from having been recently founded, had existed long enough to grow corrupt and was in process of being reformed. This suggests a state of affairs more likely to prevail at the end of the century than in Paul's day.

and appoint elders in every town: apparently the church was widely spread but unorganised (or disorganised). It also implies that Titus had authority to appoint elders on his own initiative. We do not know of any office in the church at the end of the first century that would confer such wide authority on its holder. It is possible, however, that the church in Crete had originally been founded from Ephesus, and that this would give a church leader from Ephesus some sort of wider than local authority in the Cretan church. Or it may even be that the author is wishing to claim such authority for himself. In fact the word *presbyteros* as the term for an office in the church never occurs in the genuine Paulines. But Luke in Ac. 14:23 represents Paul and Barnabas as re-visiting the churches they have founded in Cilicia and appointing presbyters in every town. Brox thinks this verse is actually inspired by Ac. 14:23. Hasler claims that the author is 'painting a picture which is purely imaginary', but makes no suggestion as to why he imagined Crete rather than anywhere else. J. P. Meier (*CBQ* 35 [1973], p. 338) and A. Cousineau (*ScEsp* 28 [1976], p. 159) claim that the church in Crete is less developed because recently founded, but there does not seem to be much evidence for this; the idea is dismissed by D–C. W. Stenger (*Kairos* 16 [1974], p. 264) draws a parallel with 1 Tim. 1:3. In each case a colleague of Paul has been

assigned a post, but now is called away from it. The aim is, he
believes, to emphasise the continuing nature of Paul's authority. **as
I directed you:** this implies that Paul had already made provision for
this when he and Titus last met; now he writes in order to repeat his
instructions. Historically this does not seem very likely, since, if
relations between Paul and his assistants were such as they seem to
be in the genuine Paulines, there would be no need for this emphasis.
Paul's colleagues would understand his wishes and seek to fulfil them.
But it does seem to suggest that the author was anxious that some
scheme of reform should be carried out in the Cretan church.

6. The list of qualities requisite in a bishop which follows in this
and the following verses can almost entirely be reproduced if we
compare the list of qualities desirable in a bishop in 1 Tim. 3:2–7. It
is also worth while comparing the list of the qualities requisite in a
church leader in 2 Tim. 2:24–6, and the description of what a deacon
should be like in 1 Tim. 3:8–12. Though these last two lists are much
less full, they have nothing that cannot be paralleled in the first two
with the unimportant exception of **not double-tongued** of the deacons
in 1 Tim. 3:8. There are also three epithets at the end of our list here
in v. 8, 'lover of goodness', 'upright' and 'holy', which are not
paralleled elsewhere. But one could hardly claim that there is anything
peculiar to bishops in these qualities. The conclusion is inevitable
that the author is drawing on an existing source for all four lists, and
that it makes little difference which office he is describing, the same
qualities appear. It is not surprising that there is only one quality
which appears without fail in all four lists, the ability to teach Christian doctrine competently, though moderation in drinking, having
well-behaved children, and not being avaricious come a close second.
But even Onosander in his list of qualities necessary for a general has
'the ability to speak', which reminds one of the concern for teaching
ability which the author manifests. Lemaire (*Les Ministères*, pp. 125–
6) rightly claims that the use of the phrase **if any man** in this verse
points to the existence of a source. Several editors have argued that
vv. 7–9 are a later interpolation inserted when monepiscopacy was
universal in order to make the letter apply to contemporary conditions. There is no textual evidence for this; D–C, Bartsch (p. 84),
and Brox rightly conclude that there is no need for any such
hypothesis.

7. For a bishop: we take the view that the author uses this ambiguous language, passing from presbyters to a **bishop** without indicating
any change of subject, because he wishes to give advice about monarchical bishops as they were beginning to emerge in some of the
churches he knew, without prejudice to the fact that there were no
such officials in Paul's day. **as God's steward:** the phrase is probably

taken from 1 C. 4:1, where Paul describes himself and his colleagues as 'servants of Christ and stewards of the mysteries of God'. There is a very interesting passage in Lk. 12:42–48, where Jesus utters a parable in which he compares the community of his followers to a household: 'Who then is the faithful and wise steward (*oikonomos*, as in this verse), whom his master will set over his household. . . ?' The word for 'set over' is *katastesei*, the same verb as is used for **appoint** in v. 5 above. Moreover, Luke gives us a thumb-nail sketch of the bad steward, who proves to be both a **drunkard** and **violent**. Compare also 1 Pet. 4:10, where the whole Christian community are to be 'good stewards (*oikonomoi*) of God's varied grace'; and in 1 Pet. 5:2–3 the presbyters are warned against seeking for shameful gain (*aischrokerdōs*) cognate with **greedy for gain** (*aischrokerdē*) here, and against 'domineering over those in your charge', which reminds us of **arrogant**, **quick-tempered**, and **violent** here. In all these passages we seem to have quite a full picture of the temptations to which the church leadership at the end of the first century was exposed. **greedy for gain:** this might mean that he should not follow a trade which would distract him from his task of oversight, one of Jeremias' suggestions. But the bishop had charge of the church's funds, so it probably means that he must be scrupulous in his handling of church finances.

8–9. a lover of goodness: D–C observe that this is a quality often attributed to rulers in contemporary inscriptions. **holy:** the word is *hosios*, already used in 1 Tim. 2:8 of **lifting holy hands** in prayer. Paul uses it in 1 Th. 2:10 of the behaviour of himself and his colleagues in Thessalonica. Houlden renders it 'devout'. **he must hold fast to the sure word as taught:** this slightly obscures the sense of the original, which is literally 'holding fast to the sure word according to the teaching'. D–C point to 1 Tim. 5:17 where **word** means oral teaching. In that case 'teaching' (*didachē*) here refers to the church's tradition of doctrine. Several editors see a connection with the *pistoi logoi*, the 'faithful word' formula that runs through the three letters. **give instruction** is *parakalein* in Greek and **doctrine** is *didaskalia*. Both words are Pauline; the author seems to use them interchangeably. **and also to confute:** this last word is *elenchein* in Greek. It is remarkable that these two verbs, *parakalein* and *elenchein*, are the two characteristics of the Paraclete in the Fourth Gospel. The author of that Gospel certainly had the teaching activity of the contemporary church in mind as he composed the great discourses about the work of the Paraclete. It looks as if we are getting in the Pastorals a worm's-eye view of the same activity as John views from the point of view of the Holy Spirit. After v. 9 one Greek minuscule (109, or 460, in Venice, 13th–14th cent.) has the following additions: 'They should not ordain those who have been married twice nor make them dea-

cons; nor should they themselves take wives in a second marriage;
nor should (such people) approach the altar for divine service; rebuke
as a servant of God those rulers who are insensitive and rapacious
and liars and merciless.' It reflects church conditions of at least a
hundred years later.

CONDEMNATION OF HERETICS (INCLUDING A QUOTATION FROM A CRETAN PROPHET)

1:10–16

10. insubordinate men: this implies that they were Christians;
when he goes on to describe them as **the circumcision party** we must
conclude that they were Jews who had accepted Christianity (so
Spicq, Dornier, Hasler). We know from Philo and Josephus that
there were many Jews in Crete; Josephus' second wife was a Cretan
Jewess. D–C perceive that the author has provided more local colour
for Crete, but suggest that he has invented it all. They confess that
they cannot discover why. But perhaps they are asking the wrong
question. The question should rather be: why was the author interested in Crete? Jews from Crete were present at Pentecost as described
in Ac. 2:11. **deceivers:** the word is *phrenapatai*, a rare one. Paul uses
the cognate verb in Gal. 6:3 for those who deceive themselves. **especially the circumcision party:** if we follow T. C. Skeat (*JTS* ns 30
[1979], p. 174), we shall render this: 'I mean Jewish Christians'. *RSV*
has imported the notion of **party**; the Greek is literally 'those from
the circumcision'. Paul uses 'the circumcision' simply to mean Jewish
Christians without any particular emphasis on the fact of their being
circumcised; see Rom. 15:8 (where it just means 'the Jewish people');
Gal. 2:7–9, 12.

11. they must be silenced: probably by excommunication rather
than by closely reasoned argument, which is not the author's strong
point. **they are upsetting whole families;** cf. 2 Tim. 3:6. They upset
them perhaps by dividing the members of the family against each
other and introducing the idea that those who did not observe strict
food-laws were defiled. **teaching for base gain:** this is probably a
purely conventional accusation, but the heretics may have expected
support in return for their privileged instruction. **what they have no
right to teach:** nearly the same phrase as we find in 1 Tim. 5:13.
There are three possible explanations of what is meant: (a) 'indecent
behaviour'; A. R. C. Leaney accepts this; (b) 'superstitious practices';
the parallel with 1 Tim. 5:13 supports this; Spicq and Holtz believe
this is what is meant (c) 'false doctrine', which they **have no right to
teach** (because they are not clergy). On the whole this seems most
likely, if we must restrict ourselves to one meaning, which is not

necessarily the case. Hasler relevantly refers to Ignatius, *Eph.* 7.1: 'Some people are accustomed to bear the name [of Christ] with culpable deceit, and practise other things unworthy of God. We must avoid them as we would wild beasts, for they are rabid dogs who bite secretly. Since they are very difficult to cure, we must guard against them.' Ignatius at least was confronting real adversaries. We notice that his have in common with those we meet in the Pastorals the suggestion of discreditable secrecy, and of immoral behaviour, and the comparison with wild animals (see v. 12 below). This on the whole imparts more credibility to the author's picture of his opponents.

12. **One of themselves:** this should mean one of the heretics; but this can hardly be the case, since the prophecy goes back to legendary times. The author must mean 'one of the Cretans'. He is however associating the heresy with Crete, and he wishes to use this prophecy as a means of discrediting the heretics. Hence we cannot agree with Brox's argument that there is nothing particularly Cretan about the heresy, and that the quotation in v. 12 has been brought in simply to discredit the heretics (see Brox on 1:10). This attributes an extraordinary deviousness to the author of the Pastorals: one of the anti-heretical letters must be directed to Crete, not because the heresy is Cretan, but because a useful tag to use against the heretics is associated with Crete! Unless there was an already existing connection between the heresy and Crete, the introduction of this quotation is pointless. The author then proceeds to quote a hexameter line which he attributes to a **prophet of their own**. This line, which here appears for the first time, is attributed to Epimenides by Clement of Alexandria, Jerome, and Augustine. Some scholars would prefer to attribute it to Callimachus, a poet of 305–240 BC. We do have two lines from Callimachus written in defence of Zeus. He calls the Cretans liars because they claimed to possess Zeus' tomb:

> Cretans are always liars, for the Cretans have
> invented thy tomb, O king. But thou
> didst not die, but art for ever.

The Cretans had a reputation for lying (*krētizein* meant 'to lie'), perhaps because of this. They also had a reputation of stealing. Cicero complains that the Cretans do not consider it immoral to steal. Compare the attitude of the highlanders in Scotland during the eighteenth century. For a very long period during the first century BC Crete was a resort of robbers and pirates, and this no doubt accounts for their evil reputation. We can learn something about Epimenides from Plato's *Laws* (1.642.d–e). Here we are told that he was born in Crete and ten years before the Persian attack on Greece he was instructed

by an oracle to go and warn the Athenians of the impending attack
and to tell them that it would fail. He obeyed and while at Athens
performed certain sacrifices. This would place him at about 500 BC,
though it seems that this is an anachronism (whether unintentional
or deliberate) on Plato's part, and his true date is nearer 600 BC. It
does not matter as far as our author is concerned, who obviously
regarded him as a pagan prophet with genuine powers of prediction.
Plutarch, a contemporary of the author of the Pastorals, describes
Epimenides as 'the seventh of the sages of Greece . . . a man beloved
of the gods and instructed in divine matters in that which concerns
inspiration and the mysteries', which probably sums up the author's
estimate of him. We must conclude then that the author could not
resist the opportunity to use this well-known tag about the Cretans
as a way of defaming the Cretan heretics. It is quite impossible to
imagine Paul doing anything so obtuse. In so doing the author has
implicitly conceded that a pagan poet could be inspired to prophesy
truly; though he could no doubt support his case by the well-known
example of Balaam, a figure whom the author of 2 Peter uses. See 2
Pet. 2:15. There is no particular connection between Epimenides and
the Judaism which was a feature of the heresy. We must imagine,
then, a heresy which was an early form of Gnosticism, strong in Crete
(where perhaps it originated), especially among Jewish Christians.
Hasler draws our attention to Ignatius, *Mag.* 8.1: 'Do not be led
astray by heresies or ancient mythologies, which are unprofitable.
For if we go on living according to Judaism right up to the present,
we admit that we have not received grace.' Ignatius also was facing
a form of false teaching which combined Gnosticism with a Jewish
element.

13. This testimony is true: the author has to put this in. Otherwise
he is open to the objection that, since all Cretans are liars, Epimenides
must be a liar also. E. K. Simpson points out that the author wishes
to impale the heretics on a dilemma: either they accept the words of
their venerated prophet, in which case they are self-condemned. Or
they reject the oracle and condemn their own prophet. **rebuke them
sharply:** the word rendered **sharply** is *apotomōs*, the same word as
Paul uses in 2 C. 13:10. 'I may not have to be severe'. Titus is to
rebuke them, not argue with them. There is hope that some of them
may be recalled to orthodoxy. **sound in the faith:** a favourite metaphor with the author; see 1 Tim. 1:10; 6:3; 2 Tim. 1:13; 4:3; Tit.
1:9; 2:1–2. He treats the heresy as if it was a dangerous bacillus that
had infected the whole community. Hasler claims that by this period
anyone who opposes the church's official teaching can be accused of
being a Jew or a heathen; but Ignatius' careful discrimination about
the form of false teaching he was coping with belies this

14. Jewish myths: we believe this to be a reference to Gnostic theogonies propagated by Christian Jews, or by Gentile Christians influenced by a Jewish form of Gnosticism. D–C well compare Col. 2:8, 22, and suggest that reverence for angels may be an ingredient in the teaching (so also Holtz). A system of angelic hierarchies could very easily pass over into a system of related aeons such as we find in the developed Gnosticism of the second century (see Col. 2:18). **commands of men:** Houlden suggests that this might be a reference to parts of the Torah. But would the author of the Pastorals regard anything written in Scripture as merely **commands of men?** It seems much more likely to refer to the *Halaka*; cf. Mk. 7:8, where exactly this distinction is made (so Dornier).

15. To the pure all things are pure: this is not a quotation of Scripture, but it does sum up Jesus' attitude towards purely ritual defilement. See Mk. 7:19, where of Jesus it is said: 'Thus he declared all foods clean.' We should notice what D–C underline that we are not here dealing with the situation which Paul faces in Rom. 14, where Gentile Christians had to show forebearance towards Jewish Christians who wished to observe the Jewish food-laws. There is no longer any question of continuing some Jewish observances within the Christian fold. Now all orthodox Christians are on the side of those who were the enlightened in Paul's day (it seems likely that the slogan of the liberal party in Paul's Corinth was 'Everything is clean', *panta kathara*, exactly the same words as we have here – see Rom. 14:20). In the author's day anyone who tried to observe food-laws would be ranked as a heretic. **to the corrupt:** the word in Greek is the regular one used to denote ritual impurity. The author gives it a moral sense. **their very minds and consciences are corrupted:** the Greek is a little more emphatic: 'both their minds and their consciences'; it is not just pleonasm. It may be that when the author says about the heretics that to them **nothing is pure** he is referring to the Gnostic horror of physical matter: their repudiation of the physical element has reduced them to a condition in which the non-physical element in them, mind and conscience, is corrupted.

16. They profess to know God, but they deny him by their deeds: cf. Jn. 8:54–55, where Jesus is represented as telling the Jews that in fact they do not know God for all their claim that they are his people. If the author means this accusation seriously, then he must imply that the God whom they worship is really an idol, since he can hardly mean that they are secretly atheists. This is probably borne out by his use of the word **detestable**, *bdeluktoi*, which has a strong sacral overtone and is one of a group of words used in connection with blasphemy and accusations of idolatry (e.g. Mk. 13:14, where the word 'sacrilege' translates *bdelugma*).

unfit for any good deed: compare 2 Tim. 3:4, which makes a very similar accusation. 2 Tim. 3:8 describes the heretics as of 'counterfeit faith'. One would never guess that the same Greek word *adokimoi* stands behind both 'counterfeit' there and **unfit** here. Holtz well remarks that the heretics' unsatisfactory attitude towards God is indicated by their rejection of God's creatures. Compare 1 Tim. 4:4, which gives the orthodox view, and see 2 Tim. 2:21; 3:17 for phrases describing someone who is fit for **any good deed**. Brox points out *à propos* this verse that the author lays great stress on **good deeds**, especially in this letter. There is a faint echo here of Paul's great indictment of the Gentile world. See especially Rom. 1:19–24, where Paul declares that, because men refused the natural revelation of God which they could have known, he gave them up to their own evil devices.

QUALITIES NECESSARY FOR VARIOUS SOCIAL GROUPS

2:1–10

G. Lohfink (*ThQ* 157 [1977], pp. 99–100) describes these verses as the most important passage in the Pastorals as far as the *didaskalia* (orthodox catechesis) is concerned. The catechesis is, he says, 'the concrete realisation of the gospel in practice'.

1. This verse is however a purely transitional sentence. The author is passing from condemnation of heretics to give material from one of his sources, a 'domestic code'.

2. the older men: the word is *presbutas*, which could refer to presbyters, but can hardly bear that sense here. In the first place the author uses *presbuteroi* for ordained presbyters; see 1 Tim. 5:1, 2, 17, 19; Tit. 1:5. In the second place, though he requires the older men to be **sound in faith**, he says nothing here about teaching. **in faith, in love, and in steadfastness:** we have here in fact Paul's three theological virtues of 1 Cor. 13:13; but instead of *elpis*, 'hope', he uses *hupomonē*. In LXX *hupomonē* is often used to translate words that convey the sense of 'hope' in the Hebrew. This may be because *elpis* in the Pastorals always mean 'hope in life beyond the grave', whereas *hupomonē* suggests continuing steadily hopeful in this life; cf. 1 Tim. 6:11; 2 Tim. 3:10. We might imagine that the exhortation to be **be temperate** was otiose, but we must remember that contemporary pagan society often admired heavy drinkers (as is coming to be the custom in our day outside the church). Spicq quotes examples of pagan funeral inscriptions which commend the deceased as having been hearty drinkers, including one which narrates that the late lamented died as a result of a drinking bout. Brox and Hasler describe this list of qualities (not altogether fairly perhaps) as 'a popular philosophical ethic' and 'these Stoic virtues' respectively.

3–4a. the older women: There is an almost exact correspondence between the qualities required in **older women** here and those desirable for wives of deacons in 1 Tim. 3:11. It certainly suggests a common source for both lists. **reverent in behaviour:** the word for **reverent** is *hieroprepeis*, which means literally 'like those engaged in sacred service' (Moulton and Milligan). D–C suggest there may be the thought of the natural priesthood of matrons, and we may surely see a hint of the priesthood of all Christians here. Indeed it might almost be more appropriate to translate the word with 'reverend' rather than **reverent**. Knox's rendering is good: 'carry themselves as befits a holy calling'. D–C well compare Ignatius, *Trall.* 4.2, where the bishop's behaviour (*katastēma*, the same word as here) is described as 'a great source of instruction'. **they are to teach what is good:** seven words in English for one in Greek. It is *kalodidaskalous*, literally 'good teachers', hence 'teachers of what is good'. The word appears to have been coined by the author. It seems likely that their method of teaching is by their lives and behaviour; there does not seem to be any suggestion that they should be formally accredited teachers of the younger women, especially in view of 1 Tim. 2:12 (so D–C and Brox, as against Trummer, *Biblica* 51 [1970], p. 476). Hasler observes that the church is here seen to be a social group held together by an ethic rather than by an ideology.

4b–5. young women: This list of qualities in its turn offers a pretty close correspondence to 1 Tim. 5:14, which describes how young widows should behave, including even the concern for outside opinion. **to love their husbands:** this was a necessary reminder in societies in which brides did not choose their own husbands. This epithet together with **to love their children** (each representing a single word in Greek) is often found on tomb inscriptions, so, to borrow a phrase from Mrs Malaprop, the author has chosen 'a nice derangement of epitaphs'. **domestic, kind:** the Greek is *oikourgous, agathas*, which means literally 'working at home, good'. It is difficult to believe that even the author should be so banal as to demand that Christian wives should be 'good'. We should therefore take these two words as noun and adjective respectively and render 'good workers at home'. I cannot agree with Dornier that such an interpretation would break the rhythm of the sentence. There is an alternative *oikourous* for *oikourgous*, which would mean 'stay-at-home'. By Greek standards this would be a laudatory epithet for women. Philo uses this adjective, together with **sensible** and 'husband-loving', to describe the ideal wife. But *oikourgous* is better attested, the rarer word, and therefore the more difficult reading. On these grounds it should

be preferred (so Spicq). **submissive to their husbands:** see on 1 Tim.
2:11. This duty for wives is taught throughout the *NT*; see Eph.
5:22f.; Col. 3:18; 1 Pet. 3:1f. **that the word of God may not be
discredited:** this must mean simply the Christian religion. This is
Hasler's view; he contrasts 1 C. 14:34, where he believes that the
phrase 'as even the law says' refers to a specific passage, Gen. 3:16.
This is quite true; but we may still doubt whether 1 C. 14:34 comes
from Paul's pen.

6. younger men: The author really has almost nothing to say
peculiar to young men except that they should exercise self-control,
and even this is closely paralleled in 2 Tim. 2:22. J. Elliott (*CBQ* 32
[1970], pp. 377–9) suggests that *tous neōterous* (**the younger men**)
should be translated 'the newly-baptised'. But in a context where
advice has just been given to older men, older women, and young
women, this does not seem plausible. Jeremias, Holtz, and Brox hold
that Titus is regarded as a representative of the younger men, but
this would, even from the author's assumed point of view, be an
anachronism, and in any case v. 7 seems to be describing a church
leader.

7–8. the church leader: The grammar of these two verses is very
loose; we have to take **show** in **show yourself** as the verb governing
integrity, gravity, etc. *RSV* has simply repeated the verb. The characteristics commended to Titus here are very like what is required of
Timothy in 1 Tim. 4:11–12, indicating clearly that the list is drawn
from an existing document and is far from being part of a personal
letter. For a far-ranging comparison between Tit. 2–3, 1 Pet. 1–3,
and parts of Ephesians, see my *Studies*, ch. 7. I conclude that the
several authors of these three letters are drawing on the same source
containing baptismal and catechetical material. There is also an interesting parallel between Tit. 2:6–14 and 1 Pet. 5:1–5. They have in
common an exhortation to younger men, the requirement that church
officers should be examples to the rest, advice to slaves, and a reference to the appearance of the Lord. There can be little doubt that
some common material lies behind both documents.

in your teaching show integrity: the word for **integrity** is *aphthorian*;
there are alternative readings, such as *aphthonian*, which would mean
'abundance'. But the author is hardly expecting Titus to run short of
teaching! Presumably **integrity in teaching** means preserving orthodoxy pure. **sound speech:** Hasler, correctly no doubt, takes this as
a reference to preaching. **so that an opponent may be put to shame:**
not an exact translation. It should be '*the* opponent'. Who is the
opponent? Probably the pagan critic or the heretic teacher (so Spicq;
Brox thinks the latter). Holtz and Dornier, who regard the Epistle as
having some authentic connection with Paul, argue that 'the oppo-

nent' refers to the Jewish community in Crete. Holtz quotes 1 Th.
2:15 where the Jews are described as those who 'oppose all men', in
Greek *enantiōn*, whereas 'the opponent' here is *ho ex enantias*. But
this does not seem likely. We do not find Jews, as distinguished from
Jewish Christians, referred to in the Pastorals. A third possibility is
that the opponent is Satan (whom Dornier sees operating behind the
Jews). But this seems unnecessarily subtle.

9–10. slaves: There is a general resemblance between these verses
and 1 Tim. 6:1–2, where he deals with the same theme. There is
some uncertainty as to whether the author here envisages slaves as
working in Christian or in pagan households. In the other passage
where he deals with this subject he distinguishes the two groups.
Kelly is confident that Christian households are meant here but the
last clause in v. 10 seems to suggest that the slaves can commend the
faith to pagan masters by their behaviour, so probably the author is
addressing slaves in pagan households (so Holtz).

9. Bid slaves to be submissive: there is no Greek word corresponding to **Bid**, only the infinitive **to be submissive**. This suggests
an excerpt from a household code. D–C draw an effective contrast
between this passage and Col. 3:23; Eph. 6:6; 1 Pet. 2:19, where
slaves are urged to work as for Christ or for God. Here they are only
to work for their masters. No advice is given to the masters; but this
may be because they are not Christians.

10. nor to pilfer: this is an original touch; it would be a very
common temptation for slaves. **entire and true fidelity:** the word for
fidelity is *pistin*, which more commonly means 'faith', either subjective or objective. But *RSV* has certainly given the correct rendering
here. Spicq quotes an instance of nine persons, including one slave,
dedicating a statue to Pistis. For **true**, *agathēn*, one Greek minuscule
reads *love*, *agapēn*. It would be syntactically very awkward and
cannot be original, but may have been inserted by a scribe who
wished to conform the text closer to 1 Tim 6:2. **they may adorn the
doctrine: doctrine** is *didaskalian*, but it does not mean anything
different from 'the word of God' in v. 5, or indeed from 'the mystery
of our religion' in 1 Tim. 3:16, or from 'the commandment' in 1
Tim. 6:14. The author disposes of a wide variety of synonyms for
the Christian faith. **of God our Saviour:** this is a most un-Pauline
phrase. D–C and Holtz emphasise that God, not Christ, must be
meant, though indeed one might well have one's doubts about this
in the light of v. 13 below. The closest modern parallel to this piece
of advice given to slaves might be the situation of Christian coolies
today in an Indian village who are still in the social status of outcaste.
What advice would their church leaders give them today? Certainly
they would not preach social revolution, as many Christian writers

would urge them to do; but they would probably not take the subordinate social status of their flock so much for granted as all the writers of the *NT* do, with the possible exception of John the Divine. Modern Christians have learned something from Karl Marx.

LITURGICAL FRAGMENT DESCRIBING THE COMING OF CHRIST

2:11-14

In ch. 7 of my *Studies* I have argued that Tit. 2:11-14 and 3:4-7 were taken from a source also used by the author of Ephesians and the author of 1 Peter. It was of baptismal origin. The author of the Pastorals has therefore taken an excerpt from his baptismal liturgical tradition and used it to complement his letter. But, in accordance with his usual technique, he has not set it down all in one piece, but has divided it in two, inserting in the middle Tit. 2:15-3:3 (for this technique, see Introduction, section 8). It is possible that this inserted material is also borrowed, since it has affinities with 1 Peter in its exhortation to obey the ruling authorities, and with Ephesians in its lurid description of the pre-conversion pagan life of those whom he addresses. S. C. Mott (*NovTest* 20 [1978], pp. 22-48) has detected traces of the influence of Philo on the author in these two passages, both in his mention of most of the cardinal virtues and in his writing of the manifestation of God's benevolent qualities rather than of God himself. Mott may well be right.

11. the grace of God has appeared for the salvation of all men: the Greek is literally 'the grace of God salvific to all men has appeared'. **appeared** is *epephanē*, so we can claim this as another example of the author's epiphany-christology. Here he uses the verb of the whole event of the incarnation, as he uses *ephanerōthē* in 1 Tim. 3:16. But we must beware of attributing too much to the author's own originality; both this passage and 1 Tim. 3:16 are certainly taken from a source. The emphasis on God's desire to save all men is, however, typical of the author and is one of his most admirable characteristics. For the association of the language used in this section with the imperial cult see the 'Note on the Imperial Cult', after 2:14. It is difficult to understand how Spicq can possibly justify his comment that 'the doctrine and the spirit of these verses must be counted as among the most Pauline in the whole *corpus apostolicum*'. If *'le style c'est l'homme'* is true, these verses are not Pauline.

12. training us: the Greek is *paideuousa hēmas*. Paul uses this verb, but he uses it to mean 'chastise', not 'educate' as here. Pax (p. 240) has an interesting essay on this word and its cognates. He shows that in contemporary pagan moral philosophy training (*paideia*) was an autonomous activity, a form of self-improvement. The author harnesses it to his Christian belief in God's dealing with mankind. Spicq and Houlden agree that the use of *paideuein* in this sense shows the influence of Hellenistic thought. *1 Clement* 59.3 uses the verb of God's teaching us through Christ.

to renounce irreligion: several editors, such as Bernard, Dornier, and Brox, detect an implied reference to baptism in the use of this verb, no doubt rightly in view of the conclusions we have come to about the origin of these verses.

worldly passions: this phrase also appears in *2 Clem.* 17.3; cf. 2 Pet. 1:4. Cyril of Jerusalem, quoted by Holtz, understood the phrase to apply to theatres, horse-races, and hunting. He may well have hit off the author's meaning. **to live sober, upright, and godly lives:** the author's notion of the purpose of Christianity in a nutshell. It is hard to imagine anything more unlike Paul's fervent, far-reaching, and profound theology. Pax (p. 141) sees a Stoic colouring in this language. **in this world:** literally 'in the now aeon', not a Pauline phrase. The author has used it already in 1 Tim. 6:17; 2 Tim. 4:10. Hasler's comment on this verse is 'The church appears as an educational institution of grace'.

13. **awaiting our blessed hope:** cf. Rom. 5:2, which undoubtedly refers to the same event, the parousia, though using somewhat different language. Bernard well points out that **hope** has been virtually identified with the object of hope. **the appearing of the glory of our great God:** this could be a Hebraism meaning 'the glorious appearance'; cf. Rom. 8:21; 9:23; 2 C. 4:6. But it could just as well be taken literally: all agreed that the parousia would be a manifestation of Christ in glory. **our great God and Saviour Jesus Christ:** this is the most obvious and straightforward interpretation of the Greek text. The alternative reading, 'and of our Saviour Jesus Christ', is obviously a copyist's effort to avoid the theological embarrassment latent in the text. If this translation is correct, then the author describes Jesus Christ as **our great God**. Commentators are about equally divided as to whether this is correct or not. The following accept it: Bengel, Bernard, Lock, Easton, Pax (p. 242), Leaney, Higgins, Barrett, Spicq, Houlden, Dornier. It is also the translation of *NEB* and *JB*.

But others cannot accept so drastic and unqualified an attribution of full divinity to Christ at this stage in the development of the church's theology, and conclude that somehow or other we must extract from the text the meaning 'the glory of our great God and of our Saviour Jesus Christ'. Among those who take this view are Moffatt, Windisch, Jeremias, Kelly, Holtz, Brox, and Hasler (who surprisingly does not comment on the point, but translates it so as to follow this interpretation). But the difficulties of this rendering are very great. We have to conclude that the author expected God the

Father as well as Christ to appear at the parousia, which seems incredible. It seems preferable boldly to accept the fact that the author could describe **Jesus Christ as our great God and Saviour**. For the theological implications of this and a comparison with Ignatius, see Introduction, section 7.

F. J. A. Hort in his commentary on Jas 2:1 attempted another explanation. He would render it 'awaiting the appearing of the glory of our great God (that is) our Saviour Jesus Christ', **glory** being used as a title for Christ, as perhaps in Jas 2:1. But this is much too clever to attribute to the author of the Pastorals. It may be that the author inherited this phrase from the source he is using, but it is more likely that he is responsible for this actual juxtaposition of phrases. If so, he has exposed himself, no doubt through a laudable desire to counter the imperial cult, to a near-pagan doctrine of Christ as a demi-god – not that he had any such intention. Compare, for example, the phrase used by the prefect of Egypt very early in the reign of Claudius. He refers to the emperor as 'the majesty of our God Caesar' (see H. I. Bell, p. 8). And the title 'our great god the benefactor and saviour' is applied to one of the Ptolemies in the 3rd century BC (D–C 74). The phrase **great God** can be traced in the *OT*. It is, for example, Daniel's way of referring to Adonai when speaking to pagans (Dan. 2:45; 4:20, 34). The phrase is also freely used in 3 Maccabees for the God of the Jews: 3 Mac. 1:9, 16; 3:11; 4:16; 5:25; 7:2; cf. 7:22. D–C, who cannot make up their minds on the question posed by this verse, bring evidence to show that it was also a title used in contemporary paganism.

14. who gave himself for us to redeem us from all iniquity: this phrase distinctly recalls Mk. 10:45, which the author has already used in 1 Tim. 2:6. The phrase seems to go back to Ps. 130:8: 'And he will redeem Israel from all his iniquities' (I have worked the comparison out in greater detail in *Studies*, pp. 91–6). This is also a verse which bears a close resemblance to Eph. 5:25*b*–27 and to 1 Pet. 1:13*b*–19. But the comparison is best made with the whole excerpt which the author uses before us, and that means bringing in Tit. 3:4–7 also. The originally baptismal nature of the material used becomes clear here, and even clearer in 3:5–6. **a people of his own:** this phrase originally comes from Exod. 19:5; Dt. 4:20; 7:6; 14:2. But compare also Eph. 2:10; 1 Pet. 3:13, where the element represented here by **zealous for good deeds** is also reproduced. Thus we can fairly claim that the author is dependent on the *OT* for his vocabulary in a way not often paralleled in the Pastorals. But it is very likely indeed that his *OT* material came to him in the source which he (in common with the authors of Ephesians and 1 Peter) used. He is of course reiterating the universal conviction of the early Christian church that God's promises made to Israel of old have now been inherited by the church. We have here in fact an impressive theology of the church and plenty of material for a doctrine of the atonement, but the author has merely reproduced them. He cannot really be said to have made them his own.

Note on the Imperial Cult

Long before there was a Roman emperor, royal dynasties in Asia Minor, the Near East, and Egypt had been receiving divine honours. It was the demand by the Seleucid monarch Antiochus IV that the Jews should worship him as Zeus Olympios that sparked off the Maccabean rebellion in 168 BC. The Ptolemies in Egypt, inheriting the traditional deification of Pharaoh, were worshipped as gods by their Greek, as well as their Egyptian, subjects. While the Roman republic still stood, prominent Roman generals or proconsuls were offered divine honours in Asia Minor. There is evidence that Julius Caesar in his last years was planning to institute the cult of *Divus Julius* by way of undergirding the permanence of his dynasty in the sovereignty of the Roman empire. See S. Weinstock, *Divus Julius* (Oxford, 1971). This cult was fostered by his successors as a way of ensuring stability of society and loyalty to the empire among provincials. It was not emphasised in Rome itself at first. But the more neurotic emperors, such as Gaius, Nero and Domitian, took their divinity very seriously. From AD 66 till the end of his reign two years later, Nero was officially described as 'lord and saviour of the world' (Garzetti, p. 169). Domitian insisted on being addressed as *Dominus et Deus noster*, 'our Lord and God'.

The Jews had managed to secure a certain amount of immunity from this cult. While the temple stood, they offered a daily sacrifice for the welfare of the emperor. They would not apply the word *theos* ('God') to him, and tried to avoid *despotēs* ('sovereign'); but they were willing to use *divus* (divine) and *dominus* in Latin (D. Keresztes *VC* 27 [1973], p. 12). Sometimes emperors showed a certain reluctance to take the cult seriously. There is some evidence that Claudius deprecated being treated as a god in the early days of his principate, but official protocol always won in the end (Bell, p. 5). It seems likely that only by Domitian's time (reigned AD 81–96) did the church first feel the pressure of this cult. The Neronian persecution was not caused by Christians refusing divine honours to the emperor. The evidence is very obscure, but it looks as if Flavia Domitilla, the niece of Flavius Clemens, was exiled by Domitian because she was a Christian (Keresztes, pp. 14–16); and the most likely date for the book of Revelation is in the reign of Domitian. J. P. Sweet (pp. 24–5) however insists that the Domitianic persecution of Christians is an invention of Eusebius. With the accession of Nerva in 96 there seems to have been something of a reaction against Domitian's stern regime, and the threat of state action against Christians may have receded (H. Garzetti, p. 293). But in AD 112 Trajan seems to have attempted to revive the imperial cult; this appears to be the most likely date for the Pliny-Trajan correspondence (S. L. Davies, *VC* 30 [1976], pp. 174–80). This evidence, such as it is, would fit our proposed date for the Pastorals very well. They would come during that period of relative relaxation (for there is no sign of persecution in them), when the divine claims of Caesar were nevertheless a potential threat to Christianity.

It is certainly true that one can find in the Pastorals a whole battery of terms which were also used in the imperial cult: *sōtēr* ('saviour'), *epiphaneia* ('appearance', 'epiphany of a god'), *makaria elpis* ('blessed hope'), *megas theos* ('great god'), *philanthrōpia* ('humanity'), *chrēstotēs* ('kindness'), the suggestion that with the advent of the god a new aeon has begun for mankind – all these features of the Pastorals can also be paralleled in the imperial cult. It is of course perfectly true to say that the cult was already well developed during Paul's life, and there is no reason why he should not have taken notice of it, except that these terms simply do not appear in the authentic Pauline letters. For example, he uses *sōtēr* of Christ only once, in Phil. 3:20. Even the deutero-Pauline Ephesians uses it only once, and even then not as a title (Eph. 5:23). It is indeed to be noted that Pax, who in 1955 devoted a learned work to the study of the use of the word *epiphaneia*, is not inclined to think that the use in the Pastorals of *sōtēr* and *epiphaneia* indicates a desire to oppose the imperial cult. But D–C and Trummer (*Die Paulustradition*, p. 195) believe that the cult has influenced the author's vocabulary.

Most of all when we read Titus are we driven to conclude that the author was trying to counter the imperial cult. Such phrases as *hē Gaiou Kaisaros charis* ('the grace of Gaius Caesar'), which D–C cite (Introd., pp. 108f.), and *tou epilampsantos hēmin epi sōtērai tou pantos anthrōpou genous euergetou* ('he who has lightened upon us, the benefactor for the salvation of the entire human race'), which Bartsch (p. 172) quotes of the emperor Galba (who ruled only three months), make it seem very probable that the author of Pastorals was consciously attempting to present Christ as the true saviour of the human race over against the false saviour Caesar. The theological risks which he thereby ran (albeit unconsciously), we have already pointed out. We can only speculate as to why there is more sign of opposition to the imperial cult in Titus than in the other two letters. It may be that the author simply decided to make Titus the main vehicle for this material. Just as 1 Timothy is mainly a handbook for church leaders, and 2 Timothy mainly Paul's last will and testament, so Titus was planned to be the letter in which the author's counterclaim for Christ against Caesar was to be more prominent. It is interesting to note that coins from Crete dating from Domitian's reign bear the image of his baby son, who died in AD 83 and was immediately deified (E. Stauffer, *Christ and the Caesars*, p. 132).

TRANSITIONAL VERSE

2:15

15. This is one of the link passages that hold together the heterogeneous material contained in the Pastorals. It is not particularly appropriate to the immediately preceding verses, which are liturgical rather than parenetic. Some commentators emphasise the distinctive activities indicated by the three verbs. **Declare** refers to proclaiming the gosepl, says Holtz. But *lalein* is a very colourless Greek word for something which was so important in the author's eyes. It means 'talk' in classical Greek, but could be used for 'speak, utter' in *koinē*. Holtz goes on to claim that **exhort** refers to Christian instruction, and **reprove** applies to what Titus must do with the heretics. **with all authority:** the word is *epitagē*, which the author uses in 1 Tim. 1:1; Tit. 1:3 to mean 'command'. Brox remarks that the word of the bearer of church office has not optional but obligatory force. **Let no one disregard you:** not particularly appropriate to Titus, unlike the warning in 1 Tim. 4:12 that no one should despise Timothy's youth. The phrase is no doubt intended for the churches for whom the author is writing more than for their leaders (so Holtz). Spicq attempts to salve Pauline authenticity by claiming that the verb (*periphronein*) means 'defy' and the Cretans were a defiant lot.

BEHAVIOUR REQUIRED OF CHRISTIANS AS MEMBERS OF THE STATE AND OF SOCIETY

3:1-2

There is an interesting comparison to be made between these two verses and the two other places in the *NT* where the topic of obedience to rulers is treated, Rom. 13:1-10 and 1 Pet. 2:13-17. It is plainly a subject with which the early church was concerned and probably formed one of the elements in catechesis and therefore in domestic codes. The full pattern of teaching on this topic occurs only in 1 Peter and includes the following elements:

(a) Obey secular rulers.
(b) They are God's agents.
(c) Show respect to all men.

(d) Love especially the brethren.

Of these 1 Peter has (a), (b), (c), and (d); Romans has (a), (b), (c), and probably (d) in 13:8. Titus has only (a) and (c). The author may have inserted this section here by way of implying: 'You must not join in emperor worship, but that does not mean that you should not be obedient to the emperor.'

1. Remind them: Houlden points out that it is not clear to whom **them** refers, and he takes this, no doubt correctly, as an indication that the author is here using a source, probably a domestic code. **to be submissive:** Spicq claims that this word (*hupotassesthai*) means 'to obey', whereas that translated **to be obedient** (*peitharchein*) means 'allow oneself to be persuaded, voluntarily yield submission'. **to rulers and authorities:** there is no word for **and** in the best MSS, though some may have it. C. K. Barrett believes that **and** has simply dropped out from the original. It makes no difference to the sense. There is probably no distinction intended between **rulers** and **authorities**; see on 1 Tim. 2:2. *JB* renders it 'officials and representatives of the government'. **ready for any honest work:** this is almost a cliché. Dornier quotes this phrase from a law of the client-state of Pergamum in Asia Minor, and we meet it in *1 Clem.* 2.7 in a description of the Corinthians' happy condition before the discords broke out that occasioned Clement's letter.

2. Gealy points out that both **to avoid quarrelling** (an adjective, *amachous*, in Greek) and **to be gentle** (*epieikeis*) occur also in the description of the qualities desirable in a bishop in 1 Tim. 3:3. This is however primarily an indication that the lists of qualities used by the author were originally drawn up by someone who did not have the office of bishop in mind. Both *epieikeia* ('gentleness') and *praütēs* (**courtesy**) here are leading characteristics of the historical Jesus; see 2 C. 10:1. The author does not give the slightest indication to connect them with Christ, but Brox believes that the immediately succeeding reference to the incarnation is intended to connect them: the *epieikeia* and *praütēs* which are required of Christians have been manifested by God in Christ.

LITURGICAL FRAGMENT ON THE SAME THEME AS **2:11-14** BUT
INCLUDING A REFERENCE TO BAPTISM

3:3-7

3. The contrast between the old pre-conversion life and the life of the Christian convert is a familiar theme in the epistles of the *NT*; cf. Col. 3:7f.; Eph. 2:1f.; 4:17f. In *Studies* (p. 88) I list 'former pagan behaviour' as one of the topics belonging to the source which the author, in common with the authors of Ephesians and 1 Peter, was using. It is possible that this list is based on Rom. 1:21, 27–30, but it does not reproduce it nearly as exactly as does the list in 2 Tim. 3:2–4. N. J. McEleney (*CBQ* 36 [1974], p. 215) believes that the author is following Eph. 2:1f. D–C observe that a lurid description of the pre-Christian plight was part of the early Christian preaching. It should be followed either by a description of the speaker's conversion or, as here, by a reference to the saving action of God in Christ. We must agree with Hasler when he says that **we ourselves** here does not mean 'You Titus and I Paul', even accepting the author's assumption of Pauline authorship. It is simply part of his scheme. **disobedient**: this is the right rendering, as Spicq has perceived, not the other possible meaning of the word *apeitheis*, which is 'unbelieving'. Dornier well remarks that those who do not admit the authority of God are really **slaves** of their own **passions**. Brox claims that **passions and pleasures** here is the language of popular philosophy. His verdict on the verse as a whole is that it is Pauline in thought but not in language. **malice**: the word is *kakia*, which Spicq says means 'mischievousness'; it is not so very far from the modern vice of vandalism. **hated by men**; one word in Greek, *stugētoi*. It could mean 'hating' and Spicq says we cannot tell whether the active or the passive sense is intended. Dornier thinks it should be translated 'hateful'. In view of the next clause, this seems better.

4. goodness is *chrēstotēs*, a word used by Paul of God's kindness in redemption; see Rom. 2:4; 11:22; compare also Eph. 2:7, which no doubt has links with this passage. Holtz goes so far as to suggest that *chrēstotēs* is used deliberately in order to recall the word *Christos*, and that the two qualities here (**goodness and loving kindness**) are intended to be regarded as qualities of Christ in his incarnate life. But this goes beyond the evidence. **loving kindness** is the *RSV* rendering for a word which nowhere else in the *NT* is applied to God, *philanthrōpia*. It is used in Ac. 28:2 of the kindness which the Maltese showed towards the shipwrecked travellers, and the corresponding adverb occurs in Ac. 27:3 concerning the humane way in which the centurion Julius treated his prisoner Paul at Sidon. But it is a word which is freely used in the imperial cult; indeed Easton conjectured that the author lifted the two words from some inscription in honour of the emperor. Lock points out that the word is often employed in connection with redeeming captives. This makes it all the more appropriate in this context. Spicq believes that the phrase as a whole applies specifically to the birth of Christ, but this is surely to limit it too narrowly; it must apply to the whole redemptive action of God in Christ.

5. he saved us . . . by the washing of regeneration: the author does not mean that baptism alone effects salvation, but that baptism is a focal element in the process of salvation. He may however mean something more specific as well. If we follow his line of thought, we must assume that in this verse as well as the previous one he is referring to the redemptive action of God. In that case he must think of some sort of archetypal baptism as having taken place during that redemptive action. Some scholars suggest a reference to Jesus' baptism in Jordan, but it is more probable that Christ is regarded as having undergone an archetypal baptism on behalf of all Christians in the waters of death. This is what appears to be meant in Eph. 5:25–27, a passage quite similar to this, one which makes use of the same source. See my *The New Testament Interpretation of Scripture* (London, 1979), ch. 5, where I explore this passage in Ephesians.

not because of deeds done by us in righteousness: a reference to justification by faith was evidently part of the source which the author is using; cf. Eph. 2:5, 8. The author has attempted to reproduce this eminently Pauline thought, but has not hit on a very Pauline way of putting it. Paul would never use *dikaiosunē* (**righteousness**) in this way. Houlden (Introduction, p. 28) goes too far, however, in calling this 'a parody of Paul's doctrine'. Brox contents himself with saying that Paul's doctrine is not understood from the inside.

by the washing of regeneration and renewal in the Holy Spirit: we meet a problem here: does **renewal in the Holy Spirit** refer to the same thing as **washing of regeneration**? The great majority of editors believe it does; in fact only D–C among moderns suggest that two events are meant. Some MSS read *dia*, 'through', before **renewal**, which would confirm this interpretation; but the reading is unlikely to be original. If D–C were right, it would leave a loophole for those who hold that some ceremony corresponding to confirmation can be found in the initiation practice of the church even in *NT* times. J. Belser has actually made this suggestion; but it is rejected by Brox. Indeed it does not seem very probable.

washing of regeneration: the Greek is *loutrou palingenesias*: as it stands the language is startlingly reminiscent of pagan religious vocabulary. It reminds one of the *taurobolium*, the bath in bull's blood which was practised in Mithraism, and which was believed to confer new life. And *palingenesia* has an interesting background in both philosophy and religion. The Stoics used it of the periodical recreation of the universe after its periodical destruction. The Pythagoreans used it of their doctrine of metempsychosis (Spicq). E. Büchsel (*TDNT* I, pp. 686–9) says that it was a term used in the mystery religions, but it is found in this context only at a period later than that of the *NT*. In Mt. 19:28 it is used of the parousia. Both Büchsel and D–C deny any direct influence from the mystery religions. The latter suggest that *loutron palingenesias* was a phrase current in the

Christian circles in which the author moved. 'A special sort of mystical Christianity is not meant', they say. The reference is to moral,
not ecstatic experience. The word *loutron* means 'the process of washing', not the vessel in which the washing takes place, which would
be *loutēr* (so Lock). *anakainōsis* (**renewal**) is used by Paul in Rom.
12:2, and the cognate verb occurs in 2 C. 4:16; Col. 3:10. Hasler well
remarks that the Holy Spirit is not here the prerogative of the ordained ministry, but the common possession of all Christians. This
is one of the few places in the Pastorals where the Holy Spirit is
mentioned and the only place where there is anything approaching a
sketch of the doctrine of the Trinity. But we must bear in mind that
the thought-content and outline are taken from a liturgical source.
When the author refers to the doctrine of God in his own words it
does not occur to him to include more than God the Father and Jesus
Christ. Spicq enthusiastically writes that this is one of the most
elegant expressions of the Trinity in the *NT*, but Holtz is nearer the
truth when he says 'a distinct Trinitarian terminology is not present'.

6. which he poured out upon us: the verb comes originally from
the famous prophecy in Jl. 2:28; of the giving of God's Spirit in the
end time; but it is also found in Rom. 5:5, where the love of God is
poured into our hearts through the Spirit; see also Ac. 10:45. *1
Clement* uses the corresponding noun of the full effusion of the Holy
Spirit upon all the Corinthian Christians (2.2); cf. also *1 Clem.* 46.6.
And in *Barnabas* 1.3 the author rejoices at 'the Spirit poured out
among you [his readers] from the bounteous spring of the Lord'.
(Hasler gives these references.) A. R. C. Leaney claims that the
eschatological dimension of the Spirit, which one would expect in
Paul, is missing here, and points out that another essential element,
faith, is lacking.

7. so that we might be justified by his grace: this phrase has given
rise to dark suspicions among Protestant editors that the author is
not being true to Pauline doctrine. Easton complains that justification
does not come before baptism as it does in Paul. D–C suspect that
perhaps here the act of justification is not meant but rather a righteous
life in the power of grace (and their suspicions are shared by
Houlden). Hasler claims that the author understands righteousness
not forensically but statically: the baptised are not reckoned righteous
by baptism but made righteous. One is almost led to conclude that
the real trouble with the author is that he had not read Luther! Brox
attempts to dispel these suspicions, and indeed the language here is
quite Pauline; cf. Rom. 3:24; 4:16; 5:1. If we speculate as to what
the author understood himself by the language he is using here, the
Protestants may have the right of it. He is not, however, intending
to convey to us his own theology of baptism, but that of the church,

and we may well conclude that the church of his day had still retained a good deal of the Pauline meaning of justification. When we examine his last phrase **and become heirs in hope of everlasting life**, he does seem to have fallen short of the Pauline doctrine of eternal life. D–C are correct when they point out that according to the author we do not become heirs of **everlasting life**, but of **the hope of everlasting life**; compare Rom. 5:21; 6:4, 23. Brox however understands the phrase to mean that we are made 'heirs of eternal life, for which we hope'.

THE NEED FOR GOOD WORKS IN VIEW OF WHAT GOD HAS DONE IN CHRIST

3:8

8. The saying is sure: the last of the 'faithful sayings'. Almost all editors, with the exception of Spicq, who takes it with what follows, believe it applies to what precedes. G. W. Knight (p. 8of.) believes it refers to the whole passage, vv. 3–7. But, if our interpretation of the author's use of this formula is correct, we need not tie it down exactly to any one statement. He uses it as part of his technique when passing from one element in his source-material to another. **I desire:** R. F. Collins (*LTP* 2 [1975], p. 159) underlines the strong authoritarian overtone of this word; cf. 1 Tim. 2:8; 5:14. **insist on these things:** the verb, *diabebousthai*, has already been used in 1 Tim. 1:7 of the false teachers' confident assertions. We must not press his syntax too literally. He does not mean that this liturgically coloured statement about God's salvation in Christ must be strongly asserted in order that those who believe in God may be sure to devote themselves to good works. The author is simply making the transition from a liturgical piece to a parenetic piece. Perhaps we should render it: 'insist on these things; let those who have believed in God . . . etc.'. **those who have believed in God:** formally this would include all Jews and the vast majority of pagans. But the author means 'Christians'. The perfect participle of the verb he uses for 'to believe' might perhaps imply 'those who have committed themselves to belief in God'. D–C say it corresponds to **our people** in v. 14.

to apply themselves to good deeds: so banal is this sentiment that one is tempted to adopt *RSV* marginal rendering 'to enter honourable occupations'. This would be very much to the point, since we know that persons following certain occupations, such as that of an actor, were not accepted as catechumens in the early church. But the fact that the author refers to 'good' (*agathos*) or 'noble' (*kalos*, as here) deeds in 1 Tim. 2:10; 3:1; 5:10, 25; 6:18; 2 Tim. 2:21; 3:17; Tit. 1:16; 2:7, 14; 3:1, 14, must constitute a very strong argument against it. No modern editor accepts the marginal rendering as correct, though it appears in the text of *NEB*, and Barrett shows some sympathy for it. **these are excellent and profitable to men:** nowhere does the author descend lower in mere banality than here. Perhaps he was running out of material (see Introduction, section 8). It may however be somewhat redeemed if we regard the author as concerned that local Christian churches should make a contribution to the life of the whole community by their works of social welfare.

HOW TO TREAT RECALCITRANT HERETICS

3:9-11

9. The content of this verse is very much the same as what we encounter in 1 Tim. 1:4, 7; 4:7; 6:4. There is a little more emphasis on the law, though this does also appear in 1 Tim. 1:7. The general impression that the verse gives is of teachers who were always pointing to the relevance of the *OT* law for conduct and life and engaging in disputes about the *Halaka*. Paul would have replied by clarifying the place of the law in Christianity, but that is beyond the author's scope. **genealogies** we interpret in terms of systems of related aeons, and **quarrels over the law** will mean a system of careful rules, concerning diet perhaps, designed to avoid as much contact with physical matter as possible. The stronger Jewish element in Crete may account for the stronger emphasis on law here. Dornier well points out that Ignatius seems to be facing a similar situation in Magnesia. **unprofitable and futile:** the two adjectives convey exactly the same meaning. Spicq has recourse to the desperate shift of suggesting that this is an example of the prolixity of the aged Paul.

10-11. a man who is factious: the Greek **factious** is *hairetikon*, from which our word 'heretic' comes. Many editors emphasise that the word here does not have the later meaning of 'heretical' (so Bernard, D–C, Kelly). Certainly in earlier Greek the word had a good sense: it could mean 'discriminating'. In an inscription of the first century AD the title *hairesiarchēs* means 'chief of the medical profession'. In Ac. 5:17; 15:5; 24:5, *hairesis* is used of the Sadducean party, the Pharisees, and the Christians respectively (the last usage on the lips of a prosecuting counsel hired by Paul's enemies). Paul himself uses it of parties forming in the Corinthian church (1 C. 11:19). In 2 Pet. 2:1 *haireseis* is used of forms of false teaching appearing in the church. We must also note Ignatius' use of the noun in *Eph.* 6.2 and *Trall.* 6.1, where it must mean 'false teaching'. In view of this we would probably be right in translating the word 'heretic' here. **after admonishing him once or twice:** this is reminiscent of the church practice that must lie behind Mt. 18:15f. It was founded on the practice of the synagogue. **have nothing more to do with him:** this is a rather colourless rendering of the Greek *paraitou*. The author has already used the verb three times (1 Tim. 4:7; 5:11; 2 Tim. 2:23). In 5:11 it is rendered 'refuse' in *RSV*, which may be nearer the sense; 'repulse', 'turn away' might be better. Gealy offers 'refuse to enrol', but it is not clear what the man concerned is supposed not to be enrolled in. The verb seems to imply some form of church discipline, no doubt the first beginnings of the later system of excommunication is indicated here.

such a person is perverted and sinful: with **perverted**, cf. Mt. 17:17. Note that heresy is in itself a sin here, a sinister omen for the ages to come. **he is self-condemned:** because he has refused the church's summons, say D–C. But the summons to do what? To cease teaching? Or to meet the church authorities in debate? Probably he is self-condemned simply because his teaching when examined proves to be inconsistent with the official teaching of the church. That should be enough, the author holds, without the necessity of theological debate, which is anyway not the author's strong suit. Tertullian used much the same argument against heretics a hundred years later, but that did not prevent him from debating with them most effectively. Notice that there is no question of the heretics forming a separate sect, though this may follow after excommunication. They are still a party within the church. Hasler points out the difference from Paul's practice. Paul brought the offender before the whole local church. The author of the Pastorals envisages a situation in which the leader in a local church (probably the bishop) acts on his own initiative in matters of discipline. So Mt. 18:16f. is not an exact parallel. Hasler thinks the culprit is to be brought before the group of presbyters and disciplined.

DIRECTIONS ABOUT FELLOW-WORKERS

3:12–13

12. Artemas is mentioned nowhere else. There is no reason to regard him as a fictional character. But we cannot follow Spicq in his romantic speculation that his full name was Artemidorus ('gift of Artemis') and that therefore he came from Ephesus, centre of the worship of Artemis. One could claim with as much justification that Demas came from Athens, home of democracy, or that Zenas came from Cyprus because the great Zeno, founder of Stoicism, was a Cypriot. For **Tychicus**, see on 2 Tim. 4:12. **come to me at Nicopolis:** since the name means 'city of victory', it is not surprising that there were many towns bearing this name in the Roman empire – Spicq lists seven. He is very convincing however when he opts for Actia Nicopolis built by Augustus on the gulf of Ambracia to commemorate his victory over Anthony and Cleopatra in 32 BC and peopled with veteran legionaries. It seems very likely that Paul did on at least one occasion winter in Epirus (see Rom. 15:19), so the association of **Nicopolis** with his sojourn there may well be a piece of genuine historical tradition. But we cannot be sure when it happened in the course of Paul's travels. The summons to Titus to **come** is probably fictitious. Hasler thinks there is a contradiction between this detail and the instructions given in 1:5f., which would take some time to carry out. He is no doubt right here, but when he goes on to suggest that Nicopolis is mentioned because it is there that the famous philosopher Epictetus (probably a contemporary of the author of the Pastorals) spent some time there in exile, he is trying our credulity too high.

13. Zenas the lawer: he is mentioned nowhere else in the *NT*. The Greek translated **lawyer** is *nomikos*, which in Matthew and Luke means a scribe versed in the Torah, but in secular Greek simply means 'attorney'. Some have seen him as a converted rabbi, but he would hardly have retained his title. All modern editors seem to prefer the *RSV* translation. He could be an expert in the law appointed to assist a judge, who might be a general or a prominent person not expert in the law; in which case he would correspond to our clerk of the court. Or he might just be a practising lawyer, like our solicitor. D–C suggest that the author's word for 'rabbi' is *nomodidaskalos*, as used in 1 Tim. 1:7, and that therefore *nomikos* must mean **lawyer**. There has been much speculation as to why he is described as a **lawyer**. Hasler puts forward two theories. (a) This is to show that Paul is free from prison as he writes the letter, so he can dispense with Zenas' services. (b) The church in the author's day was being compelled to relate itself to society and therefore had to take cognisance of lawyers. A far simpler explanation is that there really was a **Zenas the lawyer. Apollos:** all our information about him comes from 1 Corinthians and Acts. The last we see of him in these documents is back in Ephesus after visiting Corinth just before the writing of 1 Corinthians. Several editors have suggested that **Zenas** and **Apollos** were travelling evangelists such as we meet in the *Didache*. Brox sees the reference to these two as serving two functions: to make Titus look more like a letter, and to introduce v. 14. This sounds reasonable.

CHRISTIANS SHOULD BE WILLING TO HELP THE NEEDY

3:14

14. the same problem faces us here as we meet in v. 8 above. Is it **apply themselves to good deeds**? Or 'enter honourable occupa-

tions'? Just as we decided there that the first translation was preferable, so here. This repetition may be a sign that the author's material,
or inventiveness, is running out. There is a different problem about
the next phrase: **so as to help cases of urgent need**. The Greek is
literally 'for the necessary needs'. Does this simply mean, 'Christians
ought to be urged to work, so as to be able to supply their own daily
needs'? This is how most editors take it, and how both *NEB* and *JB*
render it. But there is an alternative translation, that which we have
in *RSV*. According to this rendering, the author is urging Christians
to help those who are in need. Hasler so takes it and compares 3
John, where Christians are urged to show hospitality to visiting fellow
Christians. Holtz even suggests that the example of the Jewish community is in mind here, because Jews extended hospitality to visiting
rabbis. But there is a possible extension of this meaning: the author
may be urging the Christians to take part in relief work in the
community at large. We know that Christians in a somewhat later
age did this; for example, in times of plague it was the Christians
who were most persevering in nursing the sick. The final clause **and
not to be unfruitful** could apply to any of these three renderings, but
perhaps goes best with either of the last two. If so, the author ends
his letter on a characteristic note: Christianity is to be expressed in
practical action.

FINAL GREETING

3:15

15. Greet whose who love us in the faith: D–C point out that
papyrus letters often include a final greeting formula such as this one
(an actual example): 'Greet Tereus and all who love you'. Dornier
and Houlden both suggest that this sentence is a last implicit reference
to the heretics, in which case **in the faith** will refer primarily to the
content of Christian belief. The author uses **us** not because Paul is
being represented as using a royal or an apostolical 'we', but because
he has just referred to the fact that there is a group with him as he
writes. This is of course entirely in accord with Paul's actual practice;
he always associated others with him in his work and very often in
his letters. **Grace be with you all:** as with the endings of the other
two Pastorals, there is an alternative reading here: 'Grace be with
your [sing.] spirit'. But it is certainly an attempt by a later scribe to
make Titus end more like a personal letter. Since the author does not
intend it as a personal letter, we may be sure that the phrase **with
you all** is deliberate.

APPENDIX

A list of passages in which the author appears to be editing Pauline material.

1 Tim.		adapts	
	1:12	adapts	Phil. 4:13
	1:20		1 C. 5:5
	2:13–15		2 C. 11:3, 14
?	3:15–4:10		Col. 1:24–29
	4:12		1 C. 16:11
	5:18		1 C. 9:9
	5:19		2 C. 13:1
	6:3–5		Rom. 1:18–32
	6:12		Phil. 3:12–14
2 Tim.	1:3–4		Rom. 1:8–11
	1:6–8		Rom. 8:12–17
	1:8–9		Rom. 1:16–17
	1:9–10		* Eph. 2:4–8
	2:1–13		1 C. 9:1–27
	2:8–13		Phil. 1:12–28
	2:20–21		Rom. 9:19–24
	3:2–4		Rom. 1:29–31
	3:16–17		Rom. 15:4–6
	4:6–8		Phil. 2:16–17
	4:8		Phil. 3:12–14
	4:11*b*		Phm. 11

* Though Ephesians is not regarded in this commentary as Pauline, the author of the Pastorals probably knew it. There is no reason to think he did not take it as coming from Paul.

INDEX OF MODERN NAMES

INDEX OF SUBJECTS